Learning to read critically in teaching and learning

Edited by
Louise Poulson and Mike Wallace

Los Angeles • London • New Delhi • Singapore • Washington DC

First published 2004

Reprinted 2009

SAGE Publications Ltd
1 Oliver's Yard
55 City Road
London EC1Y 1SP

SAGE Publications Inc.
2455 Teller Road
Thousand Oaks, California 91320

SAGE Publications India Pvt Ltd
B 1/I 1 Mohan Cooperative Industrial Area
Mathura Road, New Delhi 110 044

SAGE Publications Asia-Pacific Pte Ltd
33 Pekin Street #02-01
Far East Square
Singapore 048763

Library of Congress Control Number: 2003105196

A catalogue record for this book is available from the British Library

ISBN 978-0-7619-4797-4
ISBN 978-0-7619-4798-1 (pbk)

Typeset by Pantek Arts Ltd, Maidstone, Kent
Printed in Great Britain by CPI Antony Rowe, Chippenham, Wiltshire

FSC
Mixed Sources
Product group from well-managed forests and other controlled sources
Cert no. SGS-COC-2953
www.fsc.org
© 1996 Forest Stewardship Council

Learning to read critically in teaching and learning

This series, edited by Mike Wallace, supports research-based teaching on masters and taught doctorate courses in humanities and social sciences fields of enquiry. Each book is a 'three in one' text designed to assist advanced course tutors and dissertation supervisors with key research-based teaching tasks and aims to:

- develop students' critical understanding of research literature;
- increase students' appreciation of what can be achieved in small-scale investigations similar to those which they undertake for their dissertation;
- present students with major findings, generalisations and concepts connected to their particular field.

Each book includes reports of professionally conducted research not previously published in this form. Students are shown how critically to review research literature, while the research reports provide them with extensive material on which to practise their critical reviewing skills. The research reports are selected as models of good practice, showing different national contexts, foci, research designs, methods of data collection and analysis, and styles of reporting. They are accessibly written with key concepts defined, and each contributor presents findings and explains how his or her research was carried out.

The books are suitable for:

- students on advanced courses or research training courses;
- academics responsible for designing and teaching advanced courses and for supervising students on these courses;
- academics who seek information within the field of enquiry.

Books in the series:

Learning to Read Critically in **Educational Leadership and Management** edited by Mike Wallace and Louise Poulson

Learning to Read Critically in **Teaching and Learning** edited by Louise Poulson and Mike Wallace

Contents

Notes on Contributors

Louise Poulson is a Senior Lecturer in Education at the University of Bath, UK.

Mike Wallace is a Professor of Education at the University of Bath, UK.

Hilda Borko is a Professor of Education at the University of Colorado at Boulder, USA.

Kathryn Davinroy was formerly a graduate student at the University of Colorado at Boulder, USA.

Carribeth Bliem was formerly a graduate student at the University of Colorado at Boulder, USA.

Kathryn Cumbo was formerly a graduate student at the University of Colorado at Boulder, USA.

Martin Hughes is a Professor of Education at the University of Bristol, UK.

Pamela Greenhough is a Research Fellow in the Graduate School of Education at the University of Bristol, UK.

Gary D. Fenstermacher is a Professor of Education at the University of Michigan, Ann Arbor, USA.

Virginia Richardson is a Professor of Education at the University of Michigan, Ann Arbor, USA.

Harry Torrance is Professor of Education and Head of Research in the Institute of Education at Manchester Metropolitan University, UK.

John Pryor is a Lecturer in Education at the University of Sussex, UK.

Diane Reay is Professor of Sociology of Education at London Metropolitan University, UK.

Madeleine Arnot is a Reader in the Sociology of Education and Fellow of Jesus College at the University of Cambridge, UK.

Elias Avramidis is a Lecturer in Education at the University of York, UK.

Brahm Norwich is a Professor of Educational Psychology and Special Educational Needs at the University of Exeter, UK.

Preface

The purpose of this book is to assist students working at an advanced level with learning what it might mean to be critical and how to become a more critical consumer of literature in a particular area of enquiry. It is addressed directly to students participating in masters and doctoral level programmes. The material may be studied independently by individuals and also incorporated into the formal input of a programme as a source of critical reading and writing exercises supported by tutors and supervisors. Undergraduate students, postgraduates pursuing vocational programmes and their tutors will also find useful the guidance on learning to be critical.

The book is a 'three-in-one' text, which students may use:

▶ to develop their critical understanding of research literature through a focus on reviewing empirical investigations in a particular field of enquiry;
▶ to increase their appreciation of what it is possible to achieve through professionally conducted research investigations of modest size or components of larger studies, informing their thinking about the scope and focus of their own dissertation or thesis;
▶ to learn about major findings, generalisations and concepts connected with a diversity of important topics in their field of enquiry.

Programme tutors and supervisors may also use the material as sources of critical review activities and assessed assignments, models of research, including some that are small-scale, to inform the planning of empirically based dissertations and theses, and research-based information on various substantive topics in the area covered.

The book is divided into three parts. Students are offered guidance in Part 1 on how critically to read literature in their area of study and how to build a critical approach to literature into their writing, whether of assignments, a dissertation or a thesis. A structured approach to the critical analysis of a single text is offered which is linked to two exercises in critically reviewing, respectively, either one or several texts on the same topic. Consideration is given to the process of conducting such small-scale research and of developing the written account of it that is eventually presented for examination. Throughout Part 1, we indicate where readers may find a relevant example among the accounts in Parts 2 and 3.

Part 2 consists of research reports written for publication (rather than examination) by leading academics in the field of enquiry. They provide extensive examples of an important type of literature. Students are invited to practise their critical reviewing skills on them. The research reports represent models of good practice in researching and report writing that may inform students' own investigations. But as with all research studies, it is legitimate for students and others to ask how convincing are these authors' arguments, their more detailed claims about what they have found out, and any recommendations they may offer for practice.

Part 3 consists of an exemplary critical literature review chapter, not only offering insights into a key aspect of the area of study but also demonstrating how a high quality literature review may be constructed. Here, too, it is legitimate to consider how far the reviewers' claims to knowledge embodied in their argument are convincing. Together, the reports and the review make up a collection that is international in scope, displaying different national contexts, foci, research designs, methods of data collection and analysis, and styles of reporting.

Finally, there are two appendices. The first provides reference to selected additional sources of information. The second consists of a blank form for analysing a single text that students may wish to photocopy or to use as the basis for creating a template on their computer.

We wish to acknowledge the contributions of all those whose collaborative efforts made this book possible. The authors of chapters for Parts 2 and 3 are all busy academics who were nevertheless willing to squeeze in the time required to draft and revise their chapters to a tight deadline. Ray Bolam's ideas strongly influenced our thinking in shaping the content of Part 1, though of course we take full responsibility for what we have done with them. Martin Hughes's ideas contributed significantly to elements of Chapter 2. Feedback from the students who have tried out materials connected with Part 1 within their coursework has proved invaluable in informing the development of this component of the book.

Part 1

Becoming a critical consumer of the literature

Chapter 1

Critical reading for self-critical writing

Mike Wallace and Louise Poulson

If you are a student studying for a masters or doctoral degree, you are likely to notice that the word 'critical' crops up repeatedly in phrases like 'critical understanding', 'critical evaluation', 'critical engagement', or 'critical review', together with the closely associated words 'critique' and 'criticism' – whether in the student handbook, course unit outlines or assignment titles. These words and phrases are all connected with something that course designers value, and they are giving you the opportunity to learn how to do it to the literature in your chosen area of study. Assessors, supervisors and examiners also value 'critical' activity. Criteria for assessing your course assignments, dissertation or thesis all convey the expectation that you will be able to demonstrate how you have learned to perform this activity in whatever written work you submit, often through some form of literature review. Demonstrating your competence in critical reading of the literature through the critical academic writing you produce for assessment will be a condition for the award of your qualification. So you will have to be critical in your reading from the point where you begin preparing to write your first assignment.

But what does it actually mean to be critical as a reader of literature and to demonstrate being critical as a writer in your area of study? And if you do not already know what it means and how to do it, how are you to learn? In our experience, many students are unsure what is involved in being critical but are unwilling to say so because they assume that they are expected already to know. Some lack confidence in their ability as 'beginners' or 'amateurs' to challenge the arguments and evidence put forward by respected academics and other professional writers, often very persuasively. Others have strong opinions about practice born of their years as practitioners in the area they have chosen to study. But they frequently find difficulty in justifying why these opinions are worth holding and in coping with challenges to their views.

In some cases, students' previous academic training has emphasised deference to 'older and wiser' authority figures. Such students may naturally perceive that writers are expert purveyors of knowledge and wisdom that should not be questioned, but rather accepted and absorbed. The cultural adjustment to critical engagement with the ideas of those in 'authority' can be disorientating, but it must be achieved in order to meet the criteria for assessing postgraduate study in the western university tradition.

The process of academic enquiry reflected in postgraduate courses has its historical roots in this tradition. But with rapid globalisation it is increasingly being adopted in higher education institutions right across the world as a way of thinking and informing practical action. Here, while all individuals are entitled to respect as people, there is a cultural expectation that any person's work may legitimately be challenged, exposed to criticism, and even rejected if there are strong enough grounds for doing so. Therefore, it is quite acceptable for students to question the ideas of leading academic figures in their area of study, as long as they can give convincing reasons for their view.

Box 1.1
Being critical: great expectations

References to being critical are commonplace in official statements describing advanced courses. Anything that applies to masters level also applies to doctorates. Here is a selection from a masters course at the University of Bath offered in 2002.

Aim
▶ to give participants opportunities to improve their skills of **critical** thinking and analysis.

Learning Objective
▶ to identify, and engage **critically** with, appropriate and representative literature in the field.

Assignment Assessment Criteria
▶ to what extent has the student made **critical** use of appropriate literature and professional experience to inform the focus of the study?
▶ to what extent has the student made **critical** use of the literature in the development of the study and its conclusions?

A national policy requirement

In 2001, the UK central government's national framework for all higher education qualifications included the following descriptors.
Masters degrees are awarded to students who have demonstrated:
▶ a systematic understanding of knowledge, and a **critical** awareness of current problems and/or new insights, much of which is at, or informed by, the forefront of their academic discipline, field of study or area of professional practice;
▶ conceptual understanding that enables the student:
  – to evaluate **critically** current research and advanced scholarship in the discipline;
  – to evaluate methodologies and develop **critiques** of them and, where appropriate, to propose new hypotheses.

Indeed, the process of developing and refining knowledge and using it to inform efforts to improve practice proceeds through a never-ending sequence of claims to knowledge and counter-claims. There is a widely held belief among academics working in this tradition that no one can have a monopoly on what is to count as knowledge or on what will work in practice. Lack of agreement among experts is especially prevalent in social fields of enquiry because of the nature of the social sciences and of their application to practice. The social sciences are intrinsically value-laden ways of understanding. It is possible to adopt an explicitly value-oriented stance – positive or negative about the phenomenon being explored. It is equally possible to adopt a relatively impartial stance, but not one that is wholly neutral. Decisions on the focus for study reflect values about what is worth investigating in the first place. Carrying out a study will be implicitly and often explicitly underpinned by positive or negative values about the topic, about ideas informing which aspects of the topic should be attended to or ignored, and about the choice of methods of investigation. The practical use to which findings may be put through related policies is bound to reflect particular political values. Unsurprisingly, there is rarely consensus among academics or practitioners on the values informing their views. Nor is there any means of proving to everyone's satisfaction which values are the right ones to hold.

Therefore, learning to be critical as you engage in academic enquiry implies accepting a particular approach to your work. We are probably all familiar with being critical in the sense of not accepting things that happen in our family, social and working lives with which we disagree, whatever our cultural background. But for students who do not have a western university cultural background it may require a bigger cultural step to feel comfortable with being publicly critical, according to the implicit rules of academic enquiry and debate, than it will be for students who have been immersed in this tradition.

A place for being critical in academic enquiry

Postgraduate courses and research programmes leading to academic qualifications are an induction into the world of academic enquiry, writing and ways of thinking. Your participation in them offers you a form of academic apprenticeship. There are many opportunities to learn from experts by observing how they contribute to this process, whether by interacting with them face-to-face or through the medium of their writing. Even more important is the extended opportunity for you to learn-by-doing through trying out academic activities including critically reviewing literature, presenting an argument at a seminar, applying an idea to see if it works in practice, and receiving expert feedback.

Your own academic expertise will develop through this apprenticeship experience. Your habitual way of thinking about your area of study will probably become more sophisticated. You will find yourself gaining knowledge about the field including some which is at the leading-edge of what any expert knows, about topical areas of debate where experts disagree, about the limits of what is known, and about the extent to which prescriptions for practice derived from one context can be applied to another. You will also develop insights into the critical nature of the academic enquiry that produces this knowledge and its areas of controversy. You will become familiar with the ways in which academics holding very different views about the same phenomenon will put forward their own argument persuasively while seeking to counter or to refute the arguments of other academics who oppose their view.

One aspect of your thinking that you will surely notice changing is your ability to adopt a critical stance towards others' claims to knowledge about aspects of the area of study, and a self-critical stance towards your efforts to produce knowledge through your research and writing. The notion of 'being critical' tends to have a particular meaning in the academic world, reflecting values deriving from the western university cultural tradition. Here is our definition. Being critical in academic enquiry means:

▶ *adopting an attitude of scepticism* or reasoned doubt towards your own and others' knowledge in the field of enquiry (e.g. a theory, research findings or prescriptions for improving practice) and the processes of producing this knowledge (e.g. 'armchair' theorising, research investigations, reflecting on practice);
▶ habitually *questioning* the quality of your own and others' specific claims to knowledge about the field and the means by which these claims were generated;
▶ *scrutinising* claims to see how far they are convincing in the light of checking (e.g. whether the components of a theory are logically consistent, whether there is sufficient evidence to back a generalisation based on research findings, or whether the values underlying prescriptions for improving practice are acceptable);
▶ *respecting* others as people at all times. Challenging others' work is acceptable, but challenging their worth as people is not;
▶ *being open-minded*, willing to be convinced if scrutiny removes your doubts, or to remain unconvinced if it does not;
▶ *being constructive* by putting your attitude of scepticism and your open-mindedness to work in attempting to achieve a worthwhile goal. Challenging others' work to find a better way of doing things is acceptable, but indulging in destructive criticism of others' work just to demonstrate your intellectual prowess at their expense is not.

Easier said than done, of course. But the more you learn to be critical, the more you take responsibility for your academic learning activity and efforts to inform your own and others' practice (rather than being merely the passive receiver of others' wisdom, or the over-active promoter of your unjustified opinions that leave others unconvinced). Through engaging critically with the literature relating to your field of enquiry in a constructive way, you develop your capacity to understand and evaluate practice, research, theories and policies. You may also inform your efforts to conduct research and possibly to commission investigations, and to apply practical prescriptions derived from the literature.

Your ability to take responsibility for your academic learning rests on becoming a critical consumer of literature who is also a self-critical writer. In our view, it is essential that you apply to your own work the same critical approach that you are learning to apply to others' writing. For the academics who assess your work will be critical readers of what you have written. The assessment criteria will in all probability include the extent to which your work demonstrates your ability to be critical in engaging with the literature.

In Table 1.1 we have highlighted the link between elements of your endeavours in your academic apprenticeship as a critical reader and their application to your writing for assessment by other critical readers. Those entailed in critical reading will be discussed in the remainder of this chapter, and their reflection in self-critical writing will be considered in Chapter 2. For now, we wish to draw your attention to the way each element of critical reading has its counterpart in self-critical writing. Whatever you look for as a critical reader of literature, your assessors will also look for in your writing when judging the extent to which your account of what you have read meets the assessment criteria.

Table 1.1 *Linking a critical approach to your reading with a self-critical approach to your writing*

As a critical reader of the literature, you:	As a self-critical writer of assessed work, you:
▶ consider the authors' purpose in writing the account	▶ state your purpose in what you write to make it clear to your readers
▶ examine the structure of the account to help you understand how the authors develop their argument	▶ create a logical structure for your account that assists you with developing your argument, and make it clear to your readers
▶ seek to identify the main claims the authors make in putting forward their argument	▶ state your own main claims clearly to help your readers understand your argument
▶ adopt a sceptical stance towards the authors' claims, checking whether they support convincingly what they assert	▶ assume that your readers adopt a sceptical stance to your work, so you must convince them by supporting your claims as far as possible
▶ question whether the authors have sufficient backing for the generalisations they make	▶ avoid making sweeping generalisations in your writing which you cannot justify to your readers
▶ check what the authors mean by key terms in the account and whether they use these terms consistently	▶ define the key terms you employ in your account so that your readers are clear what you mean and use these terms consistently
▶ consider whether and how any values guiding the authors' work may affect what they claim	▶ make explicit any values that guide what you write
▶ distinguish between respecting the authors as people and being sceptical about what they write	▶ avoid attacking authors as people but are sceptical about what they write
▶ keep an open mind, retaining a conditional willingness to be convinced	▶ assume that your readers are open-minded about your work and are willing to be convinced if you can adequately support your claims
▶ check that everything the authors have written is relevant to their purpose in writing the account and the argument they develop	▶ sustain your focus throughout your account, and avoid irrelevancies and digressions in what you write
▶ expect to be given the information that is needed for you to be in a position to check any other literature sources to which the authors refer	▶ ensure that your referencing in the text and the reference list is complete and accurate so that your readers are in a position to check your sources

For instance, you may wish to know what the authors' purpose was in writing their account of, say, some research they have conducted. Knowing their purpose will help you to identify whatever argument they are developing and why they are developing it, and how they are attempting to support their argument through their claims to knowledge based on what they have found. You should similarly clarify and state your purpose in what you write as a self-critical writer reviewing this research. Your assessors will wish to know what your purpose was in writing your account to help them identify what argument you are developing and why you are developing it, and how you have attempted to support your argument through your critical evaluation of these researchers' work. Make it easy for your assessors to find out!

Box 1.2
A sense of audience: profile of the typical academic who assesses your writing

Age	Anyone's guess.
Lifestyle	Busy – appreciates writing with a logical structure, clear focus and fluent writing style that communicates efficiently.
Attitudes	Fair and respectful – concerned solely with the quality of your writing. Sceptical – will not accept your argument unless you can prove your case. Open-minded – ready to be convinced.
Favourite subject	The area of study – knowledgeable about the area in general but not about detailed issues or about your professional experience, so welcomes a brief description but only insofar as it is relevant to your argument.
Likes	Books – so knows the literature well and expects you to have read the literature you write about and to report it accurately. Reading high quality writing – carefully constructed, well-argued, balanced, meticulous on detail and reflective.
Pet hates	Waffle – ill-structured writing whose focus is diffuse and which leads nowhere. Avoidable errors – whether typographical, punctuation or grammatical, which careful proofreading could have picked up. Over-generalisation – wild claims that go far beyond any backing they may have. Poor referencing – failure to acknowledge authors, inaccurate or incomplete reference lists.
Most likely to say:	'Address the question or task set in your assignment!' 'Keys to writing success are a logical structure and a clear focus.' 'Take the criteria for assessment into account when planning your written work.' 'Your literature review should be critical, not just descriptive.'

As you read down the list of elements of self-critical writing, you will see that they relate to meeting the needs of your readers so that they can grasp what you are trying to communicate. But just as important, they also maximise your chances of convincing your readers that whatever argument you are putting forward is compelling. Both meeting your readers' needs and convincing them will help to ensure that your account meets their assessment criteria. So it is vital to develop a strong sense of the audience for whom you are writing.

When reading the literature, it is worth making a habit of noticing what other writers do that helps or hinders your attempt to grasp whatever they are trying to communicate to you. Emulate the good and avoid the bad practices in your own writing, because your top priority is to communicate to your readers. The chapters in Parts 2 and 3 incorporate various techniques designed to assist readers, like dividing the text into a series of sections separated by subheadings (e.g. Chapter 3), or providing an indication in the introduction about what will be covered in the remaining sections of the chapter (see page 86). As you read these chapters, look out for techniques that give you clues about what their authors are trying to communicate to you. Build these techniques into your own writing.

A mental map for navigating your way around the literature

It will be helpful to develop a mental map to guide your thinking when engaging critically with literature in your area of study. The literature will probably represent unfamiliar and potentially confusing territory, especially when you are just starting out on your intellectual journey. A map enables you to find a route through the sheer quantity and complexity of the literature by working out what you need to know and then navigating your way towards the answer you seek. We will define a set of tools for thinking that form a key to this map, and then outline four of its most significant components. We will exemplify how these components contribute to people's ability to make sense of the social world and indicate how they interrelate. Together, these tools and components can be used like a map to guide you in making sense of what you read. You may refer back to them at any point to help you see what the authors of the literature are doing as they attempt to convince you through their writing. But you should also be aware that our attempt to provide you with a mental map has its own limitations. We have greatly simplified complex ideas that philosophers spend their lives critically thinking and arguing about, so you will need to consult other sources if you want to learn about such ideas in depth. (Our attempt at mental map-making is, of course, as open to critique as any other academic writing.)

Tools for thinking are necessary for understanding the social world, because your experience of it and your ability to communicate that experience do not rest solely on your senses. The social world is also interpreted through language – as we are doing here to communicate with you about engaging critically with the literature. The notion of 'education', for example, is a social construct: education is an idea employed by convention to refer to various experiences, activities and even the state of being of the educated person. But there is not a one-to-one correspondence between the social world out there and people's interpretation of it in their minds. In common experience, different people understand what may be the same social world in different ways using a variety of terms to interpret and evaluate their experience. One person's valuable educational activities (say, opportunities for children to learn through play) may be another person's deplorable waste of time (if opportunities for learning through play are interpreted as merely encouraging playing around, without learning).

We will consider how our set of tools for thinking – the key to the mental map – is incorporated in finding out about the social world through:

▶ two dimensions of variation among claims to knowledge;
▶ three kinds of knowledge generated by reflecting on, investigating, and taking action in the social world;
▶ four types of literature whose authors are attempting to develop and convey different kinds of knowledge;
▶ five sorts of intellectual 'project' in which people engage who are working in a field of enquiry, leading to the creation of literature.

One set of tools for thinking...

These tools for thinking are embedded in the language through which people communicate by means of literature. They enable you to understand the social world and they have a hierarchical structure. But be warned: writers vary in what they mean by each of these tools for thinking, how they employ each tool, and how they conceive the relationship between the tools. No idea, even a tool for thinking, has an absolutely fixed and universally agreed meaning. Here is our version of what these tools are.

What are concepts?

Ideas like 'education' are *concepts*: terms used for classifying, interpreting, describing, explaining and evaluating aspects of the social world. The meaning of any concept may be defined using other concepts, so 'education' may be defined using concepts like 'instruction', 'creativity', 'training' or 'skill formation'. But there is no guarantee that everyone will define any concept in the same way. If no one has a monopoly on the possession of knowledge or prescriptions for practice, no one has a monopoly on the meaning of any concept either. Consequently, there is great potential for confusion and failure to communicate if the implicit definition of key concepts adopted by authors does not match their readers' implicit definition of these concepts. What authors can do, however, is to offer a 'stipulative definition' of concepts to indicate what they mean when using particular terms (e.g. pages 88 and 111). We, as authors, are giving a stipulative definition of concepts for making sense of the social world to provide you with your map. (But we cannot guarantee that all authors would define them according to our stipulation.) For clarity in communicating about ideas, it is important to consider what you and others mean by particular concepts. Otherwise you may find yourself unclear, as a reader, about what authors mean when they use undefined terms that are central to their argument. As a writer, you may confuse your readers unless you give a stipulative definition of the core concepts that you are employing.

Since the social world is infinitely complex, it is not humanly possible to focus on all aspects of social phenomena like education at the same time. Concepts may be grouped in various ways, and used as symbols where a concept (like the idea of a 'map' to guide your thinking) is used to represent something else (here, a multiplicity of concepts and ways of using them to structure thinking about aspects of the social world). Grouping concepts has the advantage of enabling you to attend closely to certain parts of the phenomenon you are studying. But to do so carries the inevitable disadvantage that you are likely to ignore other parts of the phenomenon that another group of concepts would have drawn to your attention. There seems to be no single best way of making sense of the social world. All ways entail compromises because no one is capable of attending to everything at once. Let us examine more closely how concepts are used in the creation of different sorts of knowledge that you will find represented in the literature.

What are perspectives?

Sets of concepts are often combined to form *perspectives*: selected facts, values and assumptions forming a screen for viewing social events and processes. A cultural perspective focuses on facts, values, assumptions, and codes governing what can be thought and done connected with the central concept of culture (Firestone and Louis, 1999). People may pick out different features of the social world through different screens, but they cannot look through all possible screens simultaneously. Any perspective, such as the cultural orientation, forms a lens for interpreting phenomena in the social world. So a cultural perspective on education might constitute a screen, directing your attention to the way educational activities contribute to moulding the beliefs and values of those being educated. It incorporates a bundle of related concepts that draw attention to some aspects of the social world while downplaying others. Cultural concepts include the sharing of beliefs, values, and 'norms' or rules of behaviour. An important concept within this perspective is the notion of ritual, where an activity symbolises something else. Degree ceremonies in higher education institutions are a celebratory ritual. The procession of academics and the award event symbolise how academics are publicly acknowledging the achievement of their students who have successfully completed their degree studies, and are now welcoming them into the ranks of graduates of the university or college. The degree certificate that each successful student receives is physically just a piece of paper with her or his name on it. Yet it also symbolises the student's achievement. This particular piece of paper can be acquired only by passing the assessment requirements for the award of the degree.

What are metaphors?

A *metaphor* is a way of describing one thing as something else that is perceived to be like it in some way. Where a screen for interpreting the social world is viewed as centring on a particular idea, key concept or image, this screen is often viewed as a metaphor for those aspects of a social phenomenon to which it draws our attention. The notion of a metaphor is a good example of an idea or concept whose meaning varies between writers. Some use the term metaphor interchangeably with the term perspective to highlight a central concept forming a particular screen, as where reference is made to the 'cultural metaphor'. Others implicitly define metaphor more narrowly, to capture in a single concept the image of some activity in the social world. Our image of tools for thinking as a key to a map for navigating your way around the literature is an example of such a metaphor. They do not literally provide you with a physical key, nor is there a physical map, but we hope that the image sums up for you what we are actually trying to offer.

A well-known metaphor in organisation theory is March and Olsen's (1976) image of a 'garbage can', created to sum up the process of decision-making in organisations. They wished to draw attention to a particular aspect of the phenomenon of organisational decision-making: the extent to which there may be ambiguity and unpredictability over why opportunities for making decisions arise, who participates in which decisions, and why they do or do not participate. The 'garbage can' metaphor captures the aspect of decision-making on which they wish to focus in a single image. Streams of different kinds of rubbish, representing opportunities for decision-making or organisation members who are entitled to participate, are thrown into a garbage can or dustbin. What eventually emerges from the mix is tipped out in the form of decisions. Notice that by drawing attention to ambiguity in decision-making, this metaphor draws attention away from other aspects of the phenomenon – not least the extent to which organisational decision-making may be orderly and predictable. As a critical reader, you will often find yourself engaging with an account where a particular perspective or metaphor has been adopted. It is important for you to reflect on which aspects of the social phenomenon being discussed are highlighted, and which underplayed or ignored altogether.

More than one perspective or metaphor may be used to interpret the social world in the same analysis. A common approach is to examine a phenomenon first from one perspective, then from another. Difficulties can arise when the two perspectives embody concepts that are not compatible with each other. If a cultural orientation emphasises how people share beliefs and values but, say, a political perspective emphasises how they use power to achieve their personal goals at others' expense, which explanation are you to accept? Another approach is to combine two or more perspectives by adopting stipulative definitions of the concepts from each perspective that are compatible with each other. A combined cultural and political perspective may use a stipulative definition of power that allows for power to achieve goals by working together as well as power to achieve goals through conflict. But employing combined perspectives becomes difficult because of the large number of concepts that may be involved. There is a limit to human capacity to keep a large number of ideas in mind at one time.

What are theories and models?

These terms refer to explanatory and often evaluative accounts of some aspect of the social world, incorporating a bundle of related concepts defined in a particular way. *Theories* are widely viewed as a coherent system of connected concepts, sometimes lying within one or more perspectives. They may be used to interpret, explain or, more normatively, to prescribe what should be done to improve an aspect of the social world, as in a 'progressive theory of education'. Such a theory may be couched within a psychological perspective on individual development embodying the metaphor or image of 'nurturing growth'. *Models* generally entail a small bundle of concepts and their relationship to each other. They tend to refer to a specific aspect of a phenomenon, which may be incorporated as part of a broader theory. A model of progressive education may concern a specified sequence of activities designed to provide a progressive education in a particular setting. Theories and models may or may not be informed by research or practical experience.

What are assumptions and ideologies?

Any interpretation of the social world rests on certain *assumptions*: taken-for-granted beliefs of which a person making a claim about the social world may be unaware. A progressive theory of education, for example, may rest on the assumption that learning how to learn is more important as a preparation for adult life than learning lots of facts. The validity of any assumption may always be questioned, often by considering whether there is evidence to support or challenge it, or by checking whether the assumption is logically consistent with associated claims being made about the social world.

The term *ideology* implies a system of beliefs, attitudes and opinions about some aspect of the social world based on particular assumptions. An ideology guides action to realise particular interests or goals. This action may entail preventing others from realising their interests. The 'educational philosophy' espoused by many teachers and lecturers is an ideology comprising their system of beliefs, attitudes and opinions about education, as in the view that 'education is about developing a lifelong love of learning'. It will be intrinsically value-laden, because any view of the purposes, content and methods of education, and of the ideal balance of control between the different groups involved, entails considerations about what should and should not be done that reach beyond facts. As we illustrated above, people may disagree over the values governing their view of what makes for good education.

The notion of an ideology is sometimes employed neutrally, referring to any system of beliefs whether true or false. But it is sometimes used more critically to imply a false or distorted set of beliefs, belying a partisan interest or goal that is not being made fully explicit. Marxists suggest that the content of people's ideology is at least partly determined by economic conditions, and in a capitalist society this ideology reflects their position of advantage or disadvantage within a hierarchy of social classes. The educational philosophy that 'the purpose of formal education is to provide the skilled and compliant workforce necessary for our nation's economic competitiveness in a global economy' may be interpreted critically as protecting employers' position of advantage, insofar as members of today's and tomorrow's workforce come to accept this ideology and are deflected from acting to better their economic position in respect of employers. In your critical reading, it is important first to identify where writers' claims about the social world reflect their ideology, and then to question the assumptions and values that underlie the ideology itself.

Two dimensions of variation among knowledge claims...

Arguments assert conclusions about what does, should, or should not, happen in relation to some aspect of the social world. These conclusions are drawn from one or more *claims to knowledge*, assertions that something is, or normatively should be, true. Such claims to knowledge are supported, in turn, by some form of evidence that warrants the conclusion being drawn. Knowledge claims are made with varying degrees of certainty, but note that it is a separate issue whether the degree of certainty is justified. The academic literature is not short of examples of highly speculative claims to knowledge of the social world made with enormous confidence that they are certain truths. Yet no knowledge of the social world can ever be beyond all doubt, as we discussed above. It is always appropriate for you critically to ask whether there is sufficient evidence to support the degree of certainty with which a claim is made.

Uncertainty whether claims are true is often made explicit when writers state that claims are tentative or cautious. A formal means of signalling tentativeness is through *hypotheses*. A hypothesis is a claim consisting of a proposition or statement that something is the case, but which is as yet unproven. An enquiry into an aspect of the social world might begin with a hypothesis whose validity is then tested to check whether evidence supports it or not. Alternatively an enquiry may produce hypotheses as outcomes, amounting to speculations that could be tested in future. However, many hypotheses in the study of the social world are so general that they are not amenable to straightforward testing. How, for example, could the hypothesis be convincingly tested that 'learning how to learn is a more effective preparation for adult life than learning lots of facts'? What would count as sufficient evidence to warrant the conclusion that the hypothesis was disproved or supported?

Claims are also made with varying degrees of *generalisation* from the context of practice or experience from which they were derived to the range of other contexts to which they are supposed to apply. For example, a claim about the effectiveness of progressive education might be made solely in relation to British primary schools, or alternatively in relation to all schools and other educational arrangements anywhere. Frequently, sweeping generalisations are not explicit about the range of contexts to which a claim applies. The extent of the claim is implied rather than stated, as in the assertion that 'learning how to learn is a more effective preparation for adult life than learning lots of facts'. Implicitly, this claim is asserted to have universal applicability – to all children everywhere, past, present or future. But note that generalisations are, in themselves, just assertions that something is known, not proof that it is known. Anyone can make generalisations – we have just done exactly that at the beginning of this sentence! It is another matter whether there is sufficient evidence that whatever is claimed really does apply to all the contexts to which the claim is explicitly or implicitly asserted to apply. So you may always, appropriately, ask the critical question whether there is sufficient evidence to support the degree of generalisation in the claim being made.

The broader the generalisation that some claim has *applicability* to a wider range of contexts, the more difficult it is to demonstrate that there is sufficient evidence from all these diverse contexts to support the claim. But generalisations also vary over their *level of abstraction* from the intricate details of any specific context. The broader the generalisation, the more likely it is to be at a high level of abstraction, glossing over details of individual contexts to make a claim about some quite abstract feature that is supposedly common to them all. The generalisation 'learning how to learn is a more effective preparation for adult life than learning lots of facts' glosses over the multiplicity of details that may vary between different contexts. They include:

- learning environments, whether a computer-equipped classroom or simply an open space;
- the characteristics of learners, whether adventurous or quietly reflective;
- the diversity of stakeholders involved in learning, whether students, parents or teachers;
- purposes for promoting learning, whether for its own sake or to contribute to society;
- values reflecting ideologies about what is learned, how it is learned, and what learning is for;
- features of adult life, whether work is pleasurable or harsh, and leisure plentiful or scarce;
- the nature of facts, whether an ethnocentric series of historical dates or the arithmetical relationships used in calculating earnings and spending.

We have mapped these variations among claims to knowledge in Figure 1.1. Note that we are putting forward a model here, offering a diagrammatic representation of relationships between concepts that we have selected and whose meaning rests on our stipulative definitions. We suggest that the degree of certainty and the degree of generalisation are key dimensions of variation. The more certainty is asserted about a claim, the more vulnerable it is to the critical question whether there is sufficient evidence to support this degree of certainty. The broader the generalisation embodied in a claim, the more vulnerable it is to the critical question whether there is sufficient evidence to support this extensive degree of generalisation. The claims to watch are those particularly prevalent in literature about the social world embodying recommendations for improving practice. They tend to make the strongest claims to knowledge, often combining a high degree of certainty with implicitly or explicitly a high degree of generalisation, at a high level of abstraction (represented in the lower right hand cell of the diagram). Conversely, least vulnerable to critical questioning are those that make the weakest claims to knowledge: tentative assertions about a specific context that avoid generalisation beyond this context (represented in the upper left-hand cell of the diagram).

Figure 1.1 *Dimensions of knowledge claims and their vulnerability to critical questioning*

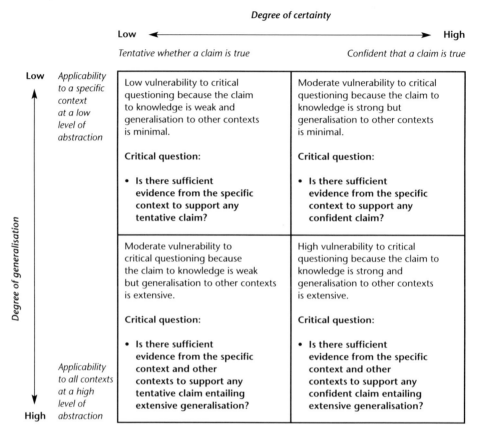

As a critical reader, you will find it useful to identify the degree of certainty and degree of generalisation of the claims to knowledge you come across in the literature, giving you clues about the sorts of critical questions to ask before you are convinced. As a self-critical writer you will wish to protect your writing from the criticism of the critical readers who are assessing it. You should be cautious about asserting greater certainty over your claims to knowledge than you have evidence to support, and about making broad generalisations except perhaps at a high level of abstraction.

Three kinds of knowledge – theoretical, research and practice...

Tools for thinking are intrinsic to developing the different kinds of knowledge that you will find expressed in the literature, and to your capacity to be critical about them. We have summarised the relationship between the tools for thinking and our typology of three kinds of knowledge in Figure 1.2 (another model). The tools for thinking are employed in contrasting ways to generate and question the three kinds of knowledge we have distinguished.

Figure 1.2 *Tools for thinking and the creation of three kinds of knowledge about the social world*

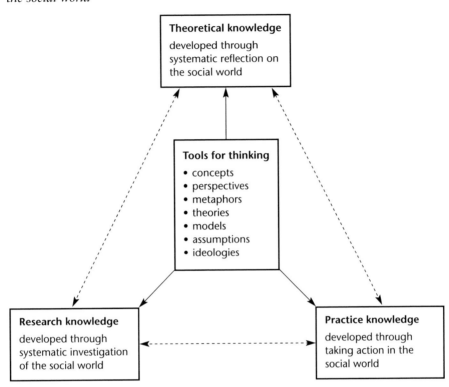

What is theoretical knowledge?

Tools for thinking are most overtly implicated in *theoretical knowledge* – you cannot have a theory without a system of connected concepts. Theoretical knowledge implies a theory about some aspect of the social world based on particular claims about what is or should be the case, as in a progressive theory of education. Theoretical knowledge is, in other words, not just a theory but a theory about something. You can always critically question how the concepts in a theory are being implicitly or explicitly defined and whether the system of concepts in a theory is coherent.

Generating this kind of knowledge may involve variable linkage with the other kinds. At one extreme, 'armchair' theorising entails reflection on personal experience in an area of practice, sometimes supported by reflection on what has been read in the literature and so potentially drawing on others' theoretical, research or practice knowledge. Where the links with other kinds of knowledge are weak, armchair theorising can lead to interpretations, explanations or even prescriptions for practice that are not backed by evidence. Anyone can dream up a theory. But since there is not a direct correspondence between the social world and interpretations of it, the strength of the claims made about the social world according to any theory can always be critically questioned by asking how far they are supported by evidence from research or practice. At the other extreme, as we shall see, theorising can be intimately linked to seeking evidence about what actually goes on out there.

What is research knowledge?

Research in the social world is a focused and systematic empirical investigation of an area of practice and experience to answer a central question about what happens and why, and sometimes also about how to generate improvement. *Research knowledge* consists of claims about what happens that are supported by evidence gathered through data collection and analysis in the course of an investigation. Research may be atheoretical, where it is not explicitly linked with any perspective, theory or model. But because research cannot be conducted without using tools for thinking, it is inevitable that particular concepts or groups of concepts will be employed. They may be undefined and employed unsystematically, but concepts will inform choices about what evidence to gather and how to interpret findings. Alternatively, one or more perspectives, theories or models may be used consciously to inform data collection and analysis (e.g. pages 153–4), whether in guiding decisions on what data to collect or in developing explanations of the findings.

The research approach may vary, from an investigation by professional researchers who do not attempt to intervene in the phenomenon they study, through an *intervention* where researchers work in partnership with those they study to help them improve their practice, to practitioners' action research where they investigate their own practice. The research process proceeds through the application of particular *methods* or techniques for focusing the investigation, collecting data as the basis of evidence, analysing it and reporting the results. These detailed methods tend to reflect a particular *methodology*, the researchers' philosophical assumptions about the nature of the social world (for example that social phenomena are or are not subject to universal laws). The results of an investigation embody researchers' claims about what happens and why, and possibly about how to make improvements. They are typically made public, commonly by publishing an account of the research in the literature. This account may be more or less descriptive, explanatory or evaluative, depending on what central question the researchers were attempting to answer.

The research reports in Part 2 of the book are all undertaken by professional researchers. They all employ tools for thinking, focus on an aspect of practice in the area of study, attempt explicitly or implicitly to answer a central question, and contribute to research knowledge by making claims about what happens on the basis of their findings. Some investigations are explicitly informed by a theory or a perspective, and some are concerned with improving practice according to the researchers' values.

What is practice knowledge?

You know a great deal about practice in your domain of the social world, but you may not be aware of just how much you know. Practice implies everyday activity. The practitioners involved interpret and evaluate their practice, guided knowingly or unknowingly by tools for thinking related – however loosely – to theoretical knowledge. Part of *practice knowledge* is tacit, the know-how entailed in skilful performance of practical tasks which practitioners use without necessarily being aware of how they do it. But some of this know-how can be raised to consciousness by reflecting on practice, possibly informed by theories, and by investigating and challenging habitual practice, as in some versions of action research. Knowledge of practice that is made explicit embodies claims about what does or should happen in the practical domain concerned. Some of this explicit practice knowledge is summarised in the literature, as when experienced practitioners write an account of their practice or where informed professionals, like inspectors, report on their work in evaluating practice. The basis of practice knowledge claims appearing in such literature is open to critical questioning for the same reasons as the other kinds of knowledge. Anyone can dream up an account of what she or he does and claim that it is good practice. But you can always question what meaning is being given to concepts used, whether the concepts are used coherently, and whether the account is supported by evidence.

Your motivation for studying may be to inform your attempts to improve your own and others' practice in your organisation. As you read this sentence you are actually using tools for thinking to raise your awareness of the nature of tools for thinking, and of how they relate to your and others' practice knowledge and the research and theoretical knowledge contained in the literature. Informing your practice through becoming a critical consumer of the literature involves engagement with the claims that you, other practitioners, theorists and researchers make in the literature about your practical domain.

Four types of literature – theoretical, research, practice and policy...

Theoretical, research and practice knowledge that is written down and published, whether in paper or electronic form, constitutes much of the literature that you will read for your study. When you first come across a text, say a book or an article, it is worth identifying what type of literature it is. Different types of literature tend to emphasise claims to different kinds of knowledge. Each type of literature is also subject to particular limitations affecting the validity of the claims it embodies. The potential strengths or weaknesses of these claims are likely to depend on different factors. By identifying the type of literature at the outset you can alert yourself to what you should look for in the text to help you decide the extent to which any claims are convincing, including any generalisation about the extent of their applicability to different contexts.

Box 1.3:
Practice makes perfect – or does it?

Which of these statements do you agree with, and why? Your answers will reflect your assumptions about the relationship between different kinds of knowledge and their ability to influence your own and others' practice.

1 'Research and theory merely tell practitioners what they know already, but perhaps hadn't thought about in that way.'
2 'Practitioners should do as they are told; policy makers know best.'
3 'There's nothing so practical as a good theory!' (A favourite saying of the social psychologist Kurt Lewin.)
4 'Research gets at the truth but practice is biased because it is driven by ideologies.'
5 'Great talkers are not necessarily effective practitioners; knowing what to do in theory is not the same as knowing how to do it in practice.'
6 'Good practice involves making choices about action; theory and research help to inform those choices.'
7 'Researchers simply identify patterns in practice so there's no need to inform research with theory.'
8 'You don't need to know any theory to be an effective practitioner.'
9 'Trainers have the solutions to practical problems so put their prescriptions faithfully into practice.'
10 'Theory is bunk – practitioners need to know what to do, not why they should do it.'

Each kind of knowledge is commonly expressed through an associated type of literature, as summarised in Table 1.2. As you would expect, theoretical, research and practice knowledge are to be found in literature with the same name. The additional type is *policy* literature, which emphasises practice knowledge since policy makers are essentially concerned with improving some domain of practice. They base their vision for improvement on their evaluation of the present situation according to the values and assumptions underlying their political ideology. Their evaluation of what is wrong with the present situation, and predictions about what will work better, may or may not be informed by the findings of research. For each type of literature, we have included an indicative list of limitations that may affect claims made. These potential limitations underline just how open to challenge and alternative interpretation knowledge of the social world may be. Becoming a critical reader entails developing the habit of questioning whether these sorts of limitations affect claims made in the literature you come across during your studies. Potential limitations such as these will be incorporated in guidance on developing a critical analysis of any literature text that we will be offering at the end of this chapter.

Table 1.2 *Types of literature and indicative limitations of claims to knowledge expressed in them*

Types of literature	Common features	Some potential limitations of claims to knowledge
Theoretical (emphasises theoretical knowledge)	Academic theorists develop a system of related concepts and apply them to understand an aspect of the social world, and sometimes to advocate improvement in practice	▶ Key concepts may not be defined ▶ Concepts may not be mutually compatible ▶ Assumptions about the social world may be false ▶ Attention may be drawn away from important features of the social world ▶ A supposedly impartial theory may be affected by implicit values reflecting a particular ideology ▶ Explicit values underlying any advocated improvement may be unacceptable ▶ Evidence from the social world may not support the theory
Research (emphasises research knowledge)	Academic researchers or practitioners on advanced or undergraduate courses report on the conduct and outcomes of a systematic investigation into an aspect of the social world, and sometimes make recommendations for improving practice and policy	▶ The focus of the research may be diffuse ▶ The research may be atheoretical, yet employ theoretical ideas unsystematically ▶ Any theoretical framework may not be rigorously applied to inform data collection and analysis ▶ The design and methods may not be given in sufficient detail to check the rigour of the investigation ▶ The design and methods may be flawed ▶ Generalisations about the applicability of the findings to other contexts may lack sufficient supporting evidence ▶ The findings may contradict those of other research investigations ▶ Recommendations for improving practice and policy may not be adequately supported by the findings ▶ Values connected with an ideology about the aspect of the social world under investigation may affect the choice of topic for investigation and the findings
Practice (emphasises practice knowledge)	Academic tutors, informed professionals, trainers or experienced practitioners offer an account of lessons for good practice in an aspect of the social world, based on personal experience or on the evaluation of others' practice	▶ Significant factors affecting the capability to improve practice may be ignored ▶ Criteria for judging the quality of practice may be implicit and unjustified ▶ Generalisations about the applicability of any advocated practice and means of improvement to other contexts may lack sufficient supporting evidence ▶ Values connected with an ideology about good practice and how most effectively to improve it may affect recommendations for practice and how to improve it ▶ The evidence base may be flimsy, narrow and impressionistic
Policy (emphasises practice knowledge)	Policy makers and their agents articulate a vision of improved practice in an aspect of the social world and the means of achieving their vision	▶ Implicit or explicit assumptions about the need for improvement and the content of the vision may be based on values connected with a political ideology which is unacceptable ▶ Any analysis of the current situation, the vision and means of achieving it may be uninformed by research and may contradict research findings

The distinctions we draw between types of literature are, of course, very crude. Most texts, whether an original study or a textbook summary, give greatest emphasis to one kind of knowledge. But many will reflect more than one, as in, say, a report of research which was informed by a particular theory, involved interviewing practitioners to gather their verbal accounts of their practice, and culminated in recommendations for policy makers that might indirectly lead to future improvement of that practice. Even here, we suggest that the authors' main purpose was to develop research knowledge. So we would categorise this report as research literature. You are sure to find a diversity of other texts relating to more than one kind of knowledge, such as:

▶ theoretical literature which draws on research findings about the practice of policy making to develop a theory of the policy process;
▶ research literature based on data drawn from practice literature (e.g. research to determine the patterns, across a large number of inspection reports, of inspectors' judgements on particular domains of practice in individual organisations);
▶ research literature exploring the nature of the practice knowledge that practitioners are capable of making explicit (e.g. an investigation of practitioners' perceptions of good teaching);
▶ policy literature comprising a statement of policy makers' vision for good practice that was developed in consultation with representatives of practitioners and with researchers.

...And five sorts of intellectual project for studying that produce literature

The authors' purposes determine which kinds of knowledge they draw upon and generate in creating any type of literature. Many areas of study that relate closely to a professional practice, such as education, are *applied fields* of enquiry. These fields take concepts, models and theories from various *social science disciplines* including sociology, psychology, philosophy, or economics. But academic study in applied fields is largely driven by a concern with improving practice, and so reflects whatever range of values those engaged in this study hold about practice and its improvement. A useful way of alerting yourself to the different purposes for producing literature is to consider the intellectual project undertaken by any author of a text. Drawing on the classification offered by Bolam (1999), we have distinguished between five intellectual projects for studying the social world (Table 1.3). They serve different purposes that affect the nature of the knowledge claims and associated literature that is produced. By a project here we mean a scheme of enquiry to generate the kinds of knowledge that will achieve specified purposes. The five intellectual projects are:

Table 1.3 *Five intellectual projects for studying aspects of the social world*

	Intellectual project for studying an aspect of the social world				
	Knowledge-for-understanding	Knowledge-for-critical evaluation	Knowledge-for-action	Instrumentalism	Reflexive action
Rationale	To understand policy and practice through theory and research	Critically to evaluate policy and practice through theory and research	To inform policy makers' efforts to improve practice through research and evaluation	To improve practitioners' practice through training and consultancy	To improve practitioners' own practice through evaluation and action for improvement
Typical mode of working	Social science-based basic research and theory	Social science-based basic research and theory	Applied research, evaluation and development activity	Designing and offering training and consultancy programmes	Action research, basing practice on evidence
Value stance towards an aspect of the social world	Disinterested towards policy and practice	Critical about policy and practice	Positive towards policy and the possibility of improving practice	Positive towards policy and the possibility of improving practice	Critical of practitioners' own practice and positive about the possibility of improving it
Typical question about the social world	What happens and why?	What is wrong with what happens and why?	How effective are interventions to improve practice?	How may this programme improve practice?	How effective is my practice and how may I improve it?
Place of theoretical knowledge in the study	Informed by and generates social science theory	Informed by and generates social science theory	Informed by and generates practical theory	Largely atheoretical, informed by a practical theory of training	Variably atheoretical and developing a practical theory
Common types of published literature produced	Academics' social science-based theory and research (reference may be made in associated policy literature)	Academics' critical social science-based theory and research	Informed professionals' practice and academics' applied research (reference may be made in associated policy literature)	Trainers' and consultants' practice literature (reference may be made in associated policy literature)	Practitioners' practice literature
Main target audience for published literature	Policy makers, academics, practitioners on advanced education programmes	Policy makers, academics, practitioners on advanced education programmes	Policy makers, academics, trainers, practitioners on advanced education programmes	Practitioners, other trainers, those practitioners on education and training programmes	Practitioners themselves

 ▶ *knowledge-for-understanding* – attempting to develop theoretical and research knowledge from a disinterested standpoint towards an aspect of the social world, in order to understand, rather than improve, practice and policy and their underlying ideologies;
 ▶ *knowledge-for-critical evaluation* – attempting to develop theoretical and research knowledge from an explicitly negative standpoint towards practice and policy, in order to criticise and expose the prevailing ideology underlying existing practice and policy and to argue why it should be rejected, and sometimes advocating improvement according to an alternative ideology;
 ▶ *knowledge-for-action* – attempting to develop theoretical and research knowledge with practical application from a positive standpoint towards practice and policy, in order to inform improvement efforts within the prevailing ideology;
 ▶ *instrumentalism* – attempting to impart practice knowledge and associated skills through training and consultancy from a positive standpoint towards practice and policy, in order directly to improve practice within the prevailing ideology;
 ▶ *reflexive action* – attempting to develop and share practitioners' own practice knowledge from a constructively self-critical standpoint towards their work, in order to improve their practice either within the prevailing ideology or according to an alternative ideology.

If you are a participant on an advanced education programme, such as a masters degree or professional doctorate, you will be engaged in your own intellectual projects as you study for your assessed work. The emphasis of such programmes tends to be on developing your capacity to undertake the *knowledge-for-understanding, knowledge-for-critical evaluation* and *knowledge-for-action projects*, where critical reviewing of literature plays a central part in supporting or challenging claims to knowledge.

As a critical reader of the literature, identifying which intellectual project authors have undertaken is an invaluable way of giving yourself an overview of what they are trying to do, why and how they are doing it, who they are trying to communicate with and how they are attempting to convince their projected audience. An insight into their intellectual project offers clues about potentially profitable directions for your critical questioning. The intellectual project pursued by any authors whose literature you review will display certain features:

 ▶ Their *rationale for undertaking the study* – indicating how explicit or implicit values about some aspect of the social world, theorising, research methodology and methods may affect their focus and the nature of the knowledge claims they make;
 ▶ Their *typical mode of working* – suggesting which kinds of knowledge they are attempting to develop and how they make use of different types of literature;
 ▶ Their *value stance* towards the aspect of the social world they are studying – reflecting their attitude towards policy and practice and attempts to improve them;
 ▶ The *typical question* or questions they ask about the social world – determining which aspects they attend to or ignore and the focus of the answers they obtain;
 ▶ Their *assumptions about the place of theoretical knowledge* in the study – guiding whether they employ any explicit definition of individual concepts or those grouped into a theory, and influencing the extent to which ideas are drawn from the social sciences or practice;

▶ The *types of literature they produce* – reflecting their rationale for studying, the kinds of knowledge they are attempting to create, and the audience with whom they are trying to communicate;

▶ The *target audience* being addressed – the people concerned with the aspect of the social world whose understanding or practice they wish to inform.

We have compared the five intellectual projects and their features in Table 1.3. When reading literature, you may identify the authors' intellectual project by considering each feature in turn to check which project it best fits. Bear in mind that these categories are crude and that intellectual projects are not always pursued separately in reality (e.g. pages 65–6). You may expect to come across authors whose activity spans more than one intellectual project, as where an account of social science-based research designed primarily to generate knowledge-for-understanding includes in the conclusion some recommendations for improving policy and practice (reflecting a knowledge-for-action agenda). However, even in such cases, we contend that you will be able to identify the main emphasis of a study as being connected with a single intellectual project.

We have now presented the key and components of your mental map for making sense of the literature you may be expected critically to read. Before considering how you may use this map to help you conduct a critical analysis of a particular text, you should be clear how your critical analysis of each individual text might contribute towards your review of a multiplicity of texts relating to the aspect of the social world you are studying. But what exactly is a literature review?

Reviewing the literature

A review of the literature is something personal. It is a product of the intellect of whoever took charge of their academic learning activity by deciding the focus, selecting texts for review, interpreting and engaging critically with them, ordering and synthesising what was found, and writing the final account. We define a literature review as:

> *a reviewer's critical account designed to convince a particular audience about what published (and possibly also unpublished) theory, research, practice or policy texts indicate is and is not known about one or more questions framed by the reviewer.*

Note what this definition excludes. We have all too often come across what students have called their literature review, but which consists of no more than an unfocused summary description of the content of diverse texts relating to some aspect of the social world, relying heavily on lengthy direct quotations. Such efforts would scarcely count as a literature review, according to our definition, because the students have not taken charge of their learning activity. Such attempts at a review are uncritical, merely restating what is in the texts; they are not built round the development of any argument; they are not obviously targeted at any identifiable audience; they fail to establish both the extent and the limits of what is known; and they are not demonstrably devoted to answering a specified question or issue. Avoid these pitfalls when you come to conduct a literature review!

Professionally conducted literature reviews that you are likely to read, like the one in Part 3, are written for publication. They are self-contained and designed to bring together knowledge that is dispersed within the literature on an aspect of the social world. Any literature review that you conduct for a course assignment, dissertation or thesis will be designed similarly to synthesise knowledge. But your review is a significant element of your academic apprenticeship, so it is also written for critical academic readers to assess. You have to communicate effectively, meet the assessment criteria, and convince your assessors of the claims you make. For a dissertation or thesis, your review must function as an integral part of the development of your overall argument.

Whether written for publication or assessment, a literature review is integral to the knowledge-for-understanding, knowledge-for-critical evaluation and knowledge-for-action intellectual projects. It has several features. First, its *purpose* dictates its focus: an academic review relates to a review question or issue that may be:

▶ *substantive* (about some aspect of the social world);
▶ *theoretical* (the concepts, theories or models informing the substantive question or issue);
▶ *methodological* (the approach to conducting the study).

The attempt to address this question or issue drives the reviewing process. It provides a criterion for selecting some texts for inclusion and rejecting others; the rationale for reading selectively within a text; the basis for a critical analysis of what has been read; and the focus for synthesising findings into a logically structured account putting forward a convincing argument. Second, the review synthesises claims to knowledge contained in a range of relevant texts in answering this question, attempting to demonstrate to the target *audience* the basis of reviewers' informed judgement about what is known, how strong the evidence is, and what is not known from others' work relevant to the identified substantive, theoretical or methodological question. Third, it also enables reviewers to demonstrate the *significance* of their question and why an answer is worth seeking. The significance of a substantive question may be for the development of research or practice knowledge in the field of enquiry; that of a theoretical question may be for theory development; and that of a methodological question for justifying the choice of research methods. Finally, it enables reviewers to *locate their own work within the wider body of knowledge* in the area to which the substantive, theoretical or methodological questions are applied.

Producing a high quality literature review is a challenging task. One secret of success is to clarify the guiding question or issue at the outset (we suggest that framing an issue as a question will help you to focus with precision on answering it) then sustain that focus right through to the conclusion. Another secret is to remember always to be constructive when evaluating the literature, ensuring that your judgements are clearly backed by what you have found. If it turns out that what is known in relation to your question is not particularly robust or conceptually coherent, state this and justify your assertion. But then be prepared to suggest how, in your best, literature-informed, professional or academic judgement the knowledge base could be enhanced, related practice improved, or theory developed.

In our view, a high quality literature review is likely to be:

▶ *focused* on an explicit substantive, conceptual or methodological question or issue;

▶ *structured* so as to address each question, perhaps broken down into sub-questions, in a logical sequence (see Chapter 9);
▶ *critical*, evaluating the extent to which any theoretical orientation is clear and coherent and any knowledge claims and the arguments they support are convincing;
▶ *accurately referenced*, so that each source can be followed up by readers of the review;
▶ *clearly expressed* to help your audience read the review easily;
▶ *reader-friendly*, introducing each question to be addressed;
▶ *informative*, providing synthesis through a strong conclusion which summarises a reviewer's answer to each question or sub-question according to the literature cited, and its strengths and weaknesses, and arbitrating between any opposing positions reviewed;
▶ *balanced*, indicating that whatever range of viewpoints expressed in the literature about each question have been carefully weighed, and that the reviewer's judgements are demonstrably based on a careful assessment of the relevant strengths and limitations of that literature.

These characteristics of a high quality literature review are worth applying self-critically to your own writing which results from your critical reading of the literature for your assessed work. For more detailed general guidance on reviewing the literature, we recommend that you consult the sources in the annotated list in Appendix 1.

Taking charge: developing a critical analysis of a text

Since a literature review is built up by synthesising material from different sources, a useful starting point is to do a critical analysis of each selected text as you read it. You may guide your reading and reflection by asking the ten critical questions and, as appropriate, their sub-questions set out in the critical analysis form reproduced here (Figure 1.3). They relate to the mental map we offered for charting your way through the literature and to our advice on developing a high quality literature review. Most questions or sub-questions are followed by examples of more detailed prompts (in brackets) that you could use in examining the text in search of your answers. The questions are grouped to form a sequence:

▶ Question 1 encourages you to think about why you have selected the text and how your critical analysis of it may contribute to your enquiry.
▶ Questions 2, 3 and 4 guide you in determining what the authors are attempting to do and in summarising whatever content of the text is of significance to you.
▶ Questions 5, 6, 7, 8 and 9 help you critically to analyse different aspects of this content to see how far it is convincing.
▶ Question 10 invites you to form a conclusion, in the light of your critical analysis, based on your informed judgement about the extent to which any claims relating to the focus of your enquiry are convincing, and why.

In Figure 1.3 we have introduced each question or group of questions in this sequence (in bold italics). We have given a brief commentary on each question (in italics) and have referred to relevant sections in the present chapter so that you may go back to them when working on the critical analysis of a text.

Figure 1.3 *Advice on making effective use of questions to ask as a critical reader of a text*

Critical Analysis of a Text

Question 1 invites you to be self-critical by justifying to yourself why you are reading the text, and how your critical analysis of it is directed towards achieving a constructive purpose. Asking this question every time you examine a text helps you to avoid the pitfalls of reading material that is not relevant to your purpose, or of writing an unfocused description of everything you read rather than a critical literature review!

1. **What review question am I asking of this text?** (e.g. what is my central question? why select this text? does the critical analysis of this text fit into my investigation with a wider focus? what is my constructive purpose in undertaking a critical analysis of this text?)
    It is crucial that you begin by identifying a question or issue that you wish to address through your critical analysis of one or more texts drawn from the relevant literature. This question or issue provides you with a rationale for selecting a particular text and a constructive purpose for reading it critically. Any text should potentially contribute to addressing the question or issue. (See the section on reviewing the literature.)

Questions 2, 3 and 4 help you to work out, in summary, what the authors of a text are trying to achieve and what they are attempting to communicate to their target audience. These questions also alert you to potentially fruitful lines of critical questioning.

2. **What type of literature is this?** (e.g. theoretical, research, practice, policy? are there links with other types of literature?)
    Identifying the main type of literature that the text belongs to will help you to predict what its features are likely to be. The type of literature will indicate the main kind of knowledge embodied in any claim, enabling you to check whether potential limitations of this kind of knowledge apply. (See the section on types of literature, including Table 1.2.)

3. **What sort of intellectual project for study is being undertaken?** *Establishing the authors' intellectual project will clue you in to what they are trying to achieve, why and how. You will be aware of whom they are seeking to convince of their argument and associated claims to knowledge. You will then be in a good position to ask critical questions about what they have done. (See the section on different sorts of intellectual project, including Table 1.3.)*

    (a) *How clear is it which intellectual project the authors are undertaking?* (e.g. knowledge-for-understanding, knowledge-for-critical evaluation, knowledge-for-action, instrumentalism, reflexive action?)
    (b) *How is the intellectual project reflected in the authors' mode of working?* (e.g. a social science or a practical orientation? choice of methodology and methods? an interest in understanding or in improving practice?)
    (c) *What value stance is adopted towards the practice or policy investigated?* (e.g. disinterested, critical, positive, unclear? what assumptions are made about the possibility of improvement? whose practice or policy is the focus of interest?)
    (d) *How does the sort of intellectual project being undertaken affect the research questions addressed?* (e.g. investigating what happens? what is wrong? how well does a particular policy or intervention work in practice?)
    (e) *How does the sort of intellectual project being undertaken affect the place of theory?* (e.g. is the investigation informed by theory? generating theory? atheoretical? developing social science theory or a practical theory?)
    (f) *How does the authors' target audience affect the reporting of research?* (e.g. do the authors assume academic knowledge of methods? criticise policy? offer recommendations for action?)

4. **What is being claimed?**
    As a basis for considering whether what the authors have written is convincing, you will need to identify any argument that they are putting forward in the text and to clarify the main claims to particular kinds of knowledge that underlie it. Concentrate on identifying a small number of major ideas by summarising the content of the text. Try to avoid getting distracted by lots of minor details. (See the section on kinds of knowledge, including Figure 1.2.) As further preparation for critical consideration of the authors' claims, it is helpful to work out the degree of certainty with which any

knowledge claim is asserted and the degree to which the authors generalise beyond the context from which the claim to knowledge was derived. (See the section on dimensions of variation among knowledge claims, including Figure 1.1.)

(a) *What are the main kinds of knowledge claim that the authors are making?* (e.g. theoretical knowledge, research knowledge, practice knowledge?)

(b) *What is the content of the main claims to knowledge and of the overall argument?* (e.g. what, in a sentence, is being argued? what are the three to five most significant claims that encompass much of the detail? are there key prescriptions for improving policy or practice?)

(c) *How clear are the authors' claims and overall argument?* (e.g. stated in an abstract, introduction or conclusion? unclear?)

(d) *With what degree of certainty do the authors make their claims?* (e.g. do they indicate tentativeness? qualify their claims by acknowledging limitations of their evidence? acknowledge others' counter-evidence? acknowledge that the situation may have changed since data collection?)

(e) *How generalised are the authors' claims – to what range of phenomena are they claimed to apply?* (e.g. the specific context from which the claims were derived? other similar contexts? a national system? a culture? universal? implicit? unspecified?)

(f) *How consistent are the authors' claims with each other?* (e.g. do all claims fit together in supporting an argument? do any claims contradict each other?)

Questions 5, 6, 7, 8 and 9 are complementary critical questions. Each helps you to focus on a different potential challenge to the claims to knowledge underlying any argument. Together, your answers to these questions provide a basis for your critical evaluation of the text as a whole and its contribution to answering your review question (Question 1 above) that guides your critical analysis as a contribution to your constructive purpose.

5. **To what extent is there backing for claims?**
   It is important to check the extent to which the main claims to knowledge on which any argument rests are sufficiently well supported to convince you, whether through evidence provided by the authors or through other sources of backing. (See the section on dimensions of knowledge claims, including Figure 1.1, and the section on types of literature, including the potential limitations of claims to knowledge listed in Table 1.2.)

(a) *How transparent are any sources used to back the claims?* (e.g. is there any statement of the basis for assertions? are sources unspecified?)

(b) *What, if any, range of sources is used to back the claims?* (e.g. first-hand experience? the authors' own practice knowledge or research? literature about others' practice knowledge or research? literature about reviews of practice knowledge or research? literature about others' polemic?)

(c) *If claims are at least partly based on the authors' own research, how robust is the evidence?* (e.g. is the range of sources adequate? are there methodological limitations or flaws in the methods employed? do they include cross-checking or 'triangulation' of accounts? what is the sample size and is it large enough to support the claims being made? is there an adequately detailed account of data collection and analysis? is a summary given of all data reported?)

(d) *Are sources of backing for claims consistent with the degree of certainty and the degree of generalisation?* (e.g. is there sufficient evidence to support claims made with a high degree of certainty? is there sufficient evidence from other contexts to support claims entailing extensive generalisation?)

6. **How adequate is any theoretical orientation to back claims?**
   Any text must employ certain concepts to make sense of whatever aspect of the social world is being discussed. Many texts will feature an explicit theoretical orientation as a framework for understanding and possibly as a basis for the authors' recommendations for improvement. You will need to decide whether the claims being made are clear and coherent, and whether you accept the assumptions on which they rest. To assist your critical reflection, check which concepts and other tools for thinking have been used, what they are taken to mean, and how they frame the claims being made. (See the section on tools for thinking, the section on types of literature, including the potential limitations of claims to knowledge listed in Table 1.2, and the section on different sorts of intellectual project, including Table 1.3.)

(a) *How explicit are the authors about any theoretical orientation or conceptual framework?* (e.g. is there a conceptual framework guiding data collection? is a conceptual framework selected after data collection to guide analysis? is there a largely implicit theoretical orientation?)

▶

(b) *What assumptions does any explicit or implicit theoretical orientation make that may affect the authors' claims?* (e.g. does a perspective focus attention on some aspects and under-emphasise others? if more than one perspective is used, how coherently do the different perspectives relate to each other?)

(c) *What are the key concepts underpinning any explicit or implicit theoretical orientation?* (e.g. are they listed? are they stipulatively defined? are concepts mutually compatible? is use of concepts consistent? is the use of concepts congruent with others' use of the same concepts?)

7. **To what extent does any value stance adopted affect claims?**
   Since no investigation of the social world can be completely value-free, all claims to knowledge will reflect the value stance adopted. So it is important to check what values have guided the authors of any text, how these values affect their claims, and the extent to which the value stance makes the claims more or less convincing. (See the section on tools for thinking, the section on types of literature, including the potential limitations of claims to knowledge listed in Table 1.2, and the section on different sorts of intellectual project, including Table 1.3.)

(a) *How explicit are the authors about any value stance connected with the phenomena?* (e.g. a disinterested, critical, or positive stance? is this stance informed by a particular ideology? is it adopted before or after data collection?)

(b) *How may any explicit or implicit value stance adopted by the authors affect their claims?* (e.g. have they pre-judged the phenomena discussed? are they biased? is it legitimate for the authors to adopt their particular value stance? have they over-emphasised some aspects of the phenomenon while under-emphasising others?)

8. **To what extent are claims supported or challenged by others' work?**
   It is highly improbable that any study of an aspect of the social world will be unrelated to others' work. A valuable check is therefore to examine whether links are made with other studies, and the degree to which others' work supports the claims being made. You may wish to refer to other texts that address phenomena related to the text you are analysing.

(a) *Do the authors relate their claims to others' work?* (e.g. do the authors refer to others' published evidence, theoretical orientations or value stances to support their claims? do they acknowledge others' counter-evidence?)

(b) *How robust is any evidence from others' work used to support claims?* (e.g. see question 5c.)

(c) *How robust is any evidence from others' research and practice that challenges the authors' claims?* (e.g. see question 5c.)

9. **To what extent are claims consistent with my experience?**
   Your own experience of the social world will probably not be identical to that being studied in the text, but it is still relevant. In considering how convincing the claims made in a text may be, it is worth checking whether these claims have significant similarities with your experience and also evaluating whether they sound feasible or unrealistic, given what you know from experience.

Question 10 requires you to sum up what you have learned from the answers you have gained from all the previous questions and to come to an overall well-informed and balanced judgement about the convincingness of the claims being made. What you have learned contributes to addressing your review question (Question 1) that led you to select the text and develop your critical analysis of it, and ultimately towards achieving your underlying constructive purpose.

10. **What is my summary evaluation of the text in relation to my review question or issue?**
    In making a summary evaluation of the text, you need to support your own best literature-informed professional or academic judgement by seeking backing from the answers you have gained to the critical questions (5 to 9 above).

(a) *How convincing are the authors' claims, and why?*

(b) *How, if at all, could the authors have provided stronger backing for their claims?*

   Both your summary evaluation and the more detailed answers to all the other questions (1–9 above) will now be available for you to draw upon selectively in writing your account of the text as you address the question or issue that has driven your critical reading activity.

There is a blank critical analysis form in Appendix 2. You may wish to photo-copy it and then complete one form for each text that you analyse in detail. If you have access to a computer, you may prefer to create a master file by typing in the content of the blank form and then use it as a template. You will be able to copy the master file for each text you critically analyse and fill in your answers to the questions. You may save each completed critical analysis form as a separate file on your computer or print it out as your record. Computerising the form in this way would offer you the flexibility to write as much as you like in response to each question.

We invite you to help yourself learn to be a more critical reader by reviewing any of the research reports in Part 2 or the literature review in Part 3. Completing the critical analysis form for each chapter you review and referring back to topics discussed in this chapter as necessary will help you to form the habit of being crit-ical when reading the literature. The form is designed to apply to most types of literature that you are likely to meet in the course of your studies, including mate-rial that you may download from the internet. You could use the form to guide you in reviewing any other literature in any area of study connected with the social world. But do not forget that you must take charge of the review process. It is your responsibility to learn how to make creative and selective use of the guid-ance we have offered, according to the question or issue you wish to address. So it is for you to decide which critical analysis questions are most important for any individual text, what your answers are to them, and how to combine what you have found into an account which will stand up to the scrutiny of your assessors.

We have included a couple of critical literature review exercises that you may either use as they stand or adapt to suit review questions that you would like to answer. They are designed to help you make the transition from being a critical reader to a self-critical writer, and both are based on the critical analysis of individual texts. We suggest that you try them out on texts which are cen-tral to a review you wish to undertake, and that you take our earlier advice about focusing and either use the questions we have supplied if they are appropriate, or else devise your own.

Exercise 1 is a *single text critical review* of a chapter or article reporting on research. Any of the chapters in Part 2 or 3 would be suitable, or you may choose an article or chapter from other literature. You may wish to focus on answering the two review questions we have suggested, or put forward your own. The suggested structure for the single text review relates directly to the ten questions contained in the critical analysis form. So you may read your text, complete the critical analysis form, then write your review of this text based on your answers to the critical analysis questions.

Exercise 1
Single-text critical review of a chapter or article reporting on research

You are invited to review one of the chapters in Part 2 or 3, or to choose an article or chapter reporting on research from other literature. Your task is to write a critical review of the article or chapter, of up to 1,000 words, to answer these two review questions:

▶

1 What does the literature reviewed suggest may be key factors promoting or inhibiting the effectiveness of (a particular aspect of practice that you have chosen in the field of enquiry)?

2 To what extent are the factors identified applicable to my professional context or one known to me?

The critical analysis questions to ask when reviewing a chapter or article are contained in the critical analysis form (Appendix 2). You are recommended to divide your written account into a sequence of sections and devise your own subheading for each section relating to the area of practice which is the focus for your critical review.

Suggested structure for your single text critical review

Title
▶ Your choice of title should include the key words that will indicate to the reader what you are doing (a critical review of a selected piece of literature) and the aspect of practice that forms your focus.

Introduction to the critical review (about 100 words)
▶ A statement of the purpose of your review – critically to review the selected text (give the names of the authors, the title of the chapter or article and the date of publication) as a contribution to answering the two review questions:
   1 'What does the selected literature reviewed suggest may be key factors promoting or inhibiting the effectiveness of (the particular aspect of practice in the field of enquiry you have chosen)?'
   2 'To what extent are the factors identified applicable to my professional context or one known to me?'

Summary of the research design – what the investigators were trying to find out and what they did – (about 200 words)
▶ A summary of the authors' purposes for the text and the kind of enquiry they engaged in, including an indication of the type of literature they produced (refer to your answer to critical analysis question 2) and their intellectual project (refer to your answer to critical analysis question 3).
▶ A brief indication of why this text is relevant to the review questions guiding your critical review (critical analysis question 1).
▶ A brief summary of how they went about their investigation (e.g. the research design, methodology, sample, methods of data collection and analysis).

The authors' main findings and any broader claims relating to the review questions for the critical review (about 200 words)
▶ A comparative summary of the main claims made by the authors of the text relevant to key factors promoting or inhibiting the effectiveness of the aspect of practice on which you have chosen to focus (refer to your answer to critical analysis question 4) – a synthesis of, say, up to five main points.
▶ An indication of the range of contexts to which the authors claim or appear to claim that their findings may apply (e.g. they imply that their claims about effectiveness apply to all contexts or do not specify any limits on the extent to which they may be universally applicable).

Evaluation of the authors' main findings and any broader claims relating to the review questions for the critical review (about 300 words)
- Your comparative evaluation of these findings and any broader claims, critically assessing how far they are convincing *for the context from which these claims were derived.* (Refer to your answers to critical analysis questions 5–9, possibly referring to additional literature to support your judgement in relation to critical analysis question 8.) In your critique, you may wish to refer back to your earlier account of the authors' purpose, intellectual project and how they went about their enquiry (e.g. you may wish to assert that the value stance of particular authors led to bias which affected their findings).
- Your comparative and critical assessment of how far the claims made by the authors of the text may be applicable to *your professional context or one known to you* (critical analysis questions 5–9, possibly referring to additional literature to support your judgement in relation to critical analysis question 8). In your critique you may wish to refer back to your earlier account of how the authors went about their enquiry (e.g. you may wish to assert that the findings from a particular intellectual project were derived from a context which is so different from yours that you consider the prescriptions for practice emerging from this work are unlikely to apply directly to your context).

Conclusion (about 200 words)
- Your brief overall evaluation of the text reviewed to assess its contribution to answering your review questions (refer to your answer to critical analysis question 10).
- The summary answer to the first review question offered by the text reviewed, including a statement of your judgement, with reasons, about how far the findings and any broader claims are convincing for the context from which they were derived.
- The summary answer to the second review question, including a statement of your judgement, with reasons, about how far the findings and any broader claims are applicable (e.g. at how high a level of abstraction?) to your professional context or one known to you.

References
- Give the full reference for the chapter or article you have reviewed.
- If you refer to any additional literature, list the texts to which you have referred, following the normal conventions for compiling a reference list.

Exercise 2 takes the review process a step further by inviting you to undertake a *multiple text review* of three or more texts reporting research which are relevant to the same aspect of practice in the field of enquiry. You will have to group and synthesise your answers to critical analysis questions for each text in writing your review. The suggested structure offers one way of doing so. As with the first exercise, you may use one or more of the chapters in Parts 2 and 3, and other texts that you choose for yourself. Either focus on the review questions we have suggested or formulate one or more alternatives. You may read your chosen texts, complete the critical analysis form for each of them, then write your review by synthesising your answers to particular critical analysis questions across all these texts. Completing this exercise will result in an in-depth account whose length will be roughly equivalent to that of many assignments for masters courses.

Exercise 2
Multiple text critical review on reports of research

You are invited to review three or more chapters from Part 2 or 3, or to choose one or more articles, chapters or books reporting on research from other literature. Your task is to write a critical review of these texts together, referring to other literature as appropriate, of up to 4,000 words. The review is designed to answer these two review questions:

1 What does the literature reviewed suggest may be key factors promoting or inhibiting the effectiveness of (a particular aspect of practice that you have chosen in the field of enquiry)?
2 To what extent are the factors identified applicable to my professional context or one known to me?

Whatever texts you choose, they should all focus on the same aspect of practice in the field of enquiry. The critical analysis questions to ask when reviewing a chapter or article are contained in the critical analysis form (Appendix 2). You are recommended to divide your written account into a sequence of sections and devise your own subheading for each section relating to the area of practice which is the focus for your critical review.

Suggested structure for your multiple text critical review

Title
▶ Your choice of title should include the key words that will indicate to the reader what you are doing (a critical literature review) and the aspect of practice that forms your focus.

Introduction to the critical review (250–750 words)
▶ A statement of the purpose of your review – critically to review the selected texts in depth as a contribution to answering the two review questions:
  1 'What does the selected literature reviewed suggest may be key factors promoting or inhibiting the effectiveness of (the particular aspect of practice in the field of enquiry you have chosen)?'
  2 'To what extent are the factors identified applicable to my professional context or one known to me?'
▶ Your justification for selecting this area of practice (e.g. its significance for improving the aspect of practice), perhaps referring to other literature to support your argument.
▶ Your acknowledgement of the scope of your critical review (e.g. an indication of the texts you will analyse in depth, giving the names of the authors, title and date of publication for each, and the reasons why you selected them for critical review).

▶ Your acknowledgement of the limitations of your critical review (e.g. that your focus is confined to these few texts and there are likely to be others relating to this aspect of practice which you will not be examining in depth).
▶ An indication of the topics to be covered in each of the remaining sections of your review so that the reader can see how you will develop your argument.

Introduction to the texts being critically reviewed (250–750 words)
▶ A summary of the authors' purposes for each of the three or more texts and of the kind or kinds of enquiry they engaged in, including an indication of the type or types of literature they produced (refer to your answers to critical analysis question 2) and their intellectual projects (refer to your answers to critical analysis question 3).
▶ A brief indication of why these texts are relevant to the questions guiding your critical review (critical analysis question 1).
▶ A brief summary of how they went about their investigation, for example:
  – for a research report, the research design, sample, methods of data collection and analysis;
  – for a research synthesis, the sequence of topics addressed and range of sources employed;
  – for a theoretical work, the main theoretical ideas, the sequence of topics and any use of evidence;
  – for a practical handbook, the sequence of topics addressed and any use of evidence.

The authors' main claims relating to the questions for the critical review (500–1,000 words)
▶ A comparative summary of the main claims made by the authors of each text relevant to key factors promoting or inhibiting the effectiveness of the aspect of practice on which you have chosen to focus (refer to your answers to critical analysis question 4) – a synthesis of, say, up to five main points for each text reviewed, indicating the extent to which there is overlap between texts in the claims made.
▶ An indication of the range of contexts to which the authors claim or appear to claim that their findings may apply (e.g. they imply that their claims about effectiveness apply to all contexts or do not specify any limits on the extent to which they may be universally applicable).

Evaluation of the authors' main claims relating to the review questions for the critical review (1,500–2,000 words)
▶ Your comparative evaluation of these claims, critically assessing how far claims made by the authors of each text are convincing *for the context from which these claims were derived*. (Refer to your answers to critical analysis questions 5–9, possibly referring to additional literature to support your judgement in relation to critical analysis question 8.) In your critique, you may wish to refer back to your earlier account of the authors' purpose, intellectual project and how they went about their enquiry (e.g. you may wish to assert that the value stance of particular authors led to bias which affected their findings).
▶ Your comparative and critical assessment of the extent to which the claims made by the authors of each text may be applicable to *your professional*

context or one known to you (critical analysis questions 5-9, possibly referring to additional literature to support your judgement in relation to critical analysis question 8). In your critique you may wish to refer back to your earlier account of the authors' purpose, intellectual project and how they went about their enquiry (e.g. you may wish to assert that the findings from a particular study project were derived from a context which is so different from yours that you consider the prescriptions for practice emerging from this work are unlikely to apply directly to your context).

Conclusion (250–750 words)
- Your brief overall evaluation of each of the three or more texts reviewed to assess their combined contribution to answering your review questions (refer to your answer to critical analysis question 10).
- The summary answer to the first review question offered by all the texts reviewed, including a statement of your judgement, with reasons, about how far the claims across all three or more texts are convincing for the contexts from which they were derived.
- The summary answer to the second review question, including a statement of your judgement, with reasons, about how far the claims across all three or more texts are applicable (e.g. at how high a level of abstraction?) to your professional context or one known to you.
- Reasons why you think, in the light of your critical review, that it may be difficult to determine effectiveness of this aspect of practice and to apply generalisations about it between contexts.

References
- The list of texts to which you have referred, including those you have analysed in depth, following the normal conventions for compiling a reference list.

In the next chapter we will consider the process and reporting of a small-scale research investigation that is to be assessed. Both the literature review and your other references to it, whether to inform the study or interpret the findings, will be crucial components of your dissertation or thesis. Your ability to be self-critical as a writer will help you to ensure that you demonstrate to the critical readers who assess your work that you have engaged critically with the literature and have developed a convincing argument of your own.

References

Bolam, R. (1999) 'Educational administration, leadership and management: towards a research agenda', in T. Bush, L. Bell, R. Bolam, R. Glatter and P. Ribbins (eds), *Educational Management: Redefining Theory, Policy and Practice*. London: Paul Chapman.

Firestone, W. and Louis, K. S. (1999) 'Schools as cultures', in J. Murphy and K. S. Louis (eds), *Handbook of Research on Educational Administration*. 2nd edn. San Francisco: Jossey-Bass.

March, J. and Olsen, P. (1976) *Ambiguity and Choice in Organizations*. Bergen: Universitetsforlaget.

Chapter 2

Designing and writing about research: developing a critical frame of mind

Louise Poulson and Mike Wallace

We have examined the process of becoming a critical reader of literature, highlighting the connection with applying that knowledge in a self-critical way to designing and writing a research study. It is important that you come to think of yourself as part of a community of critical readers and writers of research. If you are participating in a postgraduate course or research programme, this community experience is a significant part of your induction into the world of academic enquiry. Being critical is partly a frame of mind, but it is also a self-checking mechanism for your work on a research enquiry. It enables you to question your ideas and your writing, and to read it with an awareness of how others may do so.

The purpose of this chapter is to examine the nature of small-scale research, looking at what is possible within such work, and considering what it might contribute to a field of enquiry. First, we discuss challenges that small-scale researchers face, indicating the key components that contribute to high quality empirically based studies. Second, we put forward a model of the logic of the research process, distinguishing what you do from the account you write, and then discuss how researching and writing drafts of your account may be integrated as you go along. We consider some of the compromises that researchers have to make, especially when undertaking studies of modest scope. The emphasis is on applying a critical frame of mind to the dual process of conducting a small-scale research investigation and writing about it. A crucial outcome of your research will be communicating your ideas to other critical readers in the research community. You may be working on a dissertation or a thesis, a crucial part of your academic apprenticeship. Here you learn what researching is about by doing it for yourself and attempting to produce a convincing account of what you have found out. One key critical reader for your writing will be your supervisor and others will be your eventual examiners. Finally, we offer one way of structuring such a written account, consistent with our model and discussion of the research process.

Plenty of books are now available which offer detailed practical advice on the whole research process or on particular aspects of it. If you are undertaking small-scale research, we strongly recommend that you refer to such texts throughout your study. The annotated list in Appendix 1 contains several texts that you could use to supplement our general guidance.

Making the most of small-scale research

While much small-scale research is undertaken for dissertations and theses, many experienced professional researchers periodically engage in studies of similar scope. Sometimes their purpose is to explore a new idea or topic to find out whether it is feasible for a research enquiry, or to pilot a particular approach or instrument prior to undertaking a larger study. At other times small-scale research might be part of a major investigation, as where a case study is conducted of a specific aspect of the wider phenomenon being explored. Large studies often combine different components, each of which may vary widely in scope. The research reports in Part 2 offer examples of such small-scale research and also individual components of larger studies (e.g. Chapter 8), some of which are more ambitious than you could realistically attempt for a dissertation or thesis. However, whilst the context in which such studies were done may be different from that of an individual completing a research investigation for a dissertation or thesis, many principles and procedures are similar. In the physical and natural sciences, doctoral theses may be written about an aspect of a much larger study when students work with their supervisor as part of a team in a laboratory. But in the humanities and the social sciences it is more likely that as a student you will work alone, perhaps researching a problem or an issue arising from your professional context.

A key question for all small-scale researchers is: how much is it possible to achieve in work of modest scope? Even if small in scale, a tightly focused study that is well designed and executed can contribute to the delineation of an issue or problem in the field of enquiry. It may open up a new avenue for investigation, illuminate and exemplify a substantive topic already identified within the field, or approach a familiar substantive issue from a different theoretical perspective. Less commonly, it might even develop a new methodological approach to a topic.

For a dissertation or thesis, one of the first things to do is to clarify the focus and define the parameters of the research. In short, you should identify your intellectual project: consider what you will concentrate on, and what is practicable for a lone researcher with limited resources and a tight time-scale. A challenge facing you is to design a study that is both practicable and of sufficient scope and significance to yield worthwhile data. Be wary of pre-judging what you will find.

Someone may be interested in an example of national policy change and how it impacts on practice in organisations affected. Obviously, a wide-ranging empirical investigation of the national context of policy implementation in a representative sample of organisations would be beyond the scope of most individual dissertations or theses. But an individual researcher could reasonably undertake a clearly delineated study of implementation in a locality, or even a single institution within a bounded time-scale. While the scope of such a study might be limited, if it were carefully thought out and conceptualised it would still have the potential to make a contribution to understanding of the phenomenon. To do so, it would have to be narrowly focused, with a clear specification of what was being undertaken and an explanation of how it would be done. The specific problem or topic being studied would have to be linked to the wider context of the field of enquiry, indicating why it was a significant problem to study. In the example above, this linkage might be to the wider policy context, and perhaps to changing notions of practice in the organisations to implement the change.

A further means of strengthening the significance of a small-scale study is by making clear links between the work being conducted and existing literature in the field and, if appropriate, related fields. These links can be made in relation to three aspects of your enquiry (paralleling the focus for an academic literature review outlined in Chapter 1):

1 the *substantive* focus of the study – the particular topic or issue that constitutes the substance of the investigation within a field of enquiry;
2 the *theoretical* issues – how particular concepts, or theoretical perspectives, may guide and inform the study, and what the strengths and limitations of such perspectives are;
3 *methodological* approaches – in a particular field a methodology might be accepted as standard practice. You may use this approach in your study, or turn to a different methodology, perhaps by attempting to gain in-depth knowledge of a phenomenon in a particular context.

If the investigation makes strong substantive, theoretical and methodological connections with other studies within the field, its potential value will be enhanced. In relation to a dissertation or thesis, you might ask:

▶ How is my study similar to other work in substance, theory or methodology?
▶ In what ways does it build upon or extend previous work and is there other research that confirms the direction of my findings?
▶ What does my study do that has not been done before?

It is important to remember that small-scale research need not always generate its own data. The collection of *primary data* direct from the subjects of your research is often the most time-consuming, expensive and difficult part of an investigation. There are numerous statistical databases and other archive materials now accessible through the internet which could be used as the basis for a study. Gorard (2001) exemplifies how he undertook a piece of small-scale research using *secondary data:* statistical information that had already been collected and was easily available through the internet from government sources. He explains that he started by questioning the assertion made in research literature that schools in Wales did not perform as well as their counterparts in England. He then set out to test this assertion by using existing statistical data to reanalyse the comparative results of equivalent schools in both countries.

Gorard outlines how using secondary data sources enabled him to tackle an important topic that would have been impossible had he attempted to collect the data himself:

> *The findings of this simple value-added analysis ran contrary to the schooled for failure hypothesis (about schools in Welsh LEAs). They defended children, teachers and schools in Wales, and met with considerable local media and some political interest…The complete study, including data collection, transcription and analysis took me one afternoon at an additional cost of less than £10 for photocopying and access to census figures. I would have been very happy to conduct this study for my masters' dissertation instead of traipsing round schools conducting yet another survey (which is what I actually did). I would have saved time, money and produced more interesting results for my discussion section.*
>
> *(Gorard, 2001: 48)*

Note that Gorard had a clearly focused idea for a study. It led to the formulation of a clearly specified hypothesis, firmly grounded within existing research literature. He then tested this hypothesis, not by attempting to collect new evidence himself, but by careful analysis of existing data. The outcome was an example of small-scale research that had wider significance and impact. It also showed how a key to successful small-scale research is achieving a balance between a tightly focused topic embodying a practicable design, and making connections with the wider context in which the problem has arisen.

What makes for a high quality final written account of a small-scale study? Here are the top ten components we, as critical readers, would look for:

1 a clearly-focused substantive topic, with the focus sustained throughout, incorporating a well defined broad central question leading to detailed research questions or hypotheses;
2 a critical review of literature in the field, and clear connections drawn between existing knowledge and the small-scale study (in terms of the substantive topic, theories and concepts, and methodology);
3 an appropriate methodological approach and detailed methods for answering the research questions or testing the hypotheses;
4 a well-structured and explicit design for the study whose methods are fit for their purpose;
5 data that is analysed thoroughly, with the processes of data preparation, summary and analysis clearly set out;
6 discussion of the analysis or findings that relates back to the original research questions or hypotheses, and to the critical review of literature;
7 a reflective summary of what the study has achieved, its strengths and weaknesses, any problematic issues that arose, and any implications for future research (and policy or practice if appropriate);
8 accurate referencing, both in the text and in the reference list so that, in principle, any reference may be followed up;
9 clear expression with attention to writing style, punctuation, spelling and grammar, so that the account may be easily understood;
10 the development of a logical argument from the title to the end of the account, providing as much backing as possible for the claims being made.

Make the most of your small-scale research by bearing these components in mind, together with the principles of self-critical writing outlined in Table1.1 in the previous chapter, when planning the structure and presentation of your dissertation or thesis. It is also advisable to refer from the outset to the statement of criteria used in assessing your work that is likely to be included in the students' handbook for the programme. Ensure that your written account meets each of these criteria.

Box 2.1
Ten pitfalls to be avoided in a small-scale study

1   Too diffuse a focus for the study or attempting to collect too much data to analyse.
2   A descriptive or uncritical review of the literature ('X said this; Y said that.')
3   Lack of linkage between the research questions and the review of literature.
4   No connection made between the research questions and the methodology and detailed methods of data collection chosen for the study.
5   Failure to make explicit how the study was designed: its time-scale, how the research subjects or sites sampled were chosen, how research instruments were designed and tested, or how the data were analysed.
6   Data not analysed in sufficient detail or depth to provide an answer to the research questions.
7   Inadequate description or explanation of what the data showed.
8   Lack of discussion of the findings and their significance, how they answered the research questions, tested the research hypotheses, or illuminated the issues studied.
9   Weak conclusions, and failure to return to the original questions or hypotheses and say what the study has achieved, what problems were encountered, and what issues arose from the work.
10 Over-ambitious or over-generalised recommendations for policy or practice that are not backed by evidence from the study.

Experiencing the reality of the research process

There is bound to be a difference between your experience while you are working through the research process and the final written account of it that you eventually produce at the end of your investigation. Early on, it is not uncommon to feel quite confused. Clarification comes with time because you are learning as the enquiry unfolds. At first, the focus may be diffuse, perhaps based on a hunch that some social practice needs improving. As you start on your literature review and each source leads you to further sources, the amount you feel you should read may seem to be ever expanding. Later on, the research methods you adopt may turn out to produce a mass of data that seems impossible to analyse. Even when writing up your findings you may be unclear how one section fits in with your other sections. Your fullest understanding about what you are doing comes only when you complete the final written account, because you have been learning throughout your research experience.

Yet this account of what you have done and what you have learned must be focused and logical, progressively developing and providing backing for the argument you are putting forward. Everything you have written should be linked to this focus. In our experience as supervisors, the more carefully planned and focused a research enquiry is from the outset, the easier students find it to conduct the research while writing draft sections of their account as they proceed, always working towards a defensible final written account that will stand up to the critical scrutiny of examiners. It is crucial to begin drafting your account from the outset of your study, amending and adding to it as your understanding of what you are doing and knowledge of the field increase. Expect to revise the draft of your introductory chapter several times as you gain clarity about your focus, but to revise the draft conclusion chapter only once.

One possible structure for organising the content of what you write in your dissertation or thesis will be offered at the end of the chapter. But first, we will guide you through a structured approach to the research process, where focusing and writing draft sections of your account are integral parts of your work from beginning to end.

Identifying a practicable topic and focusing your research

Most students begin work for a dissertation or thesis with a general idea of the area they are interested in researching, or a particular issue that they want to address. It is likely that you will begin by identifying a substantive topic. Sources might include:

- your personal or professional experience;
- your current situation;
- your reading of literature in the field;
- a policy context or initiative;
- pilot or exploratory work;
- your supervisor's advice.

You can sharpen up what may start out as a vague idea for a topic by reformulating it as a *central question*, still expressed in general terms, that your investigation will make some contribution towards answering. If, say, you are interested in improving some area of practice in a particular organisation, you might pose this central question in such terms as: how effective is the area of practice in these kinds of organisation, and how may it be improved? Note that the central question is not specific to practice in any particular organisation. It may even help to adopt the central question as your title for your dissertation or thesis as a way of focusing your effort and indicating to your eventual readers the focus of your enquiry.

It is a good idea at this early stage to ask yourself *why* you are interested in the particular topic, and *from where* has the idea come. You might be intrigued by a topic or concerned about a problem that has arisen from your professional practice. It might be a more theoretical issue that you have come across in your reading, which you want to explore in a practical setting. You might want to examine an aspect of policy, or the relationship between policy and practice.

Working out three more specific *aims* for your research will help you further to sharpen your thinking about how you will address this topic and make a contribution to answering the central question:

▶ your *substantive* aim focuses on exactly what you intend to find out about the substantive topic (e.g. to determine factors affecting the effectiveness of some aspect of a policy or practice in a specific context);
▶ your *theoretical* aim focuses on what concepts and, perhaps, over-arching theory you intend to employ to realise your substantive aim (e.g. to employ a particular set of concepts as a framework for investigating your chosen aspect of the policy or practice in this specific context);
▶ your *methodological* aim focuses on how you are going to find out what you will be seeking to realise your substantive aim (e.g. to employ a particular methodology, research design and methods of data collection and analysis to address your central question by investigating the aspect of the policy or practice in this context).

Once you have identified why you are interested in the topic, a further question is: why is this topic important, or worth addressing as a piece of small-scale research? Its significance might relate to your intellectual project, depending on whether you are concerned with understanding the nature of policy and practice, developing a critique, improving practice by informing policy-makers, developing guidance for practitioners, or informing your own practice. Initially, it may not be easy to identify your intellectual project, but as you begin to define and refine your research topic and central question, referring back to our classification of intellectual projects (Table 1.3 in Chapter 1) will help you to clarify the purpose of your study.

In attempting to fulfil your three aims, you will need to think through how you will address related *issues or problems* to which your effort will give rise. Fulfilling your substantive aim will entail deciding exactly which aspects of your substantive topic you will be investigating in detail in the specific context for your investigation. Fulfilling your theoretical aim will entail considering the strengths and limitations of the theory or set of concepts you will be employing to help you focus on particular aspects of the substantive topic. Fulfilling your methodological aim will entail reflecting on the strengths and limitations of the methodological approach to understanding the social world and the methods you will employ to investigate the substantive topic.

The next stage in your thinking is to try expressing the specific aspects of the substantive topic that interest you as initial ideas for more detailed and specific *research questions or hypotheses* that link with your broader central question (e.g. page 177). Suppose it is a policy, or the relationship between a policy and practice. Which particular aspect of that policy are you interested in? Over what period of time? In relation to whom or what? While you may identify research questions early on, you will probably continue clarifying your focus as you read and review the relevant literature, refining your research questions or hypotheses as you proceed.

It is important to make explicit your own *value stance* towards the substantive topic that will affect your intellectual project in undertaking your investigation (see Chapter 7), as we highlighted in the first chapter. Surfacing your value stance is not always easy. People are not always aware of their own beliefs, values and assumptions because they are frequently held as a part of a world-view, or ideology, within which particular practices or beliefs are taken to be normal or natural. However, part of becoming a critical reader and self-critical writer is to raise your awareness of the implicit beliefs, values and assumptions that you hold, and how they might be different from those of others. Your value stance will affect the nature of your central question and so the content and outcomes of your enquiry.

Framing your ideas as a central question and perhaps initial ideas for more detailed research questions is an important step in clarifying what you are aiming to do, and in assessing whether you have identified a practicable study. The gradual process of identifying, refining and answering research questions connected with a more general central question will drive the research process and the associated structure for writing it up, as outlined in Figure 2.1. The logic of the process is first to ask worthwhile focusing questions and then to answer them through your enquiry.

Potentially insightful research questions are characteristically:

▶ capable of being stated clearly and concisely;
▶ answerable because they are specific enough to be investigated convincingly;
▶ new, not having been asked by others already;
▶ practicable, so that they can be answered within the time, resources and methodologies available;
▶ linked to theory, policy or practice.

When starting to frame your thoughts about the central question as specific research questions, you can ask yourself of each one: am I asking a research question that I can feasibly answer within the limits of small-scale research? If the question does not seem possible to answer, then you might ask how you could modify it so that it becomes answerable. Experiment with the formulation of your research questions until they are clear, succinct and focused. You will probably find that your initial ideas for research questions are soon revised. As you begin to review the literature, or undertake pilot work (a preliminary investigation), the research questions may become more specific, or subsidiary questions may be generated. Sometimes the focus of these research questions may shift as you learn more about the topic. Whatever your approach, it is worth reviewing your research questions regularly, and considering whether they should be revised in the light of what you have done or learned. Through doing so, you avoid a situation where you have done interesting work, but the outcome bears little relationship to the original questions with which you started. As you work on identifying a set of research questions, it will be helpful to remind yourself how your questions reflect your intellectual project (Table 1.3).

Figure 2.1 *The logic of the research process as reflected in the written account*

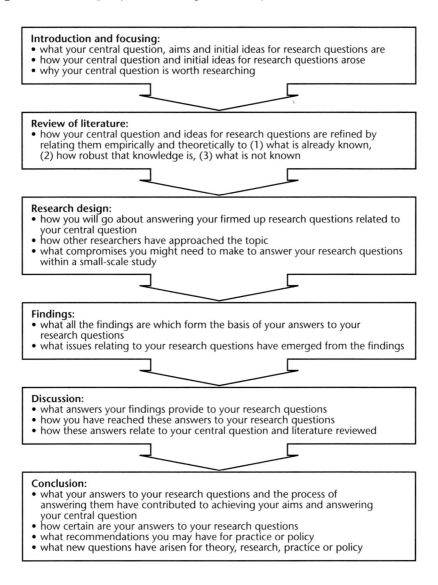

Defining a topic, a central question, a set of research aims, and research questions contribute to developing a critical frame of mind. Examining ideas and possible research questions critically and reflexively will help you to clarify what you want to do, and to justify why your topic and research questions are important and worth studying. This initial thinking provides the basis for writing the first draft of the introductory chapter, where you outline what you are doing and why. In explaining your focus and its justification to your readers, you will also need to provide a background to the topic and the central question. So if you are writing about practice in a particular organisation, you will need to describe what it is, how it operates, and the context in which it is located. You may also explain how it is similar to or different from other comparable organisations. If you are examining an aspect of policy you will need to outline briefly the purpose of the policy and the context of implementation. Alternatively, if you are examining an aspect of policy in a particular national context then you will also need to provide relevant information about it. But the watchwords here are *brevity* and *relevance*. Consider the question: what is the minimum of information that readers require to make sense of my work? Always bear in mind the readers for whom you are writing, and the conventions and expectations of the cultural context in which it will be read.

As a self-critical writer, constantly bear in mind the question: what do the readers need to know next? Provide them with clear signposts to enable them to make connections between one section or chapter and whatever follows (e.g. page 174). There is an old saying: 'First, tell them what you are going to tell them. Then tell them. Finally, tell them what you have told them!' You can provide signposts at the end of your introductory chapter and the beginning and end of each chapter that follows. At the end of the introduction and the end of each subsequent chapter, offer a brief summary of what has been discussed or presented, and (except for last chapter) an indication of what will come in the next chapter. At the beginning of each chapter after the introduction, give an outline stating what topics will be covered in that chapter.

Applying critical reading to your own ideas for research questions

As you identify a practicable topic and define the parameters of a possible study, you will need to find out what is already known about the topic, and whether similar research questions to yours have been asked before. This is where your skill as a critical reader will be applied in reviewing existing research literature. An important part of the process will involve the development of a mental map to guide you through what initially may appear to be a complex, diverse and even contradictory body of work. The mental map outlined in Chapter 1 consisted of:

- one set of tools for thinking;
- two dimensions of variation in claims to knowledge;
- three kinds of knowledge generated;
- four types of literature;
- five sorts of intellectual project.

You will be applying the tools for thinking to ask review questions about the chapters, books and articles you read. These review questions will be related to your research questions. You are likely to ask the same review question of a group of relevant texts, as with Exercise 2 in Chapter 1. There, the two review questions we suggested you seek to answer in each exercise were concerned with the substantive focus of a study, concentrating on the factors promoting or inhibiting the effectiveness of a particular aspect of practice in the field of enquiry. Your central question and initial research questions will enable you to identify your own review questions to inform the substantive focus of your enquiry.

A part of the literature review that many students find difficult is that which concerns the theoretical or conceptual focus of a study. The theoretical orientation for your investigation consists of the tools for thinking embodied in theoretical knowledge that others have used to analyse substantive issues, and that you might wish to consider for your framing your own analysis. You might generate a review question about the theoretical orientations of authors who have done research relevant to your substantive focus. Review questions and sub-questions that you might ask of a group of texts could include:

▶ What are the main *concepts* that different authors are using or developing in this group of texts?
  – Do they offer a clear stipulative definition of the key ideas?
  – If they do not do so, are there any implicit definitions?
  – Do different authors within the field differ in their stipulative definition of key concepts?
  – How do these concepts relate to my research questions – are some more helpful than others?
▶ What are the main *perspectives* evident in work in this field of enquiry?
  – Are any perspectives associated with particular disciplines (e.g. social psychology, sociology) and so likely to make particular assumptions about the social world?
  – Which perspectives appear to fit best with my research questions?
  – How do the perspectives relate to my intellectual project and to my values?
▶ Are any *metaphors* used to interpret or represent the social world?
  – What do these metaphors indicate about their users' assumptions about the social world?
  – How accurately do these metaphors reflect the aspect of the social world that they are used to interpret?
▶ What *theories* or *models* are used?
  – Are these theories and models made explicit?
  – Are they descriptive or normative, and if the latter, do I share their authors' values?
▶ What *assumptions* or *ideologies* can be detected within the group of texts (and these are often the least explicit aspects of authors' theoretical or conceptual orientation)?
  – What is the value-stance of the authors?
  – How does the value-stance of these authors relate to my values?

You will also need to evaluate the claims to theoretical, research or practice knowledge made in groups of related texts, and to identify what kind of knowledge is being claimed. These claims may be made with varying degrees of certainty and assertions about their generalisability to many contexts. Remember that the greater the degree of certainty and the higher the claim to generalisability, then the stronger the evidence will have to be for such assertions to be convincing.

Whilst reviewing the literature in a field, you will probably read a large amount of material. The mental map will help you to make sense of what may appear at first to be a diverse and sometimes contradictory body of work.

Throughout, keep in mind that a review of literature is connected to the rest of the study. It is not a discrete section of a thesis or dissertation, but has a vital function within the study as a whole. The main purposes for a critical literature review are to:

▶ locate your own central question and research questions in relation to existing work;
▶ assist you in developing an argument about the substantive topic;
▶ frame your research theoretically, including the choice of concepts as tools for thinking about the substantive topic;
▶ justify your choice of methodology and methods, while acknowledging their limitations.

Once you have begun to familiarise yourself with the literature in the relevant field, you will use your understanding to inform the construction of your own study. An important part of learning to read critically involves evaluating the literature in terms of its relevance to your research questions. You may find that someone has already asked similar questions, but their research was undertaken with a different population, or from a different perspective. They might also have highlighted areas that need further work, gaps in what is known, or limits to current methodologies. Such work can help you to refine your research questions, locate your study theoretically and conceptually, and make some claim to an original contribution within a field.

A further stage in the process is that of synthesising critical reading of many texts from the literature into a persuasive argument within your own written account (see Chapter 6). Here you are not merely identifying who said what and when about a topic, but rather guiding your writing by asking yourself, and answering, review questions that summarise what you have learned from the literature in relation to your central question, including:

1 What is known about the topic I am researching, and from what types of literature?
2 What are the most important 'landmark' works within the field?
3 Which areas of this work are centrally relevant to my topic and research questions?
4 How robust is the claim to knowledge in particular texts and across groups of texts?
5 What range of positions and approaches exist in relation to this topic?
6 What are the major relevant debates and disagreements among researchers within the field?
7 What have been the main approaches and methodologies used in researching relevant problems in this field?
8 What is my own position in relation to the way relevant problems in the field have been researched, and my justification for taking it?
9 Where are the relevant gaps and weaknesses within the field (substantive, theoretical and methodological)?
10 How will answering my research questions make a contribution to the literature in this field of enquiry?

The review of literature should lead smoothly into the next chapter of a dissertation or thesis, which is an explanation and justification of the methodology, research design and methods of data collection and analysis you have adopted.

Methodology and research design

You will probably begin writing in draft about your research design long before you implement it. Here we will concentrate on what should go into the final written account, and so, by implication, what you should have thought through before actually collecting your primary or secondary data. Communicating your research to others will involve stating how you did it, how you arrived at particular conclusions, and on what basis you are making any claim to knowledge. For any empirical study, it is necessary to make clear the process by which you conducted the research and to justify why you took your approach. Decisions about methodology and methods of data collection and analysis are not made in a vacuum. A justification of methodology needs to be made in relation to the firmed up research questions, to the kind of knowledge to which you are seeking to contribute, to your values and philosophical assumptions about the nature of the social world, and to accepted or established ways of conducting research within your field of enquiry. The theoretical framework of a study also informs the way in which that work will best be conducted (e.g. pages 153–4).

Amongst common weaknesses in discussions of methodology in dissertations or theses are three particularly to avoid. First, there is a tendency to rehearse 'paradigm war' debates. Such discussions describe the key features of different methodologies used in educational research and their underlying ontological and epistemological assumptions, but only discuss the strengths and weaknesses of different approaches in very generalised terms. Second, many discussions outline possible methodological approaches, but then assume that there is an obvious approach to take for a particular topic without justifying why it is the accepted way of proceeding. They offer little discussion of any alternative approaches that might have been taken. Third, sometimes the discussion of methodology is largely unconnected to the substantive research questions addressed by the investigation, a theoretical framework, existing work within the field, or to the researcher's philosophical assumptions about the nature of the social world. As we stated earlier, there should be explicit links between each section of any research report. As each section, or chapter, is drafted and revised, try to keep in mind a clear sense of its purpose in the overall text.

A brief review of relevant literature relating to the methodological issues or problems arising from your attempt to find an answer to your research questions will help you justify what you are doing by reference to others' approaches. Following from the discussion of methodology, a good research report will make explicit the overall design of the empirical investigation, and how the design relates to the firmed up research questions. In effect the research design is how you operationalise those questions. Whether researchers follow a largely quantitative or qualitative methodology, readers need to know how the investigation was conducted and the structure that guided it. Ideally, the account should give readers enough information for them to be in a position to do the same or similar research. It is sometimes suggested that in studies which are largely qualitative and interpretative, research design is either unnecessary or less important: researchers do not set out with any pre-specified questions, but wait to see what emerges from the research setting, and then interpret what they have experienced. In exploratory studies the research design is often more flexible, allowing for the inclusion of elements at a later stage of the research process, but this is not the same as having no design! Miles and Huberman (1994: 16-17) raise exactly this issue, cautioning against the problems arising from under-designed qualitative projects, especially for inexperienced researchers:

> *Contrary to what you might have heard, qualitative research designs do exist. Some are more deliberate than others...Any researcher, no matter how unstructured, comes to fieldwork with some orientating ideas...Highly inductive, loosely designed studies make good sense when experienced researchers have plenty of time and are exploring exotic cultures, understudied phenomena, or very complex social phenomena. But if you are new to qualitative studies and are looking at a better understood phenomenon...a loose inductive design may be a waste of time...Tighter designs also provide clarity and focus for beginning researchers worried about diffuseness and overload.*

All researchers set out with some idea of what they are aiming to do, why, where, how and with whom. It is questions relating to the what, where, how and with whom aspects of a study that guide the research design. For relatively inexperienced researchers, it is important both to create a well-structured research design and to represent this design as clearly and succinctly as possible in the final written account of the work. The research design offers readers a map of your investigation. It enables them to see how all the elements of the study fit together, over what period of time the study was conducted, what instruments or methods were used to collect data and at what intervals, who the research subjects or informants were, and why and how they were chosen.

In small-scale research it is crucial to have considered at the design stage what you could feasibly do, and what compromises you should make to ensure that a project was practicable but also rigorous. Such compromises might relate to the design of the study, the range of data collected and the population or sites sampled. A small number of research sites or respondents might be chosen, particularly if it were a labour-intensive qualitative or mixed-method study (see Chapter 3). Here the trade-off is likely to be between depth and breadth. The number of sites or people would need to be chosen carefully to ensure that the research questions could be adequately answered from the data gathered, and the potential for generalisation from them made clear. However, a strong study can still be undertaken with a limited number of sites. Whilst there are many examples of experimental studies being undertaken for theses and dissertations (especially in psychology) with a large number of research subjects, the potential is limited for a single researcher to undertake larger-scale experimental or quasi-experimental designs, such as intervention studies or evaluations.

It is important in writing about the research design to give an account of particular choices or compromises made, and the reasons for so doing (e.g. page 160). Explaining such decisions, discussing the problems encountered and indicating how you have attempted to address them all help your readers to understand the rationale for your design. You also demonstrate to them that you are capable of reflecting self-critically on your work and evaluating the strengths and limitations of particular choices. The strongest dissertations or theses are not necessarily ones in which no difficulty was experienced. They may be ones where challenges are discussed, how they were met is explained, and a reflective account is offered on what was learned in addressing them. It is another aspect of the process of becoming a critical reader and self-critical writer of research.

Once the overall design of the research has been set out succinctly, you are in a position to explain in more detail the methods and instruments used in the study. They will include methods or instruments used to gather and analyse the data, an account of how you chose the population or sites that formed your sample, and how any ethical issues were addressed (such as permission to access research sites, protecting the identity of informants, or any issues related to working with children or other research subjects). Self-critical writers of research make their choices and procedures as transparent as possible, reflecting on the strengths and limitations of a particular method, instrument or approach to sampling. Here are some self-critical questions to ask as you approach writing about the conduct of your research:

1 Why were the methods or instruments used the most effective in the circumstances for generating data to answer the research questions?
2 How were the instruments designed and constructed (e.g. questionnaires, attitude scales, observation or interview schedules)?
3 How were the instruments checked to ensure that they worked as they were intended to do, or represented what they were intended to represent (e.g. whether questionnaire questions made sense to respondents, or whether items on an attitude scale adequately represented concepts being investigated, and measured adequately what they were intended to measure)?
4 What steps were taken to ensure that the instruments or procedures worked reliably, and were applied consistently across all contexts in which they were used?
5 How were any methods or instruments tested or piloted and what modifications were made as a result of any piloting?
6 What was the population studied (e.g. where the research was conducted, who the informants were, how and why they were chosen, and how access was gained to them)?
7 What were the strengths and limitations of choosing to investigate the particular research population?
8 What events or processes were studied within each site, and how frequently were they sampled (e.g. how they were selected, and the extent to which they represented the full range that could have been studied)?
9 What documents were sampled from research sites (e.g. how they were accessed, from where the documents originated and who authored them)?
10 Overall, what data was collected?

Once you have explained how, where and when you collected data, your next task is to outline the process by which you checked, summarised and analysed it. This part of the research process is easily overlooked in writing up a study, but is crucial in a dissertation or thesis to inform your examiners how you prepared the data for analysis and carried out the analysis itself (e.g. pages 180–2). How the analysis was done tends not to feature in published accounts of research because they are generally subject to strict word limits. We refer you to any of the many research methodology textbooks, including those in our annotated list in Appendix 1, which deal with checking and cleaning data sets and how to code and summarise them.

The critical readers of your work will expect you to make explicit the procedures used for checking, summarising and analysing data because they need to be convinced that the claims you make on the basis of your analysis are well grounded in the procedures you adopted. If the data set is quantitative, or rather has quantifiable variables, then you will need to explain what statistical procedures and tests were conducted and why, from the most basic, such as analysis of frequencies, to the more complex. It is inadequate merely to state that the data set was analysed using a computer software package. Such packages are tools to help organise data and do operations speedily, but it is you, the researcher, who decides what forms of analysis will be done and in what order. Equally, there are several computer software packages that will help you analyse qualitative data, but they do not make the decisions for you about how a data set will be analysed. Procedures for coding and analysing qualitative data are less standardised than for quantitative data, adding to the importance of making them explicit in a dissertation or thesis. Underpinning such explanations, as ever, should be an awareness of the audience for your writing: a good account of your analytic procedure should enable your examiners to follow exactly how the procedure was carried out. It should leave them, in principle, in a position to replicate the analysis and reach similar conclusions.

A concluding reflective consideration of the strengths and limitations of your design, in the light of your review of the relevant methodological literature, rounds off the discussion of how you did the empirical work. Let your readers know where your account is taking them next by signposting them towards the account of what you found when you implemented your design.

Presentation of findings

This part of your account is central: it sets out the evidence on which your argument will rest. As with the research design, you can help yourself by thinking through before you collect data how you are going to structure and present the written account of what you find and your analysis of the findings. The purpose of the research design is to explain how that evidence was gathered, synthesised and tested or interpreted. The account of findings should show the outcome of the research: how the research questions were answered, or the results of any hypothesis testing. The research questions, or hypotheses, will then provide the basis for structuring your presentation of your findings. Provide a signpost for your readers by explaining in an introductory section for this part of your report how the presentation of findings will be organised, what each section will address, how these sections link to relevant previous chapters or sections (especially to the section containing the specification of your research questions).

A key decision is how you will present and display the findings. Presentation of the findings should be guided by the research questions you have asked. The type of data you have collected largely determines how you display your findings, and how you will have analysed them. If you have done a study involving variables analysed quantitatively, then the presentation will involve text, graphs, tables and charts. There are conventional ways of presenting statistical analysis of data in tabular form, to which you should adhere (see Chapter 8). A simple but important step is to check that you have included all the information in the table that is necessary for your readers to interpret it. Whatever the conventions of presenting numerical data, any tables, charts or graphs need to be labelled, making clear what they represent. In the text there should be an explanation of what the table shows. To a certain extent, the content of tables, graphs or charts may be self-evident, but it is part of your academic apprenticeship to learn how to explain them accurately and succinctly.

With data that consists largely of text, any themes or patterns found in the data will be presented, together with your interpretation of them, explaining how the evidence answers the research questions (see Chapter 4). A problematic issue for many qualitative researchers is how much textual data, such as quotations from informants, to include in presenting findings. There are no hard and fast rules about this, but readers should be provided with enough evidence to see how an interpretation was reached. One tactic is to include a range of short quotations from informants that highlight a particular phenomenon or pattern of meaning and, if there are any, quotations from informants that do not fit the pattern. Another is to indicate what was the most common finding within the overall range, backed by illustrative quotations for the most common finding and the extremes of the range. Researchers presenting qualitative data need to be particularly careful not to appear to have chosen data selectively to support their pre-judged interpretation: developing an argument first, and selecting and presenting examples of data that support it later.

Some questions to ask of any textual data presented in a research account are:

▶ How and why was this example chosen?
▶ How typical is it of other events, or of comments or responses on this issue?
▶ Were there any other examples which could have been selected that might suggest a different interpretation?

Miles and Huberman (1994) argue that presentation of qualitative data in summarised forms, such as matrices or charts, can help to make clear the overall patterns. Ultimately, it depends on you, the researcher – and the questions you have asked – whether you present qualitative analysis of data in this form, or present only segments from texts of interviews, documents or observations. The key point is that you should be explicit about selecting particular data presented in a chapter on findings.

The final section of the chapter presenting findings in a thesis or dissertation should be a summary of the key findings and any issues arising. You are, in effect, reminding your readers what you have done in the chapter. It is here also that you will signal to them where these issues will be taken up subsequently.

Discussion of findings and conclusion

The chapters or sections containing the discussion of findings and conclusions often present a considerable challenge to students. Avoid the temptation to move straight from setting out the findings to conclusions and recommendations. If you find this part of the research process difficult, one possible reason is that that you will have become very familiar with your work, and assume that what you know is obvious to your readers. Another issue is that researchers often attempt to discuss the implications of findings within a section, as they are presented. There is a certain logic to this approach, especially with qualitative data. However, it is also necessary to discuss the *overall* significance of findings and their relationship to the wider issues connected with your substantive topic. Relating findings to the wider substantive, theoretical and methodological issues identified in the review of literature can easily be neglected by attempting to present findings and discuss their implications at the same time. The key to this part of the dissertation or thesis is *critical reflection*. After the findings have been presented, the discussion of them is an opportunity to take a step back from the work and exercise the critical frame of mind that you have been developing (e.g. pages 192–5). In summary, the discussion section in a research report, or chapter in a thesis is where you:

▶ highlight what was particularly important or significant about the findings in relation to your central question;
▶ comment on any unexpected, or unusual findings (depending on the extent to which the study was exploratory and open-ended);
▶ return to discuss the substantive, theoretical and methodological issues identified earlier, and link key findings from your work with the literature reviewed.

In other words, the discussion section or chapter is where you establish the links between your findings and the wider field of enquiry: the contribution that your research makes to this field. Establishing such links is particularly important for small-scale research. Whilst your study, in itself, may make only a modest contribution to the field, it might also add to the accumulation of knowledge and understanding of relevant social phenomena and practices. The wider field in which your study is located might also lend confirmatory strength to your findings. Remember to indicate how you will draw conclusions about the implications of your findings for your research questions and, in turn, your more general central question.

In the conclusion of your account, you pull all aspects of the work together, consider with what degree of certainty the study answered your research questions, and highlight what it implies for your central question. You also have an opportunity to:

▶ evaluate the extent to which you achieved your substantive, theoretical and methodological aims;

▶ evaluate the overall theoretical framework, methodology and research design;

▶ reflect on the work as a whole;

▶ identify and discuss what has been learned;

▶ consider what you might have done differently if you conducted the research again with the experience and knowledge you now have;

▶ outline any implications for future research, and set out a possible research programme;

▶ suggest any implications or make any recommendations for improving policy or practice.

You may well discover that your research has generated as many further questions as the ones it has answered, and you may be able to suggest wider implications for future research (e.g. page 195), or identify a research programme to be undertaken in the future. There may be implications for policy or practice, and it is essential that you connect any recommendations for improvement with evidence from your research. Otherwise why should your sceptical readers be convinced to accept your recommendations? It is unwise to over-generalise from your findings, for example advocating that a national policy should be reformed on the basis of one small-scale study. Here it is worth returning to Figure 1.1 in Chapter 1 and using the critical questions about claims to knowledge to help you reflect self-critically on your work and evaluate the extent to which you can generalise in making recommendations from your small-scale investigation.

Box 2.2
The 'linkage tracker test' for accounts of a research enquiry

Every part of a defensible account of research should link logically together, from the title, with its keywords indicating the focus of the study, through the central question being addressed, the literature review, the research questions, the research design, the data collection instruments, the summary of the findings, the analysis and discussion of the findings, the conclusions and any recommendations, to the reference list and any appendices.

How well do all the parts of your written account of your research link together? As critical readers of your work, dissertation and thesis supervisors and examiners are likely to look out for any digressions and for any claims or arguments that have not been adequately backed up. Ensure that your dissertation or thesis is defensible by constructing a logical account of your research, and then applying the linkage tracker test to it.

▶

The linkage tracker test for self-critical writers

First select any piece of the text, including a table, figure, reference, or appendix. Then ask yourself two questions:

1 Why is this material here?
2 How does this material relate to the stated focus of the research?

It should be clear why anything is included in your account, and how it relates to the stated focus of the research.

Second, try tracking the logical links between parts of your account, going forwards in the direction of the conclusions and any recommendations, and backwards towards the introduction and the title. There should be a logical sequence from title to recommendations or from recommendations to title. Anything that is not directly or indirectly linked might be irrelevant to answering your research questions. If so, do you think it should it be removed?

The linkage tracker test for critical readers

The linkage tracker test may be applied to any written account of research. Your supervisor or examiner may apply it to your work. But as a critical reader yourself, you will find it instructive to apply the linkage tracker test to others' work. You might try applying it to any of the research report chapters in this book.

Once you have drafted the conclusion, you have reached a point that probably seemed impossible when you were starting out on the work for your dissertation or thesis. But whilst a full draft of the manuscript has been completed, there is further work to be done. Check through the logic of your account, from title to final recommendation, and be prepared to revise earlier sections where you were not as clear about what you were doing as you have become as you near the end of the process. Pay careful attention to presentation of your work. Countless manuscripts submitted for masters and doctoral degrees, and to the editorial boards of journals, contain errors that could easily have been corrected by the writer. Sloppy presentation, inaccuracies, poor bibliographic referencing, and inattention to detail can undermine a potentially impressive piece of work. Again, remember to put your critical frame of mind to work: apply self-critically to your own writing the critical reading strategies that you have developed in relation to other texts.

Structuring the written acccount of the research

There are various ways to structure the final written account that constitutes your dissertation or thesis itself. Figure 2.2 summarises the sort of structure that is commonly employed in the humanities and social sciences for a study involving empirical research. You might wish to use it as a starting point for thinking through the structure of your account, and possibly as a checklist to ensure that you include all the necessary components. Our framework reflects the logic of the research process we have discussed. (Each chapter in the framework covers the logical ground of the ideas in the parallel arrow box in Figure 2.1.) The suggested structure contains more detail of the components of your account that might be included in a particular chapter. You may wish to adapt this structure to suit the logic of your enquiry. One issue for you may be over how much ground to cover in each chapter. You may want to separate out parts of the literature review or the findings into more than one chapter, or to combine the presentation of findings with their discussion in the same chapter. Whichever way you structure the account, the components should all be there, in a clear and logical progression that together develop and provide backing for your argument. Never lose sight of your priority to ensure that the claims you make in your written account are sufficiently backed by evidence to convince the critical readers who will evaluate your work – your examiners.

Figure 2.2 *A possible structure for your dissertation or thesis*

COMPONENTS OF A DISSERTATION OR THESIS: A CHECKLIST

Title
▶ Containing keywords that reflect the central question you are seeking to answer, expressed in general terms.

Abstract
▶ A brief summary (say, around 200 words) of the purpose of the study, any empirical work, and your main conclusions.

Acknowledgements
▶ Any acknowledgement you wish to make of the support of individuals (e.g. your supervisor, your family) and of the co-operation of informants.

Chapter 1   Introduction
▶ A statement of purpose – to contribute to answering a central question expressed in general terms, usually about a substantive topic in your field of enquiry.
▶ A summary of the more specific aims of your research.
    – *substantive* (e.g. to determine factors affecting the effectiveness of some aspect of policy or practice in a specific context);
    – *theoretical* (e.g. to employ a specified set of concepts as a framework for investigating the effectiveness of this aspect of a policy or practice in this context);
    – *methodological* (e.g. to employ a particular methodology, research design and methods of data collection and analysis to address the central question by investigating the aspect of a policy or practice in this context).
▶ A justification of the significance of the substantive topic (e.g. its importance for policy or practice).

▶

▶ A statement of your value position in relation to this topic that shapes the focus of your enquiry.
▶ A statement of the broad issues or problems linked to the specific aims of your research to be investigated in addressing the central question:
  – *substantive* (indicating which aspects of the substantive topic identified in the central question you will be investigating in detail);
  – *theoretical* (considering the strengths and limitations of the theory or set of concepts you are using to help you understand and analyse the substantive topic relating to the central question);
  – *methodological* (considering the strengths and limitations of the methodological paradigm and methods you are using to investigate the substantive topic in addressing the central question).
▶ A brief description of the context of your enquiry. If you are investigating practice in a country other than the one in which you are studying for your dissertation or thesis, you may wish to insert a section outlining the national context relevant to your central question.
▶ An outline of the rest of the study – offering signposts to the content of the remaining chapters and how they develop your argument.

Chapter 2   Review of literature
▶ An introduction which offers signposts to what will be covered in each section.
▶ A *critical and focused* review of the literature guided by review questions relating to your substantive and theoretical issues or problems in turn. It is likely that most of the emphasis will be placed on the substantive area, then theoretical.
▶ A brief summary of your position concerning your substantive and theoretical issues or problems in the light of your review.
▶ The identification of one or more detailed research questions related to the central question.
▶ An indication of how the research design chapter will take forward your work in relation to the substantive and theoretical areas and your research questions.

Chapter 3   Research design
▶ An introduction setting out what you are going to cover in each section.
▶ Your research questions and/or hypotheses focusing on detailed aspects of the substantive topic that relate to the central question.
▶ The theoretical framework you are using to help you understand and analyse the substantive topic relating to the central question.
▶ A brief critical and focused review of the literature relating to your methodological issues or problems, indicating how other researchers have approached them and have investigated similar substantive topics.
▶ A brief summary of your position concerning your methodological issues or problems in the light of your review.
▶ Your methodology and methods:
  – a justification for the methodological paradigm within which you are working;
  – detailed methods of data collection you are using and your justification for using them;
  – specification of the sample of informants and your rationale for selecting them from the wider population;

- – a summary description of your data collection instruments indicating how research questions and/or hypotheses about the substantive topic are addressed and your rationale for using the instruments chosen;
- – a summary of the data collection effort (e.g. piloting, the number of interviews or the number of individuals surveyed);
- – a summary of how data are to be analysed (e.g. statistical methods, use of matrices for qualitative data);
- – ethical factors (e.g. confidentiality of interviews);
- – the timetable for the research process (e.g. timing of first and second rounds of interviews).
- ▶ A concluding reflective consideration of the strengths and limitations of your design (e.g. reliability, internal and external validity, sample size relative to population size) and an indication that you will evaluate the design in the concluding chapter.
- ▶ An indication of how the presentation of the findings chapter will present the results of implementing this design to answer your research questions and/or test your hypotheses.

Chapter 4   Presentation of findings
- ▶ An introduction where you set out the ground to be covered in each section.
- ▶ A summary of all the findings broken down into topics relating to the research questions and/or hypotheses, possibly supported by tables and matrices, diagrams and quotations from informants.
- ▶ A concluding summary of key findings and emerging issues you have identified.
- ▶ An indication of where they will be taken up in the discussion chapter.

Chapter 5   Discussion of findings
- ▶ An introduction where you set out the ground to be covered in each section.
- ▶ A discussion of topics identified earlier relating to the substantive, theoretical and methodological broad issues or problems, linking your key findings with your research questions and the literature you have reviewed.
- ▶ A concluding summary of how the key findings together provide a response to your substantive, theoretical and methodological broad issues or problems.
- ▶ An indication of where you will draw conclusions about the contribution of your findings to answering your central question in the conclusion and recommendations chapter.

Chapter 6   Conclusion and recommendations
- ▶ An introduction where you set out the ground to be covered in each section.
- ▶ Your conclusions relating to your substantive, theoretical and methodological aims, including an evaluation of your research design and the certainty of your answers to your research questions, in the light of the findings and experience of using your theoretical framework and methods.
- ▶ Implications of your findings overall for answering the central question expressed in general terms.
- ▶ Any recommendations for different audiences (e.g. policy-makers, researchers, trainers) with reference to their backing from the evidence you have gathered.

▶

▶ Any new questions that arise from your study for theory, research, practice or policy.
▶ A final concluding statement which includes your summary contribution to answering the central question posed in the introduction and related to the title.

Reference list
▶ Containing all works to which reference is made in the text, but not background material to which you have not made direct reference.
▶ In alphabetical author order, and in the required format.

Appendices
▶ For example, research instruments, letters to informants, examples of raw data.

In this chapter we have indicated how the principles and procedures for becoming a critical reader of research can be developed and applied to the design and writing of a small-scale research study. We have offered one model of the process of designing and writing of a project that might be used to guide a dissertation, thesis, or other small-scale investigation. It is not a definitive model, but rather a pragmatic one, based on experience of doing small-scale research and supervising masters and doctoral projects.

Part 2 contains a selection of reports on small-scale research and components of larger studies by established researchers in the field of enquiry covered in this book. They include work from a range of perspectives and national contexts. Each chapter has an editorial introduction. In their research report, authors indicate how they addressed various issues connected with their research design and methods. Part 3 is the literature review chapter which exemplifies how a review may be structured. The chapters are briefer than masters' dissertations or doctoral theses. Since they were written for publication rather than examination they will not be structured in precisely the same way as a dissertation or thesis, nor will they necessarily include every component in our checklist. What you will be unable to see (but you can rest assured that it did happen) is the careful drafting and redrafting that lies behind the final accounts presented. Nevertheless, there is much you can learn from the authors' account of how they approached the research process and from the structure and content of their final written report for critical readers like yourself.

References

Gorard, S. (2001) *Quantitative Methods in Educational Research.* London: Continuum.
Miles, M. and Huberman, M. (1994) *Qualitative Data Analysis.* New York: Sage.

Part 2

Meeting the challenge of reporting research

Chapter 3

Changing instructional and assessment practices through professional development

Hilda Borko with Kathryn Davinroy,

Carribeth Bliem and Kathryn Cumbo

In this chapter, Hilda Borko and her colleagues provide in-depth analysis of the process of change experienced by two teachers as they participated in a long-term programme of professional development to encourage and support new practices in mathematics assessment. The research presented here aimed to contribute to a better understanding of how and why teachers' beliefs and practices may change – and the relationship between them in that process of change. In this respect, it can be characterised as a knowledge-for-understanding intellectual project according to the model outlined in Chapter 1. However, the study was also part of a larger project that involved collaboration between researchers, teacher educators and classroom practitioners. This larger project aimed to generate knowledge to improve practice and, therefore, can be characterised as a knowledge-for-action intellectual project, which also aimed to create knowledge-for-understanding. An important dimension of the work is the researchers' commitment to working with teachers, who were treated as active learners. This explicit value stance is highlighted in the chapter.

Borko and her colleagues outline how detailed case studies of two teachers (Elly and Lena) were constructed, making explicit the research questions and the criteria used to select the teachers and the schools in which they worked. They also explain how data from multiple sources including interviews and observation were combined within the cases, and how the process of analysis was guided by a clear conceptual framework. This framework, in turn, was informed by existing research and theory related to the study. In addition to guiding the analysis of data, the conceptual framework helped to structure the presentation and discussion of findings. The researchers highlight the unique contribution the study made to the literature on teacher learning and professional development.

One of the important substantive issues addressed in this research is the complex nature of the relationship between teachers' beliefs and practices as they attempted to change the way they assessed students' learning in the classroom. The chapter indicates how the relationship between the beliefs and practices of the two teachers differed, and how these differences partly related to their individual identity and personal biography. Borko and colleagues discuss how the introduction of new teaching and assessment practices also challenged some aspects of the teachers' wider beliefs about what it meant to be a good teacher. The chapter identifies and discusses unexpected and surprising findings. For example, although the focus of the project and professional development programme was assessment, the teachers' approach to assessment changed less than their instructional practices.*

Research background and purpose

Here we will examine the process of change experienced by two veteran teachers – Elly Marks and Lena Schwartz – during their participation in the University of Colorado (CU) Assessment Project. (All names used in this chapter are pseudonyms.) The CU Assessment Project was a multi-year staff development and research project. Its purpose was to help teachers design and implement classroom-based performance assessments compatible with their instructional goals in mathematics and literacy. Case studies of these teachers' experiences reveal what we learned about the process of teacher change and factors that facilitated and impeded that process.

The CU Assessment Project was, in part, a response to national interest in performance assessment that has grown in conjunction with the educational reform movement in the USA. There is not a single vision of reform in this country; however the reform agenda in mathematics (the focus of this chapter) has been strongly influenced by a set of documents published by the National Council of Teachers of Mathematics (NCTM), beginning with *Curriculum and Evaluation Standards for School Mathematics* (NCTM, 1989). In classrooms aligned with the vision of reform portrayed in these standards, teachers engage students in rich, meaningful tasks as part of a coherent curriculum. Students' thinking, shared orally and in writing, is used by teachers to guide the classroom community's exploration of important mathematical ideas. The teachers gather information from many sources as they assess their students' understanding of these ideas. Advocates of this reform vision call for assessments that better address educational goals, such as higher-order thinking, reasoning, problem-solving, communication, and conceptual understanding of subject matter, and that are more closely linked with instruction (Resnick and Resnick, 1992; Stiggins, 1991; Wiggins, 1989). For example, *Assessment Standards for School Mathematics,* another of the four reform documents published by NCTM, defines the mathematics education community's task with respect to assessment (NCTM, 1995: 1): 'New assessment strategies and practices need to be developed that will enable teachers and others to assess students' performance in a manner that reflects the NCTM's reform vision for school mathematics.' Assessment activities should:

* This chapter is based on an article published in the *Elementary School Journal* (Borko et al. 2000). The CU Assessment Project was part of a larger research project, Studies in Improving Classroom and Local Assessments, supported in part by the Office of Educational Research and Improvement, US Department of Education (OERI), through the National Center for Research on Evaluation, Standards, and Student Testing (CRESST). Any opinions, findings, and conclusions or recommendations expressed in this publication are those of the authors and do not necessarily reflect the views of other project team members, CRESST, or OERI.

...provide all students with opportunities to formulate problems, reason mathematically, make connections among mathematical ideas, and communicate about mathematics. Students engage in solving realistic problems using information and the technological tools available in real life. Moreover, skills, procedural knowledge, and factual knowledge are assessed as part of the doing of mathematics.

(NCTM, 1995: 11)

Performance assessments are one approach to achieving these goals. When embedded in daily classroom life, they help to ensure that teachers are evaluating the same goals that they emphasise in instruction. The extended responses that are required yield information about individual students' thinking that teachers can use in tailoring instruction to meet their needs (Wiggins, 1989).

The transformation in knowledge, beliefs, and practices required to enact these new visions of instruction and assessment is one that teachers are unlikely to make without support and guidance. As a consequence, researchers who study educational reform are calling for increased attention to support for teachers (e.g. Borko and Putnam, 1996; Cohen and Ball, 1990). There is a growing body of research on projects that support teacher change within the context of educational reform (e.g. Carpenter et al., 1996; Marx et al., 1994; Richardson, 1994a). Our project adds to that literature.

The CU team's approach to staff development was guided by the project's overall purpose – to help teachers design and enact classroom-based performance assessments compatible with their instructional goals – as well as our assumptions about teacher learning. We believed that the teachers would actively construct their assessment ideas and practices based on their staff development experiences, as well as their existing knowledge and beliefs (e.g. Prawat and Floden, 1994; Putnam and Borko, 1997). We therefore decided to meet with participating teachers in weekly workshop sessions, creating within them an ongoing forum for the joint exploration of assessment activities and issues. These sessions would be structured to foster the kinds of active participation and problem-solving that we hoped the teachers would promote in their own classrooms. We planned the workshops to take into account the teachers' existing ideas and practices as well as the educational reform community's vision of classroom assessment.

These ideas fit what Richardson (1992) referred to as a new generation of staff development programmes: those that seek to reproduce, within the professional development setting, the same features of teaching and learning that educational reformers advocate for K-12 classrooms (for students of age 5–18). Learning opportunities are often situated within classroom practice. They may take place in the teachers' classrooms, and may involve videotapes of the teachers' lessons or examples of their students' work. Teachers are treated as active learners who construct understandings based on their past experiences, and who have valid practical knowledge to contribute to the professional conversation (Putnam and Borko, 1997).

Research questions, design and methods

Our intent in constructing the case studies of Elly and Lena was to provide an in-depth account of teacher change within the context of reform-based staff development, and of the factors that facilitate and hinder the change process. We addressed the following research questions:

1 In what ways did the teachers' beliefs and practices change?
2 What factors, both personal and institutional, influenced the process of change for each teacher?
3 How did these factors interact to facilitate and hinder teacher change?

The CU Assessment Project involved a partnership between researchers from the School of Education, University of Colorado at Boulder and the 14 third-grade teachers (of students aged 8–9) from three schools in a school district on the outskirts of Denver. The CU team included faculty specialists in assessment, teacher education, literacy education and mathematics education, together with several doctoral students. The district was selected according to three criteria: it contained an ethnically diverse student population, it had a history of standardised accountability testing, and there was a willingness to grant a two-year waiver from standardised tests to participating schools. A school district in the US is a local education agency governed by a superintendent of instruction and local school board. Most school districts, including the one that participated in our project, have their own sets of curriculum guidelines that individual schools are expected to follow.

We sought volunteer school-based teams of third-grade teachers within the district and accepted the three teams that submitted written proposals. To support the project, district officials worked with the principals at these schools to provide the teams with common planning times and university course credit for their participation. Staff in two schools decided to participate in the project for a second year in order to continue their work on mathematics and literacy assessment with the support of the CU team. This chapter focuses on the teachers' experiences and learning in mathematics.

Project activities

During the first year of the project (the 1992–1993 academic year), the CU team met with teachers at each school in after-school workshops, one day a week, to develop or select and then analyse performance assessments compatible with the district instructional goals. The focus of these workshops alternated between mathematics and literacy.

Mathematics workshops followed the district's third-grade curriculum guidelines. As the teachers moved through curricular topics such as place value, multiplication and measurement, the university mathematics education specialist came to workshops with activities that focused on conceptual understanding, problem-solving and explanation. Workshop sessions often included discussions about how to incorporate these materials into the teachers' ongoing instruction and assessment. Teachers frequently used the activities in their classes and brought samples of student work to subsequent sessions. Discussions then centred on the students' work, for example on how to score the work based on rubrics the teachers developed, and how to use information about student understanding derived from individual papers to guide instruction.

Activities during the second year included monthly observations of mathematics and literacy lessons followed by informal workshop sessions. Workshop agendas were often set on the spot, based on issues that arose through teachers' experiences with performance assessments.

Data collection

During the first year of the project, graduate research assistants took written notes, audiotaped and collected artifacts (e.g. samples of assessment materials and student work) at the weekly workshops. They used these data sources to prepare detailed field notes of each workshop session. In addition, university faculty and graduate research assistants interviewed teachers three times during the year. Semi-structured interviews focused on teachers' knowledge, beliefs, and reported practices related to reading and mathematics instruction and assessment. These interviews were audiotaped and transcribed.

In the second year, faculty and graduate research assistants observed teachers approximately once a month during their teaching of mathematics and reading. Observers took detailed written notes describing the classroom atmosphere, instructional activities and materials, and teacher and student actions. Written notes were also recorded during the workshop sessions. These data sources were used to prepare detailed field notes of the classroom observations and workshop sessions. Each teacher also participated in one interview, similar in focus to the first-year interviews, towards the end of the school year.

Identification of case study teachers and follow-up data collection

We decided to construct case studies as one way of analysing the impact of the professional development project. Case studies 'offer, through the richness of singular experiences, opportunities to consider the complexities of teaching and learning by embedding them within the details of everyday life in school' (Dyson, 1995: 26; see also Yin, 1994). They are thus well suited to addressing questions such as: what enables teachers to change their practices?, what hinders their efforts?, how do institutional factors interact with teacher characteristics to shape teachers' courses of action? We decided to present two case studies as a cross-case comparison offers insights about patterns and uniqueness. We focused on strong, experienced teachers who were willing participants in the staff development efforts. Such cases provide 'images of the possible', not only documenting that significant teacher change can occur 'but also laying out at least one detailed example of how it was organised, developed, and pursued' (Shulman, 1983: 495).

Our first decision in the selection process was that both teachers should be from the same school: one of the two schools that remained in the project during the second year. This would allow us to keep the teachers' experiences relatively consistent since both would have participated in the same set of workshop sessions. We decided to select teachers from Pine Elementary School because they were most representative of the teachers who populate the classrooms of today. They exemplified good traditional teaching, and were cautious about changing their practices yet willing to participate in the project (Borko et al., 1997).

Of the teachers at Pine, Elly and Lena best fit our selection criteria. Both are veteran teachers recognised in the district for their excellent traditional teaching methods. Both were active participants in the workshops and were committed to learning about any educational reforms or innovations that might benefit their students. Yet Elly and Lena differed in several of their educational beliefs, some of their instructional practices, and their motivation to consider changing their practice. These differences affected the course of their change processes in distinct ways, making them compelling choices for comparative case studies.

We conducted final classroom observations of Elly and Lena (one in each subject area) during the fall (autumn) of the follow-up year. We also conducted a final interview with each teacher during that winter. The interview was designed to elicit the teacher's reflections on her participation in the project. In preparation, we gave each teacher transcripts of her previous interviews. We asked her to review these transcripts and think about how she had changed during the course of the project.

Data analysis

According to Anderson (1989: 312), traditional and reform-oriented classrooms differ along five dimensions that 'determine the environment within which instruction takes place'. These dimensions – the nature of the academic task, the academic goals of schooling, teachers' classroom roles, students' classroom roles, and the social environment of the classroom – provided the framework for our analysis. To fit the project's focus on assessment, we separated 'Nature of the Academic Task' into two subcategories: instructional tasks and assessment tasks.

We constructed a written summary of each observation, organised according to the six dimensions of classroom practice. We coded interviews using the same dimensions plus several codes based on our interview protocols (e.g. 'team' – working collaboratively with the third-grade team; 'change' – changes in practices or beliefs). We met frequently to discuss questions that arose during the analysis process, working to ensure consistency in our definitions and use of the coding scheme.

Using the observation summaries and coded interviews, we identified themes related to the research questions. Our list included common themes across teachers and across subjects, alongside themes that highlighted differences between the teachers. The pair of researchers analysing data for each teacher used these themes and supporting evidence to construct a narrative case that detailed characteristics of the teacher's change process. As we composed these cases, we discussed our evolving interpretations concerning the paths of change travelled by the two teachers. This analytical work led to the identification of factors that aided or impeded the change process and eventually to our cross-case analysis.

Elly and Lena: cases of teacher change

The cases of Elly and Lena tell the stories of two veteran teachers attempting to incorporate reform-based pedagogical practices into their third-grade classrooms. In this section we explore the teachers' beliefs and practices, comparing them to one another as well as to other teachers in the literature on teacher change.

Elly Marks was the leader of the third-grade team at Pine Elementary School. When she began working with us, she described herself as a veteran teacher. Far from being burned out or complacent, as is the case for some experienced teachers, she was open to new ideas. The timing of the CU Assessment Project was right for her. With her children grown up and no longer living at home, she was at a 'stage of life' when she had the time and energy to devote to experimenting with new practices. As she explained in her final interview:

> I guess one advantage I have is that I have more time than some people. If I had a family at home with young kids, I'm not sure I could have made all these changes...I can devote more time after school hours...I can go home and read and think through some of these things...That's a lot of it, I think: the stage of life I'm in.

Lena Schwarz was also an experienced third-grade teacher who was confident in her teaching yet eager to stay abreast of innovations in education. However, with two teenagers living at home, she struggled to balance her roles of teacher and mother, and she did not have as much time or energy for experimentation as Elly. Lena explained: 'I'm going to have another life. I only have three years left with my kids [before they go to college].'

At the start of the project Elly and Lena looked, in many ways, like 'traditional' teachers. Their teaching and their classrooms exemplified the skills-based, direct-instruction model of schooling captured in Anderson's (1989) descriptions of the 'traditional poles' of the five key dimensions of classroom life. Although each teacher used a variety of instructional formats and strategies, an observer walking into either classroom during mathematics instruction would be likely to see the teacher demonstrating how to solve computational problems using manipulatives (concrete materials such as Cuisenaire rods or Unifix cubes), or students practising the use of algorithms on exercise sets from their textbook or worksheets. On a test day, the observer might have seen students quickly completing timed tests of basic arithmetic facts or working independently to complete the test at the end of a chapter in their textbook.

Elly and Lena were highly respected by colleagues and district administrators for their teaching effectiveness. Both were generally satisfied with their teaching and approached new ideas with caution and some degree of scepticism. They were willing to consider new ideas, but they expected to be convinced of their worth and to be given the resources to implement them. Elly explained: 'If I need to change my teaching, I am certainly willing to, but I also need to see something concrete...I need to be made aware of resources...I'm willing to look at them if somebody can show them to me.' Their cautious attitude towards educational innovations supports Anderson's

(1989: 335) warning that curriculum developers and staff developers 'need to consider that, from the perspective of many teachers, there is no need for such [experimental instructional] programs. Therefore if programs are to influence instructional practice, a case must be made that is convincing to teachers that alternatives to present practice exist and are worth trying.'

We were able to convince Elly and Lena to try out alternative practices. These case studies explore the results of their efforts. We focus first on instruction and assessment, and next look briefly at changes in the teachers' and students' roles. We incorporate information about the other dimensions of Anderson's framework into our discussions of instruction, assessment and roles.

The right time for change: Elly's story

When the CU Assessment Project began, Elly's mathematics instructional goals for students addressed both conceptual understanding and procedural competence. Her approach to teaching multiplication had a dual focus: 'First of all, they have to have the concept, that it's repetitive addition...And then they have to start knowing their facts.' Her instructional programme closely followed the textbook adopted in her school, although she occasionally drew from other sources.

Over the course of the project Elly made a number of changes in her mathematics programme reflecting increased attention to conceptual understanding, though she did not abandon her commitment that children learn mathematics facts and computation. During the first year she worked with us, she began to rely less on the text and more on hands-on activities using a variety of manipulatives. In the middle of that year she reported: 'Probably there's a bit more hands-on than what I anticipated at the beginning of the year. Working a lot more with manipulatives.' Students also spent more time working in pairs or small groups and less time in teacher-directed whole class lessons.

One of the most dramatic changes occurred in Elly's teaching of multiplication. During the first year of the project the third-grade teachers at Pine adopted *Multiplication: Grades 3–4*, one of the *Math By All Means* replacement units authored by Marilyn Burns (1991). Each book in the series provides a three-to-five week teaching unit that aligns with NCTM standards. While not introduced by the CU researchers, the multiplication unit was easily integrated with our recommendations for instruction and assessment. Elly described the unit as 'totally different than what I'd ever been accustomed to before.' The differences included more emphasis on 'the application level' rather than 'just learning a bunch of facts', and introducing facts after working on problem-solving activities.

Elly reported in spring of the first year that she had continued to use manipulatives more than in previous years, primarily when introducing new topics. However, without materials comparable to the multiplication unit, she typically turned to the textbook for follow-up activities. 'I still use the book for reinforcement, but not so much for teaching, for the initial instruction.' By the second year of the project, Elly's shift towards a problem-based mathematics programme had become more complete. Each time we were in her class we saw students engaged in activities that entailed using manipulatives to solve mathematical problems. On no occasion did we see or hear mention of the mathematics textbook. During one visit we observed students playing The Factor Game, an activity where two teams alternate turns circling the factors of numbers that their opponents select, until all numbers up to 30 are circled. During the activity Elly circulated among groups, observing their progress and asking questions to focus attention on mathematical concepts and strategies. After about 20 minutes, she called students to join her on the classroom floor. She described several strategies she had observed and engaged students in a conversation about their games, asking questions such as 'how did you choose numbers to circle?', 'what choices are good ones?' and 'what would you do to get more points if you were to play the game again?'.

This lesson was typical of the mathematics instruction we observed in Elly's classroom in several ways. One is in her use of games as opportunities for students to explore mathematical concepts. Another is in her questioning, both as she monitored students' work in small groups and during whole class debriefing sessions, to encourage students' use of mathematical strategies and to foster their ability to explain them.

Elly reported that by spring of the second year manipulatives and small group activities played a more central role in students' learning than they had in previous years. Our observations corroborated those changes. She continued to use the text and district curriculum framework as resources 'to make sure that I touch on the skills that I want my kids to have.' However, activities largely replaced the book as a teaching tool. Nevertheless, Elly continued to see a role for facts and computation in her mathematics programme. She explained in her final interview: 'I'm not going to jump out to where I'm not going to teach the algorithm...I don't [start with the algorithm]. I start with manipulatives so they can see it, what it means.' She was also more likely to assign problems that focused on computation as homework and to use class time for activities that emphasised problem-solving and conceptual understanding.

A comment by Elly during the final interview perhaps best captures the nature of these changes: 'I think before I was an arithmetic [teacher]. Now I am a math teacher...Before I think I was strictly teaching them how to calculate. Now I'm trying to get them to think like mathematicians think. I think that's been a good change.' She believed that as a result of these changes:

> I challenge my kids a lot more than I would have ever dreamed of doing two years ago...as far as making them think through problems a lot more. I look at some of the activities that I do with my children, and I would never have dreamed of giving those problems to my third-graders two years ago, three years ago.

This shift in expectations and recognition that she could challenge the children more provided an important impetus for Elly to continue working with the new instructional and assessment ideas. Direct experience allowed her to see how the new ideas worked for her students and for herself, and in turn began to pave the way for her to be convinced of the value of the project.

Mathematics assessment

Elly's mathematics programme in the fall of the first year included several types of assessments:

▶ inventory tests and chapter tests in the textbook;
▶ a district level test consisting of two non-routine problems;
▶ district mandated timed tests of arithmetic facts.

Grades were 'based mainly on chapter tests [and] some written assignments.' Her assessment ideas and practices changed to some extent during the first year of the project. In the fall, she continued to use chapter tests from the text-book to assess students' knowledge of addition and subtraction. But she also used other tests, including a commercially produced subtraction assessment that required students to perform computations and comparisons using infor-mation from a chart of dinosaurs' weights and heights. She used chapter tests less in the spring, working with the other Pine teachers to create multiplica-tion assessments based on materials provided in the Marilyn Burns unit. These assessments included questions and statements like 'what is multiplication?', 'show me as many ways as you know to figure out 7×6' and 'how many differ-ent ways can you arrange 24 chairs?'. Elly characterised the new assessments as focused on 'an application level.' She preferred them over 'standard assess-ments' because they 'are at a higher level of thinking.' Also, 'I think you see better how the students are thinking...and how they problem-solve.'

By the second project year, Elly felt more comfortable planning and using alternative assessments, and better able to draw from various resources to revise old assessments and develop new ones. Indicatively, she changed the question about arranging chairs on the multiplication assessment '...because last year they started putting those 24 chairs in circles. So this year I think I changed it to something like "arrange 24 chairs in rows as many different ways as you can".'

During the follow-up year of the project, Elly solidified assessment ideas and practices that she had tried out the previous two years. As was true for instruc-tion, she maintained a dual focus on problem-solving and computation. When asked whether her overall approach to assessment had changed since the beginning of the project, Elly responded: 'It looks quite different...just because I don't use chapter tests.... I don't think I've given any this year.' However she assured the interviewer 'that doesn't mean that I haven't assessed them on computation, because I have – but I've made that computation a little differ-ent, with the missing digits and that type of thing.'

While Elly made a number of substantial changes in her approach to assess-ing mathematics during the project, she reported being less satisfied with her progress with assessment than with instruction. And she consistently found the assessment changes more difficult to make than the instructional changes.

Changing roles for Elly and her students

As Elly's classroom practices came to reflect a greater emphasis on conceptual understanding and higher order thinking, her role began to shift from a trans-mitter of knowledge to a facilitator of active student learning. She never wavered in her strong belief that her central responsibility as a teacher was to be an instructional guide and leader. 'Kids need teachers...You always have to hold students accountable, but it's too overwhelming without a lot of teacher support and coaching.' This belief took on new shades of meaning as she worked with new mathematics activities.

Elly gradually came to spend less time providing information and guiding students in practice activities and more time facilitating learning through problem-solving and meaning-making tasks. She noted: 'I wouldn't be at the head of the class showing and instructing. A lot more peer teaching [and] learning than what I ever anticipated in September.' Our observations of Elly's mathematics lessons confirmed this shift. Whether students worked independently, in pairs, in small groups or as a whole class, Elly rarely presented information directly. Rather, as illustrated in the Factor Game example, she encouraged and guided students in their construction of mathematical meaning through requests that they share solutions and solution strategies with their peers, and that they explain reasons for the strategies they selected.

Elly also described 'letting go' of some control in the classroom, as where she allowed students to 'call on people to answer questions – it takes me out of the loop and lets them talk more.' In her final interview, Elly summed up the relationship between new tasks and her role as teacher: 'I've changed. I think the thing I've learned the last two years, and probably in both reading and math, is I'm not as much in control. I mean I'm in control, just not as much. I am letting them go and letting them experience.'

In summary, across the five dimensions outlined by Anderson (1989) Elly's greatest changes came in her understanding and enactment of tasks, both instructional and assessment. These changes supported shifts in the roles and social environment that were necessary to accompany the new activities. Additionally, she noted that her ideas about subject matter shifted away from a skills-based approach to include higher level strategies and applications. In general, she described the project as a success.

The strength of teacher beliefs in the face of reform: Lena's story

At the outset of the project, Lena's classroom could be described as highly organised and orderly. Numerous routines were in place, students were familiar with the routines and their associated appropriate behaviours, and student engagement was high. With respect to both mathematics instruction and assessment, Lena tended to emphasise facts and skills more than conceptual understanding. Her primary goal for the first quarter (term) of mathematics instruction was that students learn their basic mathematics facts. She explained: 'I think it makes the rest of their math career in elementary school more comfortable, and they have more success. Whether they start to understand the more high level problem-solving questions, at least they can say "I know my facts", and it gives them a sense of confidence.'

A few months into the project, Lena identified getting students 'to think' and to communicate their answers as central goals for her mathematics programme.

She recognised that 'I didn't do that last year.' Lena's focus on mathematical understanding was associated with a greater emphasis on problem-solving tasks and an evolving understanding of problem-solving. A poster displayed prominently in her room listed 16 problem-solving strategies including Guess and Check, Make a Table, and Draw a Picture. At the beginning of the project, Lena defined problem-solving as knowing problem-solving strategies, and communicating mathematically as explaining the strategy you used. Similarly, when asked to describe her mathematics programme in the winter of the first year, Lena explained: 'There's a lot more problem-solving going on. I'm referring to the 16 strategies of problem-solving – draw a picture and so on.' This conception of problem-solving as applying strategies persisted into the project's second year. That spring Lena described mathematical excellence in these terms: 'They're good in problem-solving. They can decide if they need to make a table or make a graph. Also they can explain how they came up with that [strategy]. No longer do I feel [that children are] high quality in math just because they can regroup.'

As the project evolved Lena moved towards a broader conception of problem-solving, one that was not tied to the application of specific strategies and that required students to explain how they arrived at their solutions. Lena attributed these changes to the CU Assessment Project. When the project began she and the other teachers '...knew problem-solving was important but we didn't know how to teach it. We didn't know how to score it. We didn't know where to fit it in. And because of the project, we do now, we know that.'

Lena also began to use manipulatives differently during her work with us. In the spring of the first year she explained that she and the other teachers had always used manipulatives, but we didn't problem-solve with them. Instead Lena used concrete materials such as Cuisenaire rods and Unifix cubes to model mathematical procedures. She often asked the students to copy her models or use the manipulatives in similar ways on similar mathematical computations. As her understanding of problem-solving evolved, Lena began having students work with manipulatives to solve mathematical problems.

A lesson we observed that spring illustrates these changes. Students worked in small groups on the following problem:

> You are trying to find a secret door that leads to a magic garden. You know that the height plus the width of the door is 12 feet [about 3.6 metres] and that the door is twice as high as it is wide. What are the dimensions of the secret door?

When one student quickly announced to his group that the door is 8 feet [2.4 metres] high and 4 feet [1.2 metres] wide, Lena came over, listened to his answer, and then asked to see it written out with a clear explanation. The next time she joined the group, she asked each student for an explanation, probing for a way to explain the solution without using words. She encouraged the two students who understood the solution to explain it to the third. This activity, in which conceptual understanding took precedence over procedural understanding, illustrates Lena's evolving emphasis on problem-solving, explanation, manipulatives and collaboration among peers.

Lena's changing ways of thinking and talking about mathematics were not always evident in her practices, however. During a lesson in fall of the follow-up year, she used manipulatives in much the same way that she had at the beginning of the project, leading students through a step-by-step demonstration of the subtraction algorithm. Students had just completed a unit during which they measured, recorded and graphed the weights of apples. The assessment entailed comparing the weights of peeled apples on consecutive days to determine the weight change due to loss of moisture.

Prior to completing the assessment on their own, students watched Lena demonstrate the procedures they were to follow. She explained that they should build two towers with Unifix cubes: one to show 78 grams (the weight of the peeled apple on the first day), and another to show 59 grams (the weight on the second day). She stood two towers of the appropriate heights next to each other so that students could compare them, and then asked for the difference in weight from Monday to Tuesday. After several students volunteered incorrect responses, one suggested to 'take off the cubes that are higher and count them.' After praising his response, she demonstrated by taking cubes off the taller tower until the two were the same height.

Mathematics assessment

In the fall of the first year, timed tests and chapter tests were the foundation of Lena's assessment practices. Additional components included five daily computation questions and homework. Lena's regular and frequent use of timed tests reflected her belief in the importance of learning basic math facts: '[A] one-minute timed test is a pretty old-fashioned traditional way, but I find it's the only way they learn them.'

Over the two-and-a-half years of the project Lena moved away from chapter tests and began designing and using more activities that related to 'real world mathematics'. During the winter of the follow-up year she gave a subtraction assessment in which students looked up the prices of toys in a 'Toys-R-Us' catalogue and determined how much change they would receive when purchasing each toy with a specific amount of money. Lena guided students through each step of this assessment. On one problem she instructed students to 'look up on the correct page the McDonald's Magic Shake Maker that you will be purchasing and tell me how much the item costs.' The students indicated that the price was $19.99. Lena then asked how much change they would receive from $20.00. So although she situated the assessment in a real-world context, Lena transformed what might have been an authentic problem-solving task into a direct application of the subtraction algorithm.

During the course of the project, Lena also showed some evidence of changing her views about assessment: 'I think of assessment now as daily assessment instead of an assessment and a unit test being synonymous...I'm assessing daily now.' At the same time, she expressed concern about the instructional implications of daily assessment. Since this type of assessment required her to re-teach what students did not understand the first time, she worried that the time spent re-teaching concepts would prevent her from covering the curriculum completely.

The Toys-R-Us assessment and daily assessment illustrate issues that arose for Lena as she attempted to incorporate reform-based practices while still doing her job of 'teaching the students what they need to know.' They also reveal a tension between Lena's beliefs and practices. While reform-based beliefs and rhetoric were evident in her interviews, the impact of these changing beliefs was not found as consistently in what she was observed to do.

Lena did make changes in her academic goals and her instructional practices to support these goals, and she began to experiment with new forms of assessment. Some of these assessments were structured to the extent that they did not foster key aspects of problem-solving such as framing problems and evaluating alternatives. But they represented a greater emphasis on understanding and explanation than skills and procedures. Further, her use of tasks for both assessment and instruction reflects Lena's understanding of the vital connections between these two facets of an instructional programme.

Changing roles for Lena and her students

At the outset of the project Lena saw herself as a central figure in the classroom, and she characterised her 'job' as 'teaching the students what they need to know' and helping them to complete assignments successfully. We saw evidence for this conception of teaching in the way Lena structured many classroom activities as teacher-directed tasks and walked students through them in a step-by-step fashion. We also saw evidence, as the project progressed, that Lena was developing new ideas about teacher and student roles and was becoming aware of the incompatibility between these ideas and some of her existing practices. In the spring of the second year she expressed concern that she had created 'dependent monsters'. She explained: 'Last year I was doing all the work. They weren't problem-solving. I was feeding it to them.' This concern continued to surface in our conversations. In the final interview Lena noted that students 'learn more when they discover it on their own' and claimed that she was using the 'discovery method' more in her teaching.

Shifting responsibility to students was not easy for Lena, and she struggled to find a balance between teacher-directed activities and those in which students took a more active role in their own learning. She talked about these efforts during the final interview: 'I'm really trying to be more aware of not leading them along...You know, when you want to give them the answer so bad, or you want to show them how to do it. I'm a little bit more comfortable about backing off.' These evolving ideas about teacher and student roles were more apparent in Lena's interviews than in the observations of her teaching, perhaps another indication of the difficulties that shifting responsibility entailed.

The different pedagogical approaches we observed (illustrated by the contrast between the Unifix Cube Towers and Secret Door Problem lessons) may be further evidence that Lena continued to struggle with the new ideas and practices we introduced, even by the end of the project. Her beliefs seemed to change more quickly than her practices. Though Lena was able to talk about changes in her beliefs about teaching and learning, these changes took time to translate into action. Thus the transformations in Lena's practice were not complete at the time of the Unifix Cube Towers lesson, resulting in inconsistencies in style across lessons.

To summarise, Lena's teaching can be thought of as a hybrid of traditional and reform-based practices. Her struggle to incorporate new ideas about teaching and learning into her instructional programme was manifested in the seemingly inconsistent nature of her instructional and assessment practices. Sometimes they incorporated reform-based strategies that encouraged student construction of meaning. At other times they were more in line with a traditional view emphasising the role of the teacher as one who imparts knowledge and manages student behaviour. The case of Lena is an example of a veteran teacher being changed by, as well as changing, the nature of the new educational approaches she experienced through an intensive professional development effort.

The nature of change: a cross-case comparison

Elly and Lena modified their mathematics programmes during their participation in the CU Assessment Project. They moved closer to images of instruction and assessment advocated by the CU research and staff development team which were compatible with the current educational reform efforts (e.g. NCTM, 2000). This section highlights three patterns in the changes they made:

1 Instructional and assessment practices characterised by a greater emphasis on conceptual understanding.
2 Higher expectations for students.
3 A shift in teacher roles characterised by 'letting go of control' to facilitate more active student learning.

First, the goals for both teachers' mathematics programmes shifted towards *a greater emphasis on conceptual understanding and problem-solving*. By the end of the project, their instruction incorporated more problem-based activities and relied more on small group formats and hands-on work with manipulatives. Compatible with these changes, both teachers replaced chapter tests with performance-based assessments that required problem-solving and explanation.

Several recent professional development projects have focused on helping teachers modify their mathematics instructional practices to incorporate a greater emphasis on features such as conceptual understanding and active student learning. Projects comparable to ours in scope and focus include Cognitively Guided Instruction (CGI) (Carpenter et al., 1996), SummerMath for Teachers (Schifter and Fosnot, 1993), and the Purdue Problem-Centered Mathematics Project (Cobb et al., 1991). Teachers in these projects, like Elly and Lena, focused more on problem-solving and less on computation and algorithms after participating in professional development experiences. These similarities in outcomes are not surprising given that, despite differences in approaches, all four projects were based on similar underlying assumptions: children actively construct knowledge, and teachers should develop instructional practices that facilitate students' knowledge construction.

A unique contribution of our project to the literature on teacher learning and professional development is its focus on assessment in addition to instruction. While both teachers changed their approaches to assessment during the project, their assessments changed less than their instructional practices. This finding, while surprising given the project's explicit focus on assessment, becomes more understandable when we consider that teachers generally have more experience and expertise related to instruction than assessment. In fact, members of the assessment community such as Stiggins (1991) warn that many teachers lack the 'assessment literacy' necessary to implement the kinds of classroom performance assessments advocated by educational reform. As a result, it may be more difficult to help teachers change their assessment practices than their instructional practices.

Second, Elly and Lena both commented that as they introduced new kinds of activities and observed how students performed on these activities they were surprised at their students' capabilities. Their new instructional and assessment practices led to *higher expectations for students*. Fennema and colleagues (1993) reported a similar finding in their case study of Ms J. Through listening to her students, this successful CGI teacher discovered that they could do many things she did not expect. Much like Elly and Lena, Ms J. raised her expectations for children based on this discovery. For all three teachers the key to higher expectations seemed to be a combination of introducing complex tasks focused on understanding and listening closely to students as they attempted to solve these tasks – features typical of reform-based instruction.

Third, Lena and Elly both talked about '*giving up control*' to students as they organised their classroom learning environments to enable students to take a more active role in their own learning. These changes in teacher and student roles did not come easily. To differing degrees both teachers found it difficult to share control of classroom processes with students as they worked to incorporate reform-based practices into their instructional programmes.

From early in the project, Elly seemed more comfortable than Lena experimenting with new activities and new roles. Elly was more likely to have students attempt to solve non-routine mathematics problems on their own, without first demonstrating possible solution strategies. Lena was more likely to use modelling to introduce such problems, adapting the tasks to her existing instructional patterns rather than fundamentally changing her role. While both teachers remained committed to their responsibilities as instructional leaders, Elly seemed to have less difficulty than Lena making the transition from being a conveyor of information to being a facilitator of students' active learning.

Similar patterns of beliefs and practices related to shifting roles and giving up control surfaced in our review of other professional development programmes. Marx and colleagues (Marx et al., 1994; Blumenfeld et al., 1994) reported that teachers who participated in Project-Based Science 'were often unwilling to let go' of their control of students' cognition. Many held on to the belief that teachers must guide and support students as they develop new ways of learning, and they had difficulty in granting students the responsibility and autonomy to direct their own learning. Similarly, Wood and colleagues (1991: 606) quoted the teacher who was the focus of a case study in the Purdue Problem-Centered Mathematics Project: 'One of the most difficult things has been to stop talking and let the children solve a problem in their own way…[It is difficult] not to interfere or offer help before it's asked for. It's hard to hold back and not step in.' For these teachers, like Lena, efforts to give up control and share responsibility with students were associated with fundamental shifts in their conceptions of teacher and student roles.

Factors that influence teacher change

The case studies of Elly and Lena helped our research team to identify situational and personal factors that contributed to – and sometimes challenged – participants' willingness to take the risks associated with attempting to change their practices. This section explores several of these features and compares our findings with those reported by other scholars who have studied teacher learning.

Situational factors

Two situational features that supported Pine teachers' learning were the collaborative working relationship and sense of professional community shared by members of the third grade team, and the professional development experiences provided by the CU researchers. In addition to their weekly (year one) or monthly (year two) meetings with the CU researchers, these teachers met informally as a team several times a week, usually during their common planning period. They worked together well, and their collaborative efforts provided each individual with additional materials as well as encouragement through tough times of the project. Their appreciation of this support is revealed in advice that Elly offered to other teachers interested in changing their practice: 'Get a partner...so that they can brainstorm together. Bounce ideas off one another...and for support, too. It's what you need.'

Our project is certainly not the first to identify professional community as an important factor in teacher change. Indeed, McLaughlin and Talbert (1993: 15) suggested that teachers' ability to adapt their practices successfully to meet the national reform agenda depends upon 'participation in a professional community that discusses new teaching materials and strategies and that supports the risk taking and struggle entailed in transforming practice.' In a project that, like ours, centred around a longitudinal, within-school professional development experience, Grossman, Wineburg, and colleagues brought English and social studies teachers in an urban high school together for two-and-a-half years. Their task was to read together in the fields of history and English and to create an interdisciplinary curriculum. In an article (Grossman et al., 2001) focusing on the development of professional community among the teachers, the researchers noted that these teachers learned new ways of thinking about history and literature and new pedagogical practices through participation in the project. Like our teachers, they formed the kind of professional community identified by McLaughlin and Talbert (1993: 18) as central to the success of reform efforts – 'learning communities which generate knowledge, craft new norms of practice, and sustain participants in their efforts to reflect, examine, experiment, and change.'

Workshop sessions and resources provided by the CU team played a central role in teacher learning, helping the teachers to feel more willing to experiment with new ideas and practices. Both teachers commented several times about the importance of the resources. Elly explained: 'I think a lot of the reason I changed is because I had materials to look at, to get ideas from.' Teachers and researchers often engaged in thoughtful analyses of these resources during workshop sessions. Conversations were particularly effective at fostering change when they were grounded in the teachers' classroom practice (Borko et al., 1997). Such conversations frequently occurred when the CU researchers shared mathematics activities with the teachers at a workshop session, the teachers attempted to use these activities in their classrooms, and they reflected upon their experiences and their students' work in subsequent workshop sessions. Lena commented: 'The weekly support made us accountable. We couldn't slack off. We had to keep getting better because we were held accountable.'

Collaboration, weekly meetings, and resources were inextricably intertwined to provide a combination of information, support, and accountability that made teachers willing to risk trying out activities that represented fairly substantial departures from their current practice. Elly and Lena worked together closely during the first two years of the project, so it is not surprising that the situational factors influenced them in similar ways. These two teachers were, however, different individuals. And, there were differences in the roles that their personal characteristics played in the change process. The next section addresses the differences that were most salient.

Personal characteristics

The case studies examined several personal factors that were central to Elly's and Lena's experiences in the CU Assessment Project. This discussion focuses on two sets of factors to highlight the complex roles that personal factors play in teacher change: their beliefs about teaching, learning, and themselves as teachers; and the timing of the project with respect to other aspects of their lives.

Elly is a confident teacher, and she saw this confidence as central to her success: 'You need to be confident in what you're doing...No matter how you teach, if you're not confident with it, you're not going to make it.' At the same time, she expected the change process to be slow and difficult: 'It always takes me a while...to really grasp and understand how to use something new...The first time you try something, it's not going to go terrifically, and so you work out the bugs.' This combination of confidence in her teaching and beliefs about the nature of change seemed to enable Elly to accept the frustration and anxiety that sometimes accompanied participation in the CU Assessment Project.

In fact, anxiety helped push Elly to learn: 'The anxiety level can't be too low or you don't perform. That's just like with kids in the classroom, if there's no anxiety, probably not a whole lot's happening. But there has to be just – just a little bit to push kids and to push teachers.' Her advice to colleagues desiring to change their assessment practices captures these sentiments: 'Give yourself time. It takes a long time to change. It's an attitude also. You have to be ready for frustration.'

Lena's beliefs about teaching and learning played a key role in the change process. They included the belief that it was her responsibility to provide knowledge and skills to her students through instructional strategies such as explanation and modelling. When the CU team proposed activities that turned some of the responsibility for learning over to the students, Lena's beliefs sometimes acted as a filter. They caused her to adapt the new activities to fit better her conception of teacher and student roles. For example, Lena initially translated the recommendation to emphasise problem-solving in mathematics into teaching students to use each of the 16 strategies outlined on the poster in her room. She introduced each strategy using demonstration and explanation, and she provided practice in applying that strategy to a set of problems. Only then did she begin to use more open-ended tasks, as where students were responsible for determining what problem-solving strategies they would use.

These brief examples illustrate how beliefs were important determinants of change for both Elly and Lena. However, both the sets of beliefs that were most salient, and the nature of their influence, differed considerably for the two teachers. With respect to timing of the project in the teachers' lives on the other hand, the salient issues were similar although their influence differed dramatically.

We saw in the case studies how the project came at a period in Elly's life when she had the time and energy for experimentation, in part because her children were grown up and had left home. The summer before she began using the Marilyn Burns replacement units, Elly 'read the Marilyn Burns book...I was sitting by the pool while my husband was teaching – I read each chapter and I took notes on it', and she pulled together activities to use during the year. In contrast, as a mother of two teenagers who lived at home, Lena struggled to balance her roles of teacher and mother and did not have as much time or energy for experimentation.

Spencer's study of the reciprocal influence of home and school on women teachers suggests that Lena's struggles are not unique. Teachers often do not separate work and home, and many feel that 'school disrupts their personal lives' (Spencer, 1986: 284). For teachers with children living at home, multiple responsibilities of child care and household duties create more complications than are commonly experienced by teachers with no children or children who are no longer at home. Spencer's work suggests, and the cases of Elly and Lena corroborate, that when working with teachers in professional development situations, it is important to understand their personal situations: 'Teachers are human beings who have complex, multifaceted lives, and they do not neatly compartmentalise [their different] roles. Understanding the relationship between teachers' home and school lives provides a broader basis on which to analyse teachers' classroom behaviours' (Spencer, 1986: 296).

The interaction between person and situation

Situational and personal factors appear to work interactively to affect teacher change. Specific characteristics of individual teachers may make them particularly receptive to features of the environment that promote or support new ideas and practices. Equally, personal characteristics may influence the nature of the support that is provided to teachers. The interaction between Elly's attitude toward change (a willingness to try out new activities and materials combined with an expectation that these resources be supplied) and the mathematics resources provided by the CU team is illustrative. When the project began Elly expressed reservations about performance assessments, but was willing to consider them 'if somebody shows me what to do and gives me some ideas'. By providing resources, the project was able to capitalise on Elly's willingness to change and channel her motivation to improve her practice in directions that she initially resisted (like replacing chapter tests with performance assessments).

Conversely, Elly (and other teachers) influenced the project's evolution. Their insistence that we provide resources for classroom use caused the CU team to make gathering materials to share with the teachers a priority in our work.

The iterative nature of the change process

Beliefs and practices seemed to play somewhat different roles in the two teachers' change processes. For Elly, change seemed to be driven more by experimenting with new practices than by considering beliefs. When she enacted new mathematics instructional and assessment activities provided by the CU team, students' performances on these activities challenged her existing conceptions of teaching and learning and her expectations for students and led to changes in these sets of beliefs. In contrast, we noticed changes in Lena's beliefs before we noticed changes in her practices, and the change process seemed to be guided to a greater extent by changes in beliefs. Lena was able to talk about the importance of student-centred pedagogy quite articulately and convincingly in interviews throughout the first and second years of the project. It was not until the spring of the second year, however, that we saw an instantiation of these beliefs in her everyday practices, in the Secret Door Problem activity. The cases of Elly and Lena, taken together, support Richardson's (1994b: 90) suggestion that 'the process of changing beliefs and practices is interactive; that is, depending on the types of changes and the teachers themselves, the change process may begin either with changes in beliefs or changes in practices.'

Regardless of how the change process begins, beliefs and practices influence each other in multiple ways (Borko and Putnam, 1996; Richardson, 1994a). Each small change a teacher makes can become the basis for broader, more fundamental transformations. But these transformations will only occur if the small changes are supported so that cycles are recursive, with each cycle bringing the teacher to new understandings and new pedagogies.

Acknowledgements

We would like to thank the CU Assessment Project research team faculty researchers: Hilda Borko, Roberta Flexer, Elfrieda Hiebert and Lorrie Shepard. All members of the team contributed to the conceptualisation of staff development and data collection for this study. We extend special thanks to the two teachers whose stories are featured in this chapter, for opening their classrooms to us and spending countless hours on project-related activities. Without their commitment and support, the project would not have been possible.

An earlier version of this chapter appeared in the European Journal of Special Needs Education,17,1–19 at http://www<http://www>.tandf.co.uk. We are grateful to Taylor & Francis for permission to reproduce material from the original article.

References

Anderson, L. (1989) 'Implementing instructional programs to promote meaningful, self-regulated learning', in J. Brophy (ed), *Advances in Research on Teaching: Vol. 1. Teaching for Meaningful Understanding and Self-Regulated Learning*. Greenwich, CT: JAI Press.

Blumenfeld, P.C., Krajcik, J.S., Marx, R.W. and Soloway, E. (1994) 'Lessons learned: how collaboration helped middle grade science teachers learn project-based instruction', *The Elementary School Journal,* 94: 539–51.

Borko, H., Davinroy, K.H., Bliem, C.L. and Cumbo, K.B. (2000) 'Exploring and supporting teacher change: two teachers' experiences in an intensive mathematics and literacy staff development project', *Elementary School Journal* 100: 273–306.

Borko, H., Mayfield, V., Marion, S., Flexer, R. and Cumbo, K. (1997) 'Teachers' developing ideas and practices about mathematics performance assessment: successes, stumbling blocks, and implications for professional development', *Teaching and Teacher Education,* 13: 259–78.

Borko, H. and Putnam, R.T. (1996) 'Learning to teach', in D.C. Berliner and R.C. Calfee (eds), *Handbook of Educational Psychology.* New York: Macmillan. pp. 673–708.

Burns, M. (1991) *Math by all Means: Multiplication, Grades 3–4.* New Rochelle, NY: Math Solutions and Cuisenaire.

Carpenter, T.P., Fennema, E. and Franke, M.L. (1996) 'Cognitively guided instruction: a knowledge base for reform in primary mathematics instruction', *Elementary School Journal,* 97: 3–20.

Cobb, P., Wood, T., Yackel, E., Nicholls, J., Wheatley, G., Trigtti, B. and Perlwitz, M. (1991) 'Assessment of a problem-centered second grade mathematics project', *Journal for Research in Mathematics,* 22: 3–29.

Cohen, D.K. and Ball, D.L. (1990) 'Relations between policy and practice: a commentary', *Educational Evaluation and Policy Analysis,* 12: 330–8.

Dyson, A.H. (1995) *Children out of Bounds: The Power of Case Studies in Expanding Visions of Literacy Development* (Technical Report No. 73). Berkeley, CA: National Center for the Study of Writing.

Fennema, E., Franke, M.L., Carpenter, T.P. and Carey, D.A. (1993) 'Using children's mathematical knowledge in instruction', *American Educational Research Journal,* 30: 555–83.

Grossman, P., Wineburg, S. and Woolworth, S. (2001) 'Toward a theory of teacher community', *Teachers College Record,* 103: 942–1012.

Marx, R.W., Blumenfeld, P.C., Krajcik, J.S., Blunk, M., Crawford, B., Kelly, B. and Meyer, K.M. (1994) 'Enacting project-based science: experiences of four middle grade teachers', *The Elementary School Journal,* 94: 517–38.

McLaughlin, M. and Talbert, J.E. (1993) *Contexts that Matter for Teaching and Learning: Strategic Opportunities for Meeting the Nation's Educational Goals.* Stanford, CA: Center for Research on the Context of Secondary School Teaching, Stanford University.

National Council of Teachers of Mathematics (1989) *Curriculum and Evaluation Standards for School Mathematics.* Reston, VA: NCTM.

National Council of Teachers of Mathematics (1995) *Assessment Standards for School Mathematics.* Reston, VA: NCTM.

National Council of Teachers of Mathematics (2000) *Principles and Standards for School Mathematics.* Reston, VA: NCTM.

Prawat, R.S. and Floden, R. (1994) 'Philosophical perspectives on constructivist views of learning', *Educational Psychologist,* 29 (1): 37–48.

Putnam, R. and Borko, H. (1997). 'Teacher learning: implications of new views of cognition', in B.J. Biddle, T.L. Good and I.F. Goodson (eds), *The International Handbook of Teachers and Teaching.* Dordrecht, The Netherlands: Kluwer Academic Publishers.

Resnick, L.B. and Resnick, D. (1992) 'Assessing the thinking curriculum: new tools for educational reform', in B.R. Gifford and M.C. O'Conner (eds), Changing Assessments: *Alternative Views of Aptitude, Achievement, and Instruction.* Boston: Kluwer Academic Publishers.

Richardson, V. (1992) 'The agenda-setting dilemma in a constructivist staff development process', *Teaching and Teacher Education,* 8: 287–300.

Richardson, V. (ed) (1994a) *A Theory of Teacher Change and the Practice of Staff Development: A Case in Reading Instruction.* New York: Teachers College Press.

Richardson V. (1994b) 'The consideration of teachers' beliefs', in V. Richardson (ed), A *Theory of Teacher Change and The Practice of Staff Development: A Case in Reading Instruction.* New York: Teachers' College Press.

Schifter, D. and Fosnot, C.T. (1993) *Reconstructing Mathematics Education: Stories of Teachers Meeting the Challenges of Reform.* New York: Teachers College Press.

Shulman, L.S. (1983) 'Autonomy and obligation: the remote control of teaching', in L.S. Shulman and G. Sykes (eds), *Handbook of Teaching and Policy.* New York: Longman.

Spencer, D. (1986) *Contemporary Women Teachers: Balancing School and Home.* New York: Longman.

Stiggins, R. (1991) 'Assessment literacy', *Phi Delta Kappan,* 72: 534–9.

Wiggins, G. (1989) 'A true test: toward more authentic and equitable assessment', *Phi Delta Kappan,* 70: 703–13.

Wood, T., Cobb, P. and Yackel, E. (1991) 'Change in teaching mathematics: a case study', *American Educational Research Journal,* 28: 587–616.

Yin, R.K. (1994) *Case Study Techniques: Design and Methods.* 2nd edn. Newbury Park, CA: Sage.

Chapter 4

Learning from homework: a case study

Martin Hughes and Pamela Greenhough

The substantive focus of this chapter is the contribution that homework makes to student learning. Martin Hughes and Pamela Greenhough outline how their decision to research the topic was informed by three things: the policy context, their critical review of literature on the role of homework in learning, and previous research they had undertaken on a related topic. They point out that whilst policy in the UK made strong claims for homework as a key factor in raising academic standards in schools, research on the topic indicated a less clear relationship between homework and student achievement. Hughes and Greenhough identify a gap in research knowledge that they sought to address in their research: gaining a detailed understanding of the contribution made by specific homework tasks to student learning.

An important feature of this chapter is that the authors provide a detailed explanation of how they constructed the theoretical framework informing the research (which they refer to as a conceptual framework). As they point out, the need to develop a strong conceptual framework is often highlighted – particularly by supervisors of theses and dissertations. But there are few accounts of how researchers have developed their framework, or how it has been used. The authors of this chapter not only outline clearly how their framework was developed, but also how it guided the specification of research questions and the research design. They also reflect critically on the strengths and limitations of representing their framework in the form of a model.

The detailed case study of one example of a homework task completed by two students, Adam and Sophie, highlights how the researchers' conceptual framework structured the analysis of data and its presentation. Hughes and Greenhough address the issue of how it would have been possible to interpret the data on Adam and Sophie in different ways. They explain how they looked beyond the most obvious interpretation of the data relating to the two students, and probed beyond the superficial explanations that could have been given for the differences between the two young people. Their conceptual framework provided a structure that enabled the researchers to examine the complexity of factors affecting the students' engagement with the homework task in relation to their wider learning experiences in a range of social contexts. Finally, the authors reflect critically on their use of a case study approach and the extent to which the case presented in this chapter was similar to other examples of homework examined in the study.

Introduction

We have three main aims in this chapter. First, we want to present an account of research on homework which was carried out in the UK between 1999 and 2002. By homework we mean any work set by teachers to be done outside the classroom, not normally under teacher supervision. The overall purpose of the research project was to examine the contribution that homework makes to student learning, and to identify some of the conditions under which this contribution is enhanced or reduced. Although the project was concerned with homework in both primary (5–11 years) and secondary (11–16 years) schools, this chapter is based around data collected from a single secondary school. Other accounts of the research can be found elsewhere (see Hughes and Greenhough, 2003a, 2003b).

Our second aim in the chapter is to present a conceptual framework which was used to structure the design, data collection and data analysis of this project. While the importance of conceptual frameworks in research is widely recognised (e.g. Punch, 1998) there are relatively few accounts that describe how a particular conceptual framework was developed and used in a specific piece of research. This chapter will provide such an account. Our third aim is to show how the conceptual framework developed in the project was used to structure a case study of a particular piece of homework (which we call the Circles homework). This case study has been chosen as it shows how the same homework task can generate different learning outcomes in two students, whom we will call Adam and Sophie. In the chapter, we will use the framework to provide a descriptive account of Adam and Sophie's different responses to the Circles homework, and follow this with an analysis of why the homework might have generated different learning outcomes. We will also discuss the extent to which the conclusions drawn from this case study are typical of those emerging from the research project as a whole.

Rationale for the research

There were several reasons why we decided to carry out this piece of research at this point in time. The first reason lay in the educational policy context in which the research took place. Essentially, this was one in which there was a great deal of enthusiasm for homework amongst educational policymakers in the UK. In 1997, the New Labour government had come into office with a clear agenda to raise standards of attainment in primary and secondary schools, particularly in the areas of literacy and numeracy. Homework was seen as playing an important role in this agenda. For example, within weeks of taking office, the incoming Secretary of State for Education wrote that: 'Homework is not a punishment and it is not a chore. It is an essential part of a good education.' (Blunkett, 1997)

Such statements were followed by the publication of homework guidelines by the Department for Education and Employment (DFEE, 1998a). They set out how much time should be spent on homework at different ages, and gave examples of good practice. A feature of the guidelines was the clear expectation that homework should be set throughout the primary school years, as well as in secondary schools. Another document encouraged the establishment of homework clubs and other forms of study support (DFEE, 1998b). It was accompanied by the publication and promotion of research on good homework practice carried out for the government's inspection agency, the Office for Standards in Education (Weston, 1999). This encouragement of homework through official reports and documents was also accompanied by public criticism, from ministers and others, of researchers whose findings did not accord with the official position (e.g. Blunkett, 1999).

The second main reason for the investigation came from our review of previous research on homework. This review revealed a number of studies reporting an association between the amount of time spent on homework and academic attainment in secondary schools, with greater amounts of homework being associated with higher academic achievement (see Barber et al., 1997; Tymms and Fitz-Gibbon, 1992). However, there was much less evidence of such an association at primary school level (e.g. Farrow et al., 1999). Moreover, there were very few studies looking in detail at the contribution which specific homework assignments made to student learning. This gap was particularly noticeable in the UK context, where there had been virtually no previous research on this aspect of homework. Similar conclusions were drawn in two major reviews of the research literature appearing during the course of our study (Cowan and Hallam, 1999; Sharp et al., 2001), suggesting that our research would be filling an important gap.

The third main reason for this study is that it followed on directly from our own previous research. In particular, we had just completed a study which looked at young children (aged 5–7 years) carrying out 'homework-type' tasks with their parents and teachers (Greenhough and Hughes, 1998; Hughes and Greenhough, 1998a). The tasks involved sharing a reading book with the adult, playing a mathematics game together, and carrying out an activity involving electric circuits. This study suggests that there were important differences between parents and teachers in the ways in which they interacted with the children in these contexts, as well as showing some important differences within the parent group. One implication was that sending homework-type assignments home from school does not necessarily generate the intended learning outcomes, particularly if different groups of parents are involved. We hoped that our next research project would throw further light on these issues, albeit with a different age group of children.

The conceptual framework

In this section we focus on the conceptual framework which underpinned the research. We describe how it was developed, and show how it was used to generate the specific research questions which the project addressed. In subsequent sections we shall show how the conceptual framework was used to inform the design, data collection and data analysis methods used in the study.

The conceptual framework was developed as part of the process of writing the research proposal for the project. In particular, we wanted to articulate more fully what we meant by 'learning', and how we could study the contribution which homework might make to learning. Our previous work had led us to see the advantages of what we termed a 'broad socio-cultural approach to learning', drawing on theorists such as Wertsch (1991), Daniels (1993, 2001) and Rogoff (1990). In the proposal we articulated this approach as follows:

> *We assume that any attempt to understand learning needs to take full account of the social and cultural contexts in which learning takes place, paying particular attention to the purposes and intentions of the participants, the social interaction which takes place between them, the value they place on the activities being undertaken, and the material, cultural and linguistic resources available for the participants to draw on.*
> *(Hughes and Greenhough, 1998b)*

At this point, we found it particularly helpful to draw on a framework developed by Pollard and Filer (1996) in their longitudinal ethnographic study of identity and learning. Pollard and Filer propose that we ask what they call 'five deceptively straightforward' questions about learning:

1 What is being learned (learning content)?
2 When and where does learning take place (learning context)?
3 Who is learning (learning identity)?
4 What support is available for learning?
5 What are the learning outcomes?

We followed Pollard and Filer's lead and started applying these questions to what we already knew about homework, both from the research literature and from a pilot study we were carrying out in two schools (one primary and one secondary). As a result, we generated the conceptual framework shown in Figure 4.1. This framework sets out the main elements of the proposed research and the possible relationships between them.

At the centre of the framework is the *homework assignment or task*. The learning content of any particular piece of homework will depend critically on the *nature of the task*, including its intended purposes, its relationship to the ongoing curriculum, and its relationship to what the learner already knows. In addition, our pilot work, together with other studies of homework (see Wallace, 1995) suggested that we needed to pay careful attention to the *students' engagement with the homework task*, that is whether or not the homework is carried out with care, thoughtfulness and some degree of emotional involvement in the task. We were also interested in the *feedback* which the students received from their teachers on completed homework tasks, as this might be an important element in the learning process.

Figure 4.1 *Conceptual framework for the investigation*

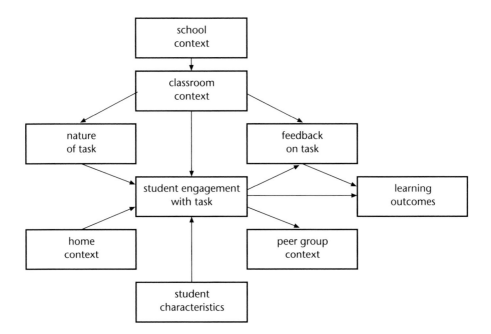

We needed to locate homework within the different contexts where it takes place. This is not straightforward, as homework – almost by definition – moves between a number of different contexts. Moreover, the values attached to homework, the practices associated with it and the assumptions made about it may differ markedly across these different contexts. In our framework, we identified four contexts as being of particular relevance:

1 *The school context.* For each school in the project, we needed to understand that school's particular approach to homework, how much it was valued at school level, and what the school's policies and practices were.
2 *The classroom context.* It is here that individual homework assignments are set, collected and returned. Thus, we needed to understand both the teacher's approach to homework, and to see how particular homework assignments related to other ongoing work in the classroom.
3 *The home context.* We assumed that much homework would be done at home, and that it was important to understand how homework was viewed within the home context, and the extent to which parents and any siblings of the student valued and supported it.
4 *The peer-group context.* We thought it was important to look at homework within the peer-group context, both in terms of the opportunities it provided for collaborative activities with peers, and in terms of its potential conflict with other peer-group activities and values.

We also needed to recognise that these specific contexts were in turn located within a range of wider social, political and cultural contexts. For example, as already mentioned, we would be carrying out our study at a time when there was considerable support and enthusiasm for homework from politicians and policymakers.

In addition to tasks and contexts, we thought it was important to include *student characteristics* as part of the framework. Earlier research had suggested that students' engagement with homework may be related to their *learning identity*, or how they see themselves as learners within the various contexts in which they are participating (Ball, 1981; Measor and Woods, 1984). In addition, Pollard and Filer suggest that learning identity is closely related to other student characteristics such as *age, gender, ethnicity* and *achievement level*, and indeed there is evidence that female students do more homework than males (Harris et al., 1993). We wanted to include factors such as students' *attitude to the subject* and their *prior knowledge* in relation to the task as these were likely to be relevant to their response to a particular homework assignment.

Finally, we wanted to look at how all these factors – tasks, contexts, and student characteristics – resulted in specific *learning outcomes*. For example, we wished to discover whether a particular homework assignment had increased any student's knowledge of the topic, provided the student with new skills or understanding, or helped her or him to make connections with out-of-school learning. Following Pollard and Filer, we were interested in looking at wider learning outcomes, such as whether the completion (or non-completion) of a homework assignment had any impact on a student's self-esteem, attitude towards the subject, or wider orientation towards learning.

The project's conceptual framework, as shown in Figure 4.1, includes the main elements described above. It also indicates possible relationships between these elements. Thus *learning outcomes* are seen as being generated primarily through an interaction between the *nature of the task, student engagement with the task*, and *feedback on the task*. Contextual factors are seen as influencing different parts of this process. It seems likely that the *school context* will not have a direct influence on a particular homework, but is more likely to exert its influence indirectly through the *classroom context*. The *classroom context* in turn is likely to influence both the *nature of the task*, the *student's engagement with the task* and the *feedback on the task*. Finally, the *home* and *peer-group contexts* are seen as having their main influence on the *students' engagement with the task*, as are the *student characteristics*.

It is important to be clear about both the strengths and weaknesses of a conceptual framework like the one presented here. The main advantage is that it can represent, in a visual form, what are regarded as the main elements of the research and how these might be related. As we will see, this representation can help directly with framing the specific research questions of the study, as well as providing a structure for data collection and analysis. The main weakness is that such a framework is inevitably a simplification of what are likely to be quite complex processes. In particular, representing elements and influences by boxes and arrows can suggest a rather mechanistic view of the learning process, which does not adequately reflect the sophistication of much socio-cultural theorising. In short, it is important to see the framework as an aid to the research process rather than as an accurate representation of reality.

The research questions (RQs) for the study followed directly from the conceptual framework:

RQ1: What kinds of task are set for homework?
RQ2: To what extent and in what ways do students engage with these tasks?
RQ3: What are the main contexts in which homework originates and is carried out, and how is homework perceived and valued within those contexts?
RQ4: What kinds of support are provided for homework within these contexts?
RQ5: What effects do pupil characteristics (such as age, gender and learning identity) have on the way homework is perceived and carried out?
RQ6: What are the learning outcomes arising from particular homework tasks?
RQ7: How do tasks, contexts and pupil characteristics interact with each other to enhance or reduce learning outcomes?

Some of the questions (RQ1–4 and RQ6) can be seen as attempts to discover more about the contents of the main elements of the study (in other words, to 'open up' one or more of the boxes in the framework). The remaining two questions (RQ5 and RQ7) are more concerned with possible influences between these elements. Indeed, RQ7 is essentially trying to identify all possible influences on learning outcomes and how these might be related.

Design and methods

The nature of our research questions suggested that we needed to carry out an in-depth study where we looked in detail at homework, and how it was perceived and valued, in a small number of research sites. This requirement indicated a qualitative research design, looking for depth and meaning, rather than a broader quantitative approach. We therefore based the research around a small number of schools, and within each school focused on a small number of students in one particular year group. We also used a range of data collection techniques in order to develop as full a picture as possible of what was going on.

The *sample* was based around four secondary schools and four primary schools in the South West of England. The secondary schools served very contrasting areas (known as catchment areas). Two schools had a high proportion of students whose low parental income meant that they were eligible for free school meals, with many of the students in one of these schools coming from ethnic minority groups. (In the UK a midday meal is provided in schools, and the number of free school meals taken up in a school is commonly used as an indicator of the proportion of students from lower socio-economic backgrounds.) The third school had a specific religious affiliation and drew students from all areas of a city, while the fourth served a large rural area. The catchment areas from which the primary school pupils were drawn were very similar to those of the secondary schools. Each primary school was a 'feeder' school for one of the secondary schools, so the oldest primary school students would transfer to that secondary school.

In each secondary school we focused on Year 8 (ages 12–13), and selected six students for more intensive study. The form tutor (or another teacher who knew the class well) grouped the students into three bands – high attaining, medium attaining and low attaining – and we selected one boy and one girl at random from each band. Data were actually collected on a larger number of students, as additional students were included either as back-up, or in order to comply with requests from staff in the participating schools. In the primary schools we focused on Year 5 (ages 9–10) and again selected six students for intensive study. We also interviewed at least one of the parents of each of these students.

In the secondary schools, a total of 64 teachers from the five subject areas of English, mathematics, science, modern languages and humanities were involved in the study. This number was larger than anticipated, mainly due to the widespread setting of students in ability groups across all subject areas. Four form tutors were interviewed. In the primary schools, seven teachers were involved. We also interviewed the headteachers of all the participating schools.

In view of our interest in the range of contexts included in the framework, we decided to carry out interviews with students, teachers, parents and headteachers. Each student was interviewed twice, usually at home. The first interview was about homework in general, and the second related to specific pieces of homework the student had been set. Each teacher was also interviewed twice, with the first interview again being about homework in general and the second about the specific piece of homework the student had been set. Parents were each interviewed once, covering areas such as their perceptions of homework in general, their aspirations for their child, and their own role in homework. A few parents also commented on the specific homework after the second interview with the student. The headteachers received a single interview focusing on overall school homework policy and practices.

All interviews were tape-recorded and transcribed. Each transcript was then checked by one of us (Pamela Greenhough) against the original tape-recording. This was a labour-intensive process, but one which was necessary to identify small but potentially significant errors in the transcription.

A variety of other methods were used. Observations were made of lessons in which homework was set in order to relate the content of the homework to the work covered in the lesson. Overall, data was collected on 65 different homework assignments at secondary level and 15 at primary level. Field notes were made in schools, homes and communities about a range of factors that might have a bearing on homework in each of these contexts. A wide range of documentation was gathered, including copies of homework policies and students' homework planners. In addition, photocopies were made of all the work produced by the students in response to the specific piece of homework which had been set.

A case study: the circles homework

In this section, we present a case study of one particular homework task: the Circles homework, set by a secondary school mathematics teacher called Donald for his Year 8 class. We will look in particular at the different ways in which two of his students, Adam and Sophie, responded to the homework.

There are two main reasons for presenting this case study. First, it provides an illustration of how the conceptual framework described in the previous section can be used in the presentation and analysis of data. Thus we will use the main components of the framework – such as *school context, classroom context* – to structure the account we provide of the homework and the students' responses to it. Second, the case study provides an interesting contrast in learning outcomes. Although the homework was the same for all students in the class, it seems that the learning outcomes for Adam and Sophie were not the same.

In the first part of the case study, we identify the *main contexts* in which the Circles homework originated and was carried out, and the *kinds of support* provided for the students in each of these contexts. This focus addresses the third and fourth of our research questions (RQ3 and RQ4). The *student characteristics* of both Adam and Sophie are also examined (RQ5). We then discuss the *nature of the task* that was set in the Circles homework (RQ1) and the two students' engagement with it (RQ2). Following this, we examine features of the classroom context after the homework was completed (RQ3) and consider the *learning outcomes* for both students (RQ6). The second part of the case study – our analysis – addresses the final research question (RQ7). Here we indicate the ways in which tasks, contexts, kinds of support and student characteristics interact to enhance or reduce learning outcomes for different students.

The school context

This secondary school was located in an inner-city area. Over 40 per cent of its students came from ethnic minority backgrounds, and around half of these students had English as an additional language. Around 25 per cent of students received free school meals, and at the time of the study, less than 30 per cent obtained the top three grades (A–C) in five or more subjects in the General Certificate of Secondary Education (the 'GCSE' examination taken at age 16+ in the UK). The school was strongly oriented towards its local community and staff placed a great deal of emphasis on celebrating cultural diversity. The school had a homework policy document containing the following rationale:

> *Homework is an entitlement for all students and it is an important element of the overall learning strategy. It provides opportunity for individual learning which extends and enhances what has gone on in the classroom. It supports development of study habits to raise achievement and lay the foundations for lifelong learning.*

The policy document made clear that all students were expected to record their homework assignments in their homework planners, and that these should be regularly monitored by parents and teachers. (Homework planners are common in the UK. They are essentially structured diaries which provide space for students to write down their homework tasks and the date by which the homework should be completed. They usually provide space for parents and teachers to comment on the students' work.) The policy document set out how much time should be spent altogether on homework each evening. For students in Year 8 this was 45–90 minutes.

The atmosphere in the school was tense during the time of our data collection. This was primarily because an external inspection by a team from the

Office for Standards in Education took place during this period. The inspection involved an intensive week-long visit to the school, during which lessons were observed by the inspectors. Many teachers were feeling stressed and there were high levels of staff absence. Despite this, we received full and generous co-operation with our research.

The classroom context: before the homework

The Circles homework was given out in a Year 8 mathematics lesson. The students in the class were aged 12–13 years and were in the upper ability band, but not in the top ability set. The atmosphere in both the lessons observed was quiet and purposeful, even when the teacher briefly left the room.

Donald had been teaching mathematics for five years. He viewed maths as 'a doing subject', believing that 'pupils progress through doing questions, making mistakes and learning how to rectify those mistakes.' He was positive about homework and considered it 'an important tool for reinforcing class-work and providing thought-provoking questions.' Donald tried to make his homework tasks 'back up' the work done in class, but tried not to make them simply 'finishing off' exercises. He considered his most successful homework tasks were a mixture of questions that both recapped the work done in class and asked some new, thought-provoking questions. For Year 8 he aimed to produce one fairly large (45–60 minutes) homework assignment, which he tried to set on the last lesson of the week to be handed in for the first lesson of the next week. He attempted to mark his homework the night it was handed in and give it back during the next lesson.

Adam: home context

Adam lived with his mother, stepfather and younger siblings in a privately-owned house which was about 100 years old. His mother worked full-time as a processing clerk. His stepfather was an information technology trainer who worked long hours of overtime in the evenings and at weekends. Adam's mother had grown up in an eastern European country and her experiences there had strongly influenced her views on education. She thought that teachers in her homeland were very strict, using corporal punishment and giving pupils a lot of homework. She had ended up hating both school and home-work. She much preferred the UK system. She thought that homework was 'very important' as it 'teaches them that they've got things to do, we got to do these first.' She made an analogy with her own work and said that homework 'teaches them to appreciate more the leisure time they've got.' Adam's mother said that Adam always did his homework, and spent about an hour a night on it. She helped him if asked, but never monitored whether he had done it since he was very conscientious.

Adam's stepfather had been brought up in the UK and his own experiences of homework were mixed. If he liked the subject or topic he would enter into it 'with a real passion and enthusiasm', while if it was something that didn't interest him he would do the 'barest minimum'. Like Adam's mother, he was also in favour of homework, saying that 'it reinforces the point of education generally...it shows the child can apply himself outside of, you know, of that learning environment.' He said he would be 'pretty depressed about it' if homework were abolished.

Adam: student characteristics

Adam's mother considered that Adam was 'a very nice chap' although he could be sulky at times. She said he was responsible and helpful in the house. She was proud of him, and said that his last report 'had just good and excellent'. Adam's stepfather considered that he just took his homework in his stride 'like everything else in life', showing little emotion. He described Adam as being 'a very, very reliable emotionally mature trustworthy boy, beyond his age in terms of his behaviour in many ways.'

Adam considered himself to be 'quite talented, sometimes a bit bossy, athletic.' He said he liked to push himself to the limits, both in his schoolwork and in his hobbies. He was a keen BMX bike rider and spent time outside with his friends building ramps for the bikes. He was also interested in fantasy war games and spent a great deal of time building scale models and then acting out war scenarios with his friends. Adam liked most subjects, especially art. He considered that 'maths I reckon is quite easy, [I can] answer a question just like that.' He wanted to move into a higher mathematics set. Adam thought it was important to do homework as it helped you learn, and said 'if you don't learn nothing there's no point of going to school is there, if you're just going to pratt [play] around.' He said that he didn't get much help at home with his homework as most of the time he found it quite easy. Occasionally he might ask his mum or dad for help, or phone a friend to find out what he had to do. Adam said he was quite confident about asking a teacher in class if he didn't understand. He put a lot of effort into maths homework 'cos I reckon that's important when you grow older.' He thought he'd be quite bored if homework were abolished.

Adam: peer group context

Adam had a small group of friends with whom he shared his interests in BMX bikes and war models. He would sometimes ask his friends for help with homework when he was stuck, but this did not seem to happen very often. He said he didn't often copy other students' work because he liked to work things out for himself. Adam said there were some students who put more effort into their homework than he did, and some who put less. He described those who put more effort in as 'the ones that are really keen on…really, really keen on doing it, like the ones that don't have anything else to do.' When asked what he thought about such students he said it was 'up to you' how much effort you put into your work. He himself put more effort into subjects he thought would be most relevant for later life. Adam described those students who put in less effort than him as 'trouble makers'. He said it was 'up to them if they want to get a bad education, they're a bit stupid aren't they…if they want to be a beggar when they're older…it's up to them.' He said that such students regarded him as a 'keener' (a local term for a student who works hard). 'They think, 'Oh, you love doing homework, you're such a keener.' And I'm, like, 'No, I just want to get a good education, I don't think *you* do though.''

Sophie: home context

Sophie lived with her mother and two sisters in a house which had been publicly-built about 50 years ago. Her mother had a boyfriend but she declined to give any details about him as she considered they weren't relevant. She was not currently working. Her last job had been working in a bar. Sophie's mother's own experiences of school and homework were not positive. She said that she 'didn't have much interest in homework...I wasn't very good at doing me homework, and I wasn't very good at going to school.' She had sometimes truanted from school but she did not want her daughters to know this. She considered that homework was 'quite important' at this stage, as it provided an opportunity to catch up if they'd missed anything in the class. She thought that Sophie did about one-and-a-half hours three or four nights a week, which she thought was about right. Her mother sometimes monitored what homework Sophie was doing, asking what she had to do and reminding her to get it done: 'It's just really giving her a prod now and again.' She said Sophie asked her for help with English, her boyfriend for help with history or geography, and her elder sister for help with mathematics and French, as she herself was not very good at those subjects. She did not think that homework should be abolished as she considered there was so much disruption in classes that students often didn't learn much at school.

Sophie: student characteristics

Sophie's mother described her as 'pretty quiet, but then on the other hand she's not!' By this she meant that Sophie was quieter than her two sisters, but that if she had something to say she would voice her opinions. She thought that Sophie took school 'quite seriously', although at the last parents' evening it emerged that she had been 'playing up' in one teacher's lesson. She thought Sophie's behaviour fluctuated a lot at this age 'because the hormones are kicking in.' Sophie herself said that she often got ear infections and that her hearing was then affected. She said that she was quite shy, especially when making friends and meeting new teachers. She said: 'I'm loud at home and I like to argue...I'm normally in bad moods when I'm at home.' Her elder sister in particular annoyed her there. When not doing her homework she would spend time reading, watching TV or listening to music.

At school, Sophie considered herself to be hard working, except when she didn't like the subject or the teacher. She liked PE, art, English and science, and disliked geography, French and maths: 'I don't like maths and if I'm stuck I just don't do the work, but I think my teacher sees me as quite a good little girl cos I sit with some quiet people.' She didn't think that homework helped her learn, as by the time she came to do it she was tired and had forgotten what she was doing: 'It doesn't help me and it doesn't help my friends, it just makes us even more tired.' Sophie said she sometimes phoned her friends to discuss homework. She seemed to be reluctant to ask teachers for help, especially during the lesson, and preferred to ask her friends 'to save embarrassment'. Sophie said she would be happy if homework were abolished, although she would be really bored without science homework.

Sophie: peer-group context

Sophie was asked whether there were some students who put more effort into their homework than she did. Her response was somewhat complex:

> In my lessons there's about three people and they're, like, goodie goodies. They're my friends, but I don't hang around with them or anything because a lot of people don't like them and they can act babyish as well and I don't like hanging round people that act babyish. And sometimes they've helped me out with my homework and it's kind of weird cos I'm in the same group as them in like every lesson, and we're, like, nearly top set in nearly every lesson. But I reckon they're so much smarter than me.
>
> (Interviewer: What do you mean when you say they act babyish?)
>
> At breaktime they spend their time playing games like 'poo touch'. They pretend they've got poo on their hands and touch people.

Sophie also said there were students who put less effort into homework than her. These were 'mostly the boys, they don't really care…they are, like, real jokers, if you look through their books all they've got is the title and the date, they don't do anything.' She thought that in general girls put more effort into their homework than boys did.

The nature of the task

The Circles homework was slightly different from Donald's normal homework in that it introduced a new topic which would be covered in the subsequent lesson. The homework was set at the end of a lesson on Friday afternoon. During the first half of the lesson the students had been completing their own Records of Achievement, and then they carried out an exercise on shape. With five minutes remaining Donald stopped the students and said: 'Right. I want your best concentration while I set the homework.'

He told them it was 'absolutely critical' that they did the homework, and repeated that it was 'vital, essential that it is done.' He asked them to get out their homework planners and write 'Homework due on Tuesday 8th February. Period 3. Complete Circles sheet'. Both the target students, Adam and Sophie, did this (see Figures 4.2 and 4.3).

Donald then gave out the homework sheet and explained that they needed to find some circular household objects and measure the circumference and diameter of each one. He checked that the class were familiar with the terms 'circumference' and 'diameter', and reinforced their understanding by drawing a cylinder on the chalkboard with arrows indicating the circumference and the diameter. Adam drew in his planner a straight arrow labelled 'diameter' and a curved arrow labelled 'circumfirance' (see Figure 4.2), while Sophie copied the diagram on the back of her sheet. Donald explained how they might use a piece of string to measure the circumference. He ended by repeating that it was vital the homework was completed by Tuesday, as they would use the measurements in class. Adam's completed homework sheet is depicted in Figure 4.4.

Figure 4.2 *Adam's planner*

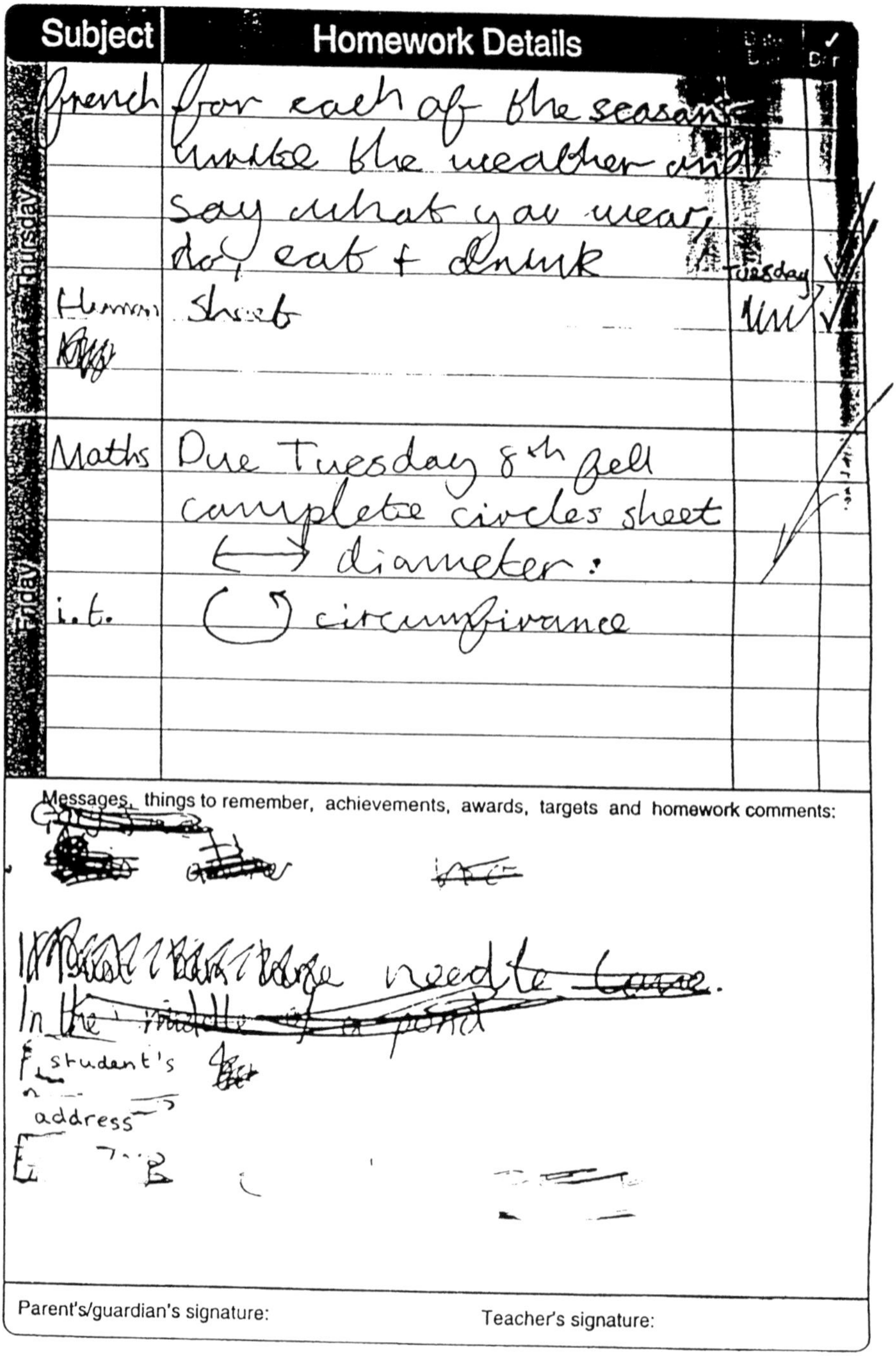

Figure 4.3 *Sophie's planner*

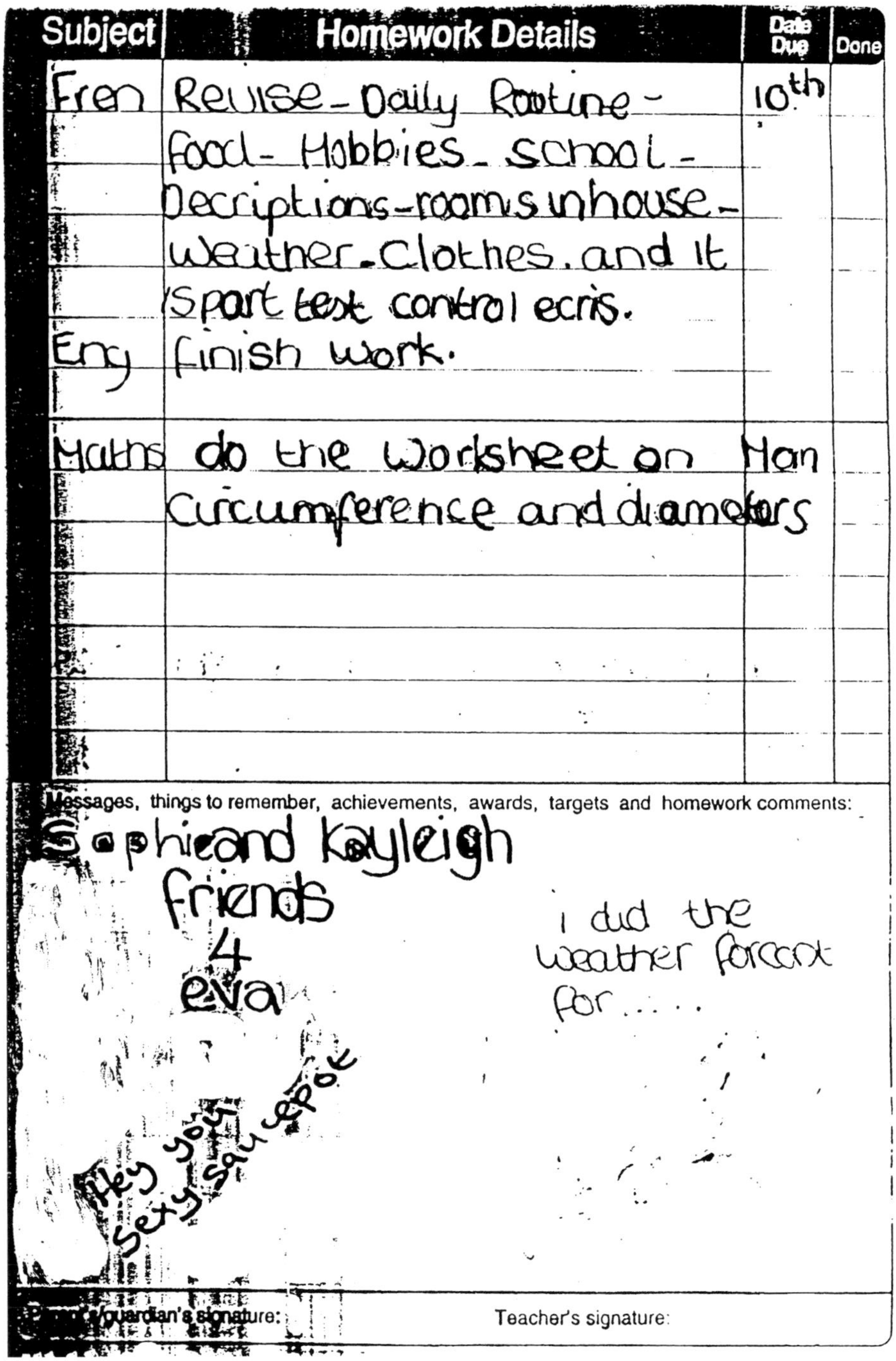

Subject	Homework Details	Date Due	Done
Fren	Revise - Daily Routine - food - Hobbies - school - Decriptions - rooms in house - weather - clothes. and it 's part test control ecris.	10th	
Eng	finish work.		
Maths	do the Worksheet on Man Circumference and diameters		

Messages, things to remember, achievements, awards, targets and homework comments:

Sophie and Kayleigh
friends
4
eva

Hey you sexy saucepot

i did the weather forecast for.....

Parent/Guardian's signature: Teacher's signature:

Figure 4.4 *Homework task completed by Adam*

Circles Homework

1) Find 10 different circular items around the house (tins, bottles etc) and then carefully measure the **circumference** (distance around the outside) and **diameter** (distance 'across' the circle) for each one. Record your results on the following table.

Item	Circumference	Diameter
can of beens	23½ cm	7½ cm
Lip Therapy tin	15 cm	5 cm
Mayo Jar	25.1 cm	8 cm
Mug	25½ cm	7.4 cm
heat mat	53 cm	19 cm
plat	60 cm	26 cm
Apple	12 cm	6 cm
Washing up Liquid	23 cm	8 cm
Pat	30 cm	8 cm
	25 cm	5 cm

2) Do you notice any link between the two measurements that you have made?

yes sume of them are Dauble the number of the diameter

3) At a fairground a 'big wheel' has a diameter of 60 metres. How long do you think the circumference might be?

~~[illegible]~~ ~~180 metres~~ 210m

Student engagement with the homework

Adam did his maths homework straightaway after school. He completed all the sections and reckoned it took him about 25 minutes. He did it in his bedroom but went downstairs to locate various objects to measure. He said he put 'quite a lot of effort' into the homework, explaining 'I tried to do quite exact measurements on, like, the circles...I thought cos I'd probably get...I'd get more marks for it.' In terms of support, Adam said at first that he found the homework easy and did not need help. However he later reported that his stepfather had helped him with the last question, because 'I didn't really know how to do that.' He and his stepfather had made a sketch together of the Ferris wheel (see Figure 4.4), and then Adam had used one of his earlier measurements to get an approximation for the wheel.

Sophie did not attempt the homework. She said it was because 'I lost my planner on that day and then I'd put a sheet into my bag but I couldn't find it anywhere, I still haven't found it.' (The researcher found it in the back of her maths book amongst other worksheets.) Sophie claimed failing to do the homework had not disadvantaged her in the subsequent lesson as she had asked her friends to explain it to her just before the lesson started.

Classroom context: after the homework

Donald started the lesson following the homework by asking the students to draw four columns in their exercise book, similar to the homework but with an extra column. He drew a similar figure on the chalkboard. He walked round the class and looked at the completed homework sheets. When he came to Sophie, she said something about losing her sheet. Donald replied that there was nothing they could do about it now.

Donald returned to the front of the class and asked the students to give him some measurements from their homework. He wrote these on the chalkboard in the appropriate columns. He then started to divide the circumference by the diameter and wrote this figure in the fourth column. The students were encouraged to join in these calculations. He drew a ring around two sets of measurements in red and said that he thought 'they were done the best'. He explained that if they had made their measurements very accurately it would always come to the same figure. He wrote on the chalkboard 'If you measured any circle really accurately and then did circumference divided by the diameter you would get 3.14 to 2 d.p.' (2 d.p. means to two decimal places.) He told the students that this quantity was called 'pi' after the Greek letter. He wrote 'C = π D' and told the students to write this in their exercise books. He then wrote some examples on the chalkboard for them to work out using this formula (see Figures 4.5 and 4.6).

Adam started work immediately and continued to do so for some time. Sophie, however, talked to her friends and did not seem to attempt any of the examples. After a while, Donald went through the first section of work, asking students for the answers and writing them on the chalkboard. It looked as if Sophie wrote the answers in her book as he did so. When Donald asked Sophie to give her answer to one of the questions she said: 'I haven't worked out them.' Later Donald came and stood in front of Sophie but did not speak to her. It looked as if Sophie did not know what to do but copied the diagrams and questions into her book so as to give the appearance of working.

Figure 4.5 *Pages from Adam's exercise book*

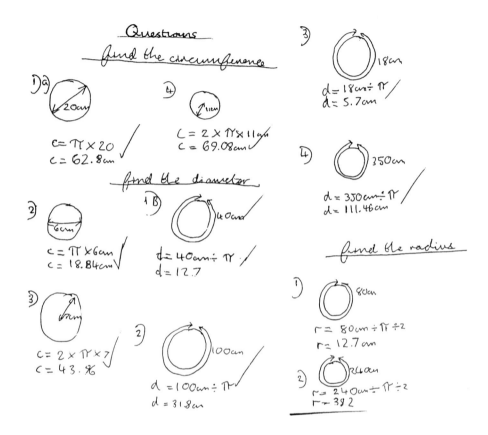

Feedback on task performance

When interviewed later about his homework Adam thought he had got 'good marks, I got them all right.' He said he was pleased as he 'didn't try exactly my hardest I've ever tried and I thought didn't take very long, and I got quite good marks for it.' He thought Donald must have marked it quite quickly, as Adam thought he'd spotted a mistake in his work that hadn't been noticed. However he thought he might have got extra marks for attempting question 3, and 'getting the closest to it'.

Donald thought Adam had done 'very well' on the task and that 'his measurements were really accurate.' He was pleased Adam had tried to do the last two questions. He seemed to think (from memory) that Adam had got around 3.1 for the second question, although Adam had actually thought the circumference was 'double' the diameter. Donald thought that Adam's performance was 'very typical' of him. Adam was an able student who would not have found much difficulty with the homework.

Figure 4.6 *Pages from Sophie's exercise book*

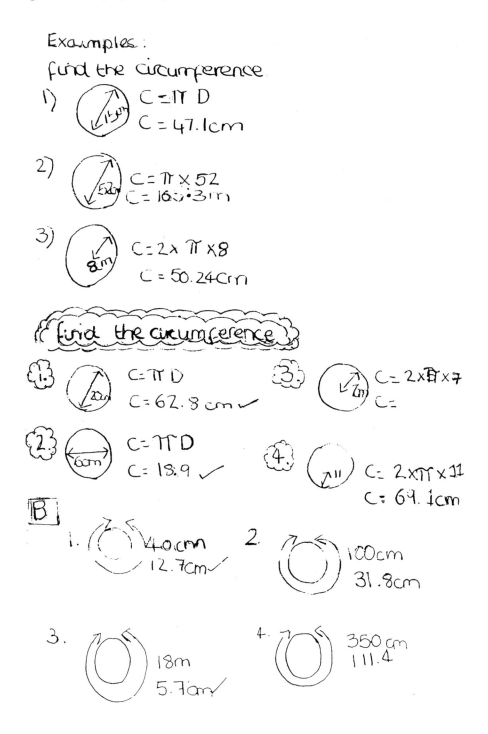

As Sophie had not done the task she did not get any feedback on her task performance. However, when interviewed later Donald thought she had done the task 'all right', although he admitted that 'I'm sorry but I can't sort of, off-hand, remember the exact sheet.' He saw her as a hard-working student whose work was always well presented, but commented that 'I don't think she always asks for extra help when she needs it.'

Learning outcomes

Adam said he knew before the homework how to measure circumference and diameter, and that he knew what sort of things to measure. He remembered from the lesson after the homework that the 'circumference was three times as much as the diameter, nearly every time.' He understood how the teacher had applied the formula to judge which sets of measurements to ring as being the most accurate. Adam seemed to have a good understanding of pi and how it could be applied, although he thought it came from Latin rather than Greek.

Adam was asked to reflect on five specific homework tasks, including the Circles homework. Of the five, he thought he had put least care into the Circles homework as it was 'just, like, not very exciting or anything, just get something and measure it and then put the answers down.' However, he also said that the Circles homework had helped him feel more confident about his work.

Unlike Adam, Sophie did not seem to have learned much from the home-work or the subsequent lesson. When interviewed after the lesson, her understanding of pi was hazy. She did not seem to understand it was a con-stant but thought of it as one of the dimensions of the circle to be measured: 'I think diameter is, er, around it and the circumference – I mean the pi is the arrow inside.' Sophie did not know why the teacher had judged the two sets of measurements as the most accurate. She said that if she kept missing lots of homework she would probably get a detention. But she didn't think she needed to catch up on this one.

Analysis of the case study

At one level, the story arising from this case study is clear and straightforward. Adam completed his homework and appeared in the process to have learned something about the underlying mathematics. Sophie did not complete her homework and there appeared to be significant gaps in her understanding. In this case at least, it would seem that doing homework can make a positive con-tribution to learning. We can, however, probe beneath the surface of this conclusion. In particular, we can ask why Adam completed his homework while Sophie did not. The data we have collected and presented according to the framework allows us to explore possible answers to this question.

The most likely answers seem to lie in what we have termed the *students' characteristics*. For a start, the two students had different attitudes towards mathematics. Adam liked mathematics, he found it easy and thought he was good at it. He wanted to move up to a higher ability set.

In contrast, Sophie did not like mathematics. She found it hard and did not think she was good at it. Thus she was approaching the homework with a mixture of negativity and lack of confidence. In addition to her negative feelings about mathematics, Sophie was also approaching the homework with some significant gaps in her knowledge. In particular, she seemed not to know the definitions of the words 'diameter' and 'circumference'. These were essential prerequisites for being able to carry out the homework. Donald assumed that the students knew these terms, although he did recap them briefly when setting the homework at the end of the lesson. Sophie did copy his diagram on the back of her sheet but her understanding of this was almost certainly limited.

The analysis so far suggests that the key differences between the two students lay in their attitude towards mathematics and their pre-homework understanding of key elements in the task. However, there were other differences as well, which might have been important. First, there were differences in the amount of support available and used in the students' homes. On the whole, Adam did not need much help with the homework. It was only when he got onto the third question – about the Ferris wheel – that he obtained some help from his stepfather. We do not know how and why his stepfather was approached, but we do know that he helped Adam draw a sketch of the wheel so he could visualise the nature of the problem. This might have been a crucial moment in Adam's understanding of the task, as he was then able to solve the problem by 'scaling up' from one of the earlier examples.

In contrast, it seems that Sophie did not seek or receive help at home. Her mother said she found it hard to help with mathematics, and Sophie asked her elder sister for help when she needed it. However, Sophie's relationship with her elder sister was clearly turbulent. She said in her interview that she was 'normally in bad moods at home', and that her elder sister annoyed her particularly. It did not seem as if this sister was a particularly reliable source of support.

Second, peer group support, another potential form of assistance identified in our conceptual framework, also played a different part for the two students. On this occasion Adam's peer group appeared to play little or no role in the homework. In contrast, Sophie's peer group played a more complex role in what happened, particularly during the lesson after the homework. As Sophie herself said, she usually sat in class with a group of friends whom she thought were much cleverer than her. Her attitude towards the group seemed quite ambiguous though, as she said that she found their behaviour immature and did not really want to be associated with them outside the classroom. At the same time, she found it useful to be in their midst during the lesson, as it helped her conceal from the teacher the fact she did not know what was going on. Whether this 'support' from the peer group was in Sophie's best interests is clearly a matter for debate.

Third, there were differences between the students in their use of the teacher as a source of help or support. Adam was described by his teacher as someone who often asked for help, although on this occasion he did not need to. Sophie, on the other hand, had the opportunity to ask for the teacher's help but did not do so. This seemed to be a common characteristic of hers, as both she and her teacher had commented on her general reluctance to ask for help.

Our analysis of this case study suggests that a number of factors might explain why homework made a positive contribution to learning for Adam, but not for Sophie. These include differences in the students' attitudes to maths, in their prior knowledge of the task, and the support they received (or did not receive) at home, in the peer group and from the teacher. The analysis thus highlights both the complexity of the learning process as well as the value of the conceptual framework in revealing this complexity.

How typical is the case study?

One question which is frequently asked of case studies concerns the extent to which they may be considered as 'typical' of whatever they are cases of. We are in a position to draw on data from the rest of our study to indicate some areas in which this case resembled other examples of homework, and areas where it did not. It should be noted that the opportunity to do this may not be available to other case study researchers – and particularly those who are carrying out a relatively small-scale study.

We start by considering the nature of the homework task. Here, the Circles homework differed from the majority of those in our study in two important aspects. First, it was set as a piece of preparatory work leading up to a lesson. The teacher's intention was that students would collect data about circumference and diameter, which could be used in the next lesson to illustrate the relationship between them. In contrast, most of the homework tasks we observed in our study arose from the lesson preceding it. These tasks usually consisted of work intended to reinforce or extend the student's understanding of concepts or skills introduced during the lesson. As the example of Sophie shows, there is a significant risk for the teacher in setting a preparatory homework. Non-completion may mean that students are unable to participate fully in the following lesson. It is possibly for this reason that preparatory homework tasks, like the Circles homework, were very much in the minority in our study.

The second atypical feature of the Circles task is that it explicitly tried to link the home and school environments. Students were asked to locate circular objects in their homes, measure their properties, and bring the measurements back into school. In contrast, the vast majority of homework tasks in our study arose directly from the school curriculum and required students to make few, if any, links with the world outside school. A more typical mathematics homework assignment would be to complete some problems similar to those worked on in class, while a science homework assignment might be to write up an experiment carried out in school. As we have argued elsewhere (Hughes, 2002), homework has the potential to help students make connections between their school learning and their out-of-school learning. But unfortunately this potential is not often realised.

While the Circles task may not have been typical of other homework tasks in our study, there were other aspects of the case that reflected our findings more broadly. For example, the fact that Sophie did not complete the homework was by no means unusual. Across the study as a whole we found that nearly one homework assignment in five was not completed. Sometimes non-completion was due to the student's absence from school, but more often it was for other reasons. Sometimes students felt there was little to be gained from doing the homework, as when they felt they already knew what it was about. On other occasions, students seemed unable to cope with the content of the homework, although they did not always express it like that. We also found several instances, like Sophie's, where students conveniently 'lost' or 'forgot about' a homework task in a subject they disliked or one with which they were likely to struggle.

A further area where we need to consider 'typicality' is that of gender. We noted earlier how homework is often considered to be gendered in that female students complete it more conscientiously than males. Indeed, Sophie herself made this same point. The present case study appears at first sight to run counter to this gender stereotyping, in that here it was the boy who completed his homework diligently, while the girl did not. However, across our study as a whole, we came across little evidence to support this gender stereotyping. We found no gender differences in students' feelings about homework, in their completion of homework, in the extent to which they worked with other students on homework, or in the amount they felt they had gained from homework. Indeed, the only area where we found significant gender differences was in the help provided at home, where there seemed to be a clear 'specialisation' according to gender. Mothers were much more likely to help with English, languages and humanities, while fathers, brothers and uncles were more likely to help with science and mathematics.

Another important issue concerns Donald's lack of awareness that Sophie was not engaging properly with either her homework or her classwork. Again, this was not untypical. Across the study as a whole we saw several instances where the student's grasp of a particular homework was hazy, but the teacher was not aware of the problem. In saying this we are not intending to be critical of the teachers in our study. Rather, we are making the point that it is difficult for any teacher with a class of 20 or 30 students to be constantly aware of the extent and nature of each individual student's engagement with and understanding of his or her work.

Conclusion: educational implications of the research

In this final section of the chapter, we draw out some implications for educational policy and practice and for researchers. We will restrict ourselves to implications arising directly from the case study, rather than from the wider project.

First, the findings of the case study make problematic the notion of a 'good homework task'. It is common to find in the literature on homework the suggestion that particular tasks can be identified as being 'good tasks', and that these are likely to make a significant contribution to student learning. Indeed, such suggestions have often been made in discussions we have had ourselves with policy-makers and practitioners. The evidence of the case study suggests that what constitutes a 'good task' may well vary significantly from student to student. In this case, the homework task worked well for Adam, but had little or no effect on Sophie's learning.

Second, the findings also have disturbing implications concerning the issue of inequality between students, and the role that homework might play in its perpetuation. The case study highlighted the differences between Adam, a student who was well motivated towards mathematics and who had good support at home, and Sophie, who was not well motivated and whose support at home was unreliable. Here, the Circles homework appeared to contribute positively to Adam's confidence and knowledge, but had little impact on Sophie. In other words, the homework appeared to be widening the differences between the two students – both in knowledge and in attitude – rather than narrowing them.

The possibility that homework can increase rather than decrease inequality, like many other aspects of school, is of course familiar to many teachers. Indeed, it was mentioned several times in our interviews with them. In response, a number of teachers suggested that their policy was to set what they termed 'can do' homework tasks, which even the lower attaining students were able to complete. While the principles underlying this policy might be laudable, its possible effects on the medium and high attaining students are open to question.

Finally, we wish to emphasise yet again the complexity of the learning process, and the need for theoretical accounts of learning which at least attempt to mirror this complexity. In the present chapter we have tried to show the value of taking a broad socio-cultural perspective and operationalising this through a theoretically based conceptual framework. The framework in turn led to a research design enabling us to collect data which illustrated this complexity, and allowed us to probe into the complex worlds of these two students and their learning. The implication for researchers would seem to be that any who adopt a more simplistic approach to studying learning are likely to overlook crucial aspects of the learning process.

Acknowledgements

The research on which this chapter is based was supported by grant R000237857 from the Economic and Social Research Council. We are very grateful to the schools, teachers, students and parents who took part in this project.

References

Ball, S. (1981) *Beachside Comprehensive: A Case Study of Secondary Schooling.* Cambridge: Cambridge University Press.

Barber, M., Myers, K., Denning, T., Graham, J. and Johnson, M. (1997) *School Performance and Extra-Curricular Provision.* London: Department for Education and Employment.

Blunkett, D. (1997) 'Turn your children off TV and on to learning', *The Mail on Sunday*, 22nd June.

Blunkett, D. (1999) *The Independent*, 20th July.

Cowan, R. and Hallam, S. (1999) *What do We Know about Homework?* Viewpoint 9. London: Institute of Education, University of London.

Daniels, H. (1993) *Charting the Agenda: Educational Activity after Vygotsky.* London: Routledge.

Daniels, H. (2001) *Vygotsky and Pedagogy.* London: Routledge.

Department for Education and Employment (1998a) *Homework: Guidelines for Primary and Secondary Schools.* London: DFEE.

Department for Education and Employment (1998b) *Extending Opportunity: A National Framework for Study Support.* London: DFEE.

Farrow, S., Tymms, P. and Henderson, B. (1999) 'Homework and attainment in primary schools', *British Educational Research Journal,* 25 (3): 323–41.

Greenhough, P. and Hughes, M. (1998) 'Parents' and teachers' interventions in children's reading', *British Educational Research Journal,* 24 (4): 383–98.

Harris, S., Nixon, J. and Rudduck, J. (1993) 'School work, homework and gender', *Gender and Education,* 5: 3–15.

Hughes, M. (2002) 'Learning in and out of school', text of inaugural lecture 4th November 2002. University of Bristol: Graduate School of Education. mimeo.

Hughes, M. and Greenhough, P. (1998a) 'Moving between communities of practice: children linking mathematical activities at home and school', in A. Watson (ed), *Situated Cognition and the Learning of Mathematics.* Oxford: University of Oxford Centre for Mathematics Education Research.

Hughes, M. and Greenhough, P. (1998b) *Homework and its Contribution to Learning.* Unpublished proposal to Economic and Social Research Council.

Hughes, M. and Greenhough, P. (2003a) 'Homework: learning at the interface between home and school cultures', in R. Sutherland, G. Claxton and A. Pollard (eds), *Teaching and Learning Where Worldviews Meet.* Stoke: Trentham Books.

Hughes, M. and Greenhough, P. (2003b) 'How can homework help learning?' *Topic,* 27. Slough: National Foundation for Educational Research.

Measor, L. and Woods, P. (1984) *Changing Schools: Pupil Perspectives on Transfer to a Comprehensive.* Milton Keynes: Open University Press.

Pollard, A. and Filer, A. (1996) *The Social World of Children's Learning.* London: Cassell.

Punch, K. (1998) *An Introduction to Social Research.* London: Sage.

Rogoff, B. (1990) *Apprenticeship in Thinking: Cognitive Development in Social Context.* Oxford: Oxford University Press.

Sharp, C., Keys, W. and Benefield, P. (2001) *Homework: A Review of Recent Research.* Windsor: National Foundation for Educational Research.

Tymms, P. and Fitz-Gibbon, C. (1992) 'The relationship of homework to A-level results', *Educational Research,* 34: 3–10.

Wallace, G. (1995) 'Engaging with learning', in J. Rudduck, R. Chaplain and G. Wallace (eds), *School Improvement: What Can Pupils Tell Us?* London: David Fulton.

Wertsch, J. (1991) *Voices of the Mind: A Socio-Cultural Approach to Mediated Action.* London: Harvester.

Weston, P. (1999) *Homework: Learning from Practice.* London: Office for Standards in Education.

Chapter 5

An inquiry into the moral dimensions of teaching

Gary Fenstermacher and Virginia Richardson

Gary Fenstermacher and Virginia Richardson outline how a set of philosophical ideas was used to underpin an empirical research project examining how students learn virtuous conduct and how teachers foster this learning (The Manner in Teaching Project at the University of Michigan, USA). The researchers aimed to interweave theories and concepts from philosophy with social science theories and methodologies. So the research aimed to address theoretical and methodological issues as well as the substantive topic. The authors highlight how they undertook a critical review of relevant literature to map the field and to identify any gaps. They suggest that there was little work that was analytical and empirical, but which at the same time did not focus on or advocate a specific approach to moral education. An important aspect of Fenstermacher's and Richardson's work is that it sought to examine how virtuous conduct was fostered in the day-to-day transactions and interaction of normal classrooms. In the chapter, the authors emphasise the importance of providing stipulative definitions of terms, particularly when they are subject to multiple interpretations, contested, or otherwise ambiguous. Fenstermacher and Richardson explain why they chose the term 'manner' in their study, rather than the more familiar term 'moral'. They also identify as problematic another widely used term in relation to teaching and learning: the notion of 'modelling'.

The researchers outline their positive ethical stance towards the teachers in whose classrooms the empirical study was conducted. Not only were the teachers fully informed of what the project aimed to do, but they were also actively involved in all stages of the project, from identification of specific questions through to the analysis and interpretation of data. Fenstermacher and Richardson point out that this approach was made possible largely because their funding allowed them to pay for teachers' time in contributing to the project. Paying for teachers' time would be more problematic for a lone researcher doing masters or doctoral research, but it might be achieved if someone were researching in her or his own institution. Another interesting methodological issue raised by the authors is that data analysis can reveal unexpected findings. Researchers need to be alert to the multiple possibilities within their data. Fenstermacher and Richardson reflect on how they almost missed an important dimension in the way teachers encouraged virtuous conduct: what they term the 'call-out'. At first the researchers interpreted call-outs as teachers keeping order in the classroom, but further questioning led them to identify that the call-out often served other functions. This example emphasises the importance of retaining a critical and questioning stance in data analysis, and of being open to other possible interpretations of data. Fenstermacher and Richardson maintain their critical stance towards the end of the chapter when they reflect on the extent to which they answered the questions they set out to address. They also comment on the degree of uncertainty still remaining in relation to some aspects of the substantive topic.*

Introduction

Hardly anyone disputes that there is a moral aspect to teaching. And most agree that teachers ought to have a moral influence on their students. The disagreements typically centre on *what kind* of moral influence teachers ought to have and *how* that influence should be exerted. These disagreements are often settled by the adoption or exclusion of specific approaches to moral education. That is, moral instruction of a particular kind is either prohibited, as is the case with sectarian, religious instruction in the public schools of the USA, or it is aimed at achieving a particular result, such as character education, positive life skills, pro-social development, or the moral dictates of a specific religious faith. Debates rage over what should be included in, or excluded from, the moral aspects of the classroom. But little attention has been paid to the actual moral character and moral sensitivities of teachers and how these become manifest in the everyday activities of the classroom. The Manner in Teaching Project, at the University of Michigan USA, was designed to study how teachers project their own moral character into the life of their classrooms.

If our work is about the moral dimensions of teaching, why do we call our endeavour 'The Manner in Teaching Project' (hereafter MITP)? There are two reasons for this name. The first and more substantive reason is that the term 'manner' points quite well to what we sought to study: those dispositions and traits of character that comprise a person's personality and, more to the point, figure prominently in accounts of a person's moral and ethical conduct. The second reason is that the term 'manner' has a certain neutrality and flatness about it that sets it apart from the term 'moral'. The latter term carries a vast range of meaning, some of it quite controversial (especially in the context of public schooling in the USA, where the research was conducted). The language of 'manner in teaching' permitted us not only to focus on the conduct of the teachers we studied, but also to avoid the controversy that would be likely to arise if we labelled our efforts as a study in the moral education undertaken by classroom teachers.

---

* This chapter expands on material, portions of which have previously appeared in Fenstermacher, 2001; Richardson and Fenstermacher, 2001.

Establishing the philosophical base

The choice of the term 'manner' was not entirely without precedent. William Shakespeare described Hamlet as 'to the manner born' (Act 1, Scene 4), referring to a cluster of dispositions and traits that are the result of a certain form of upbringing. We examine this concept of manner, not in the context of Danish royalty, but in that of the school classroom, and specifically in the actions of teachers. Our notion of manner is not very different from Shakespeare's, but we employ it for a very different purpose. We define manner as action consistent with a set of relatively stable dispositions or traits of character. For example, in everyday language, persons are referred to as tolerant, messy, funny, sneaky, generous, or thoughtful. These descriptions are based on the observation that such persons act consistently over time in ways that reflect these dispositions or traits of character. Included within the broad set of human traits and dispositions is a category known as the virtues. Among them are the intellectual virtues (such as reasonableness, regard for evidence, respect for truth-seeking, and a disciplined approach to enquiry) as well as the moral virtues (such as justice, fairness, compassion, humility and tolerance).

As we set about the study 'manner in teaching' we were most interested in that aspect of manner pertaining to the virtues, to those more noble and civilising characteristics of human conduct. Some observers might say we were interested in moral or character education, but that would be an error. We began our work not with the intent of bringing about some pre-established moral end with teachers and students, but with a desire to understand how conduct aimed at virtue manifests itself in teachers and their classrooms. That is, we used a set of philosophical ideas to set about doing empirical research. Had we called what we were up to 'moral education', we would probably have misled ourselves, the teachers with whom we worked, and any audience there might be for our work. Hence we sought a term that denoted as precisely as possible what we wanted to understand, a term that did not carry all the ideological and normative connotations of the words 'moral education' and 'character education'.

Our initial rationale for studying manner in teaching comes from the philosophical literature suggesting that one acquires virtue by being around virtuous people. These virtuous people impart a capacity for virtuous conduct when they engage the young in certain ways. In the field of normative ethics, this position is typically associated with aretaic or Aristotelean ethics. When we began work on the MITP, it was our understanding that if teachers were to contribute to the moral and intellectual development of their students, the teachers themselves had to possess and exhibit the moral and intellectual traits they sought for their students. We wanted to know whether teachers did possess such traits, how they displayed them in their conduct, and what influence they might have on students.

Once we had put forward an initial philosophical base, we turned to an empirical study of manner in teaching. Our initial focus was on how to 'make manner visible' (Fallona, 2000) so that we could gain empirical access to it. However, early in this empirical phase of the study we noted that acting virtuously is but one of a number of means teachers have for fostering virtue in students. What is more, it might not be the most powerful or compelling means that teachers have at their disposal. These observations led us to shift our attention somewhat from an exclusive focus on teachers' virtuous dispositions and how they are made visible. We now considered a broad range of actions that teachers employ, not only to develop the moral capacities of their students, but also to engender regard for the classroom as a morally nurturing and supportive community. But now we are getting ahead of the story, relating findings before fully describing the study. The first consideration in such a description is the literature that grounds the enquiry.

Examining the relevant literature

Fortunately, there is an expanding literature on the moral dimensions of teaching to aid in conceptualising how teachers foster moral conduct in their classrooms. There are philosophical writings (e.g. Carr, 1991; Carr and Struetel, 1999; Crittenden, 1990; Goodlad et al., 1990; Fenstermacher, 1992; Hostetler, 1997; Katz et al., 1999; Sockett, 1993; Strike and Soltis, 1985; Tom, 1984), as well as the beginnings of an empirical base of research on the moral dimensions of classroom teaching (e.g. Ball and Wilson, 1996; Buzzelli and Johnston, 2002; Campbell, 2002; Hansen, 1993, 2001; Jackson et al., 1993; Oser, 1986). These literatures represent different ways of thinking about how students learn virtuous conduct and how teachers foster this conduct.

For example, one approach in the philosophical literature suggests that students, in the presence of a virtuous person, will themselves acquire virtuous conduct (Ryle, 1975; MacIntyre, 1984). Within this school of thought are those who advocate moral development through modelling, role-playing, case analysis and other activities (e.g. Jackson, 1986; Oser, 1986; Solomon et al., 2001). There is another set of theories about moral development that connects becoming virtuous with the provision of specific curricula and direct teaching of desired behaviours (e.g. Lickona, 1991; Wynne and Ryan, 1997). There is also a literature on the psychology of moral development that suggests that students develop a sense of morality in stages (Bebeau et al., 1999; Rest, 1986). There is, however, little work that examines, analytically and empirically, the nature of moral education in today's classrooms without particular reference to or advocacy of one or another approach to moral education. Among the few exceptions to this claim are the work of Philip Jackson, Robert Boostrom and David Hansen (1993), the emerging work of Elizabeth Campbell and Denis Theissen at the University of Toronto (Campbell, 2002), and the MITP.

The work of Jackson et al. and that of the MITP contribute to our understanding of the moral dimensions of teaching by analysing the ways teachers and their schools sustain moral education in the course of what might be described as 'normal and ordinary' curricula and pedagogy. This work, while still quite new, suggests that many everyday teaching and schooling practices contain significant moral dimensions. That is, typical and seemingly neutral (in a moral sense) programmes and pedagogy are replete with moral initiative and import. When carefully examined, these moral aspects are apparent in such activities as classroom organisation and management, school mission, school rules and procedures, the underlying and tacit aspects of a teacher's objectives for students, and in common instructional practices employed by teachers. These more subtle, often indirect moral dimensions may have as much or more impact on the moral development of students as the more well known programmes of character education, civic education, positive life skills, or pro-social development.

The MITP represents an effort to interweave concepts and theories from philosophy with theories and methods from qualitative social science research. It is part of a relatively small body of educational research that uses philosophy to 'shape' an important and recurring theme in the education of the young into a set of questions and problems that can be investigated empirically. The relationship between the philosophical and empirical inquiries is a dialectical one, in that any gains and insights from one form of inquiry loops back through the other form, creating a metaphorical 'double helix' whereby philosophy and empirical science converse with and benefit from one another, but remain separate strands of scholarship. Thus far we have offered more background on the philosophy than on the empirical science. The next section restores the balance between the two.

The empirical study

The empirical work of the MITP was collaborative, qualitative and interpretive (Erickson, 1986). The teachers with whom we worked were involved with us in our investigations of manner, even as they and their classrooms served as subjects of the study. We believed that they had much to contribute to our understanding of the constructs we were investigating, and could aid us in determining how best to study these constructs. The qualitative, interpretive approach permitted us to remain open-ended about phenomena of interest and ensured that our explications of the critical constructs of the research would be situated in classroom and school realities.

In an effort to gain contrasting perspectives on manner, we decided to locate the research in two quite different types of schools. We have changed the names of the schools and teachers to ensure confidentiality. At one school, which we named Highlands Academy, the teachers themselves chose their own pseudonyms for the study. We were fortunate to have sufficient financial support to pay the teachers for the time they spent in meetings with us, and for the hours they spent working with us to analyse data and react to our analyses of their teaching. We believed that such payment was crucial to acknowledging the teachers as partners in our work. Also, whenever we videotaped their classrooms we immediately made copies of the tapes in VHS format and delivered them to the respective teachers.

The sites

In the summer of 1997 we began looking at elementary schools with diverse student populations that did not already have extensive, school-wide programmes making heavy demands on teachers' time. As we discovered possible sites, we made contact with the principal (headteacher), providing him or her with a detailed letter describing the study and a brief questionnaire to be completed by any interested teachers. One of the first principals with whom we made contact showed considerable interest in the study. She spoke with a number of teachers in her school, then invited us to present the study to four of them who had expressed an interest in participating in the study. All four teachers agreed to join the project. This school, Jordan Elementary, is located in a medium sized city, and has a diverse student population with just over 35 per cent of the students entitled to a free or reduced cost lunch.

Our selection of a second school, Highlands Academy, was influenced by a graduate student on our research team. She contended that an African-centred public school in the area would be an ideal location for the study of manner. After making inquiries at several such sites, one emerged where there was particular interest in what we proposed. We met with a number of teachers at this school, and as a result, gained commitments from seven of them. Highlands Academy is an elementary (primary) school of choice with an explicit African-centred curriculum (Asante, 1987). All of its students are African American, and are drawn from various parts of a large urban school district.

We did not set out to select schools that had mission statements or principals who placed such emphasis on moral ideals. Jordan Elementary became a candidate as a result of an acquaintance between a project staff member and the principal. Highlands became a site on the urging of one of the project graduate students who thought it important to include within the study a minority school in an inner city setting. It was only later that we realised we had two schools where a strong emphasis was placed on moral development, but in quite different ways (Chow-Hoy, 2001).

The teacher participants

During the first year of the study, the four white females at Jordan Elementary taught in teams – two teachers to each team. The first team taught a first through to third grade classroom, consisting of approximately 40 students, about ten of whom (with special educational needs) required extensive special education services. One of the teachers in this team was a certified special education teacher. The other two teachers shared a group of grade two and three students. The seven teachers at Highlands Academy were African American, three male and four female. One taught kindergarten, and another, grade one. The remaining five teachers taught in the upper elementary and middle grades. In these grades, teachers teach one subject, and the students move from classroom to classroom. The subjects that were covered by the remaining five teachers were computing and technology, English, physical education and social studies. Years of teaching experience for the 11 teachers ranged from three-and-a-half to 30.

The research team was fully involved with these teachers and their classrooms for two years and four months. We were frequent visitors to each teacher's classroom, and collected no less than seven hours of videotape for each teacher. We met individually with the teachers, both before and after school. We also met with the full group of teachers at each site, as well as bringing together both school groups for dinners and conversation, and an occasional half-day conference. As an example of these meetings, at one we showed the full group a videotape containing short teaching episodes from all of their classrooms. A member of the research staff introduced each episode with a short description of the context of the classroom and of the particular episode. The teachers then began to explore similarities and differences in the two schools and in their classrooms. An interesting aside about these meetings is how fascinated the teachers were to see the teaching of their fellow teachers. At Highlands, for instance, teachers who had been teaching there for a decade or more had never had the opportunity to observe one another's classrooms. Also of interest were the number of teachers who had never before seen videotape of their own teaching.

Data collection

Once the schools and teachers were identified we began to collect data. The following forms of data were used in the study reported here.

First, we conducted *research staff interviews*. Those involved in the project were interviewed by one of the staff members. This interview explored beliefs about manner in teaching, and moral and intellectual virtues. This interview was repeated at the end of each year.

Second, we conducted *teacher interviews*. Two types of interviews were used with the teachers. One type consisted of descriptive belief interviews that explored the teachers' beliefs about teaching and learning, their manner, their beliefs about the nature of their students and their relationships with them, as well as pertinent school-level issues or concerns. These interviews were relatively open-ended, with most questions focused on particular topics and guided by some general questions (Bogdan and Biklen, 1998). Several of the teachers were interviewed again as part of particular sub-studies that took place within the larger MITP. A second form of interview consisted of a teacher and interviewer observing a videotape of that teacher's classroom for the purpose of exploring aspects of the manner of that teacher. Both forms of interviews were audiotaped and transcribed.

Third, we conducted *principal interviews*. As a part of the school sub-study, the principals of the two schools were interviewed. Each principal continued to be available for follow-up questions. At one site, a second interview took place as the principal moved up and down the halls, and from classroom to classroom on her daily journey through the school. The interviews were transcribed.

Fourth, we carried out *school-level observations* where extensive notes were taken and also *classroom observations and videotaping*. All teachers were visited in their classrooms at least once before we began any videotaping. The research staff discussed the complexities of doing this and how the teachers might explain what would be going on to the students. Written notes were taken on all classroom observations. All classrooms were videotaped for at least seven hours. On nearly all occasions when videotaping, two members of the research team were involved. One handled the camera while the other took written notes on classroom activities. (It was surprising to us how much of the classroom activity is missed by the person doing the videotaping. Two people in the classroom, one taking notes, helped fill this gap.) Following each observation, reflective field notes were written describing the context of what was observed that day.

Finally, we held *group meetings with teachers*. A number of the group meetings were videotaped and/or audiotaped. In addition, extensive notes were taken at all of the sessions.

Analysis of data

As already noted, the MITP attempted to explicate the concept of teacher manner as it relates to the fostering of moral and intellectual virtues in students in the context of elementary classrooms and schools. We engaged in this effort using an 'emic' approach: one that attempts to examine the concept within the meaning-making environment of the teachers, students, and principals as they work together in classrooms and schools. The teachers were extensively involved in the selection of questions, the directions for observation, and the interpretation of the data. We selected case studies as the appropriate unit of analysis in this concept exploration.

We employed both empirical and philosophical analyses in responding to the question 'how do teachers foster moral conduct in their students?'. In the empirical analysis we relied on extensive observation and exploration of the videotapes, and on the teacher interviews. We examined, as a group, the videotapes of classroom action, developing categories of 'fostering moral virtues'. Once a draft list of categories was developed, we asked the teachers to read it and make suggestions or propose alternative perspectives. The list was then developed further and tested using examples from the observations. We also coded the teacher interviews for teachers' descriptions of fostering moral conduct in their students. The philosophical analysis allowed us to interpret the empirical findings within the broader frame of the literature on ethics and normation (the development of norms or rules of behaviour). This philosophical analysis runs through the empirical findings below, particularly the section on modelling.

Findings

How do teachers engage with the moral aspects of their work? How do they go about fostering virtuous conduct in their students? Our analyses of the data led us to answer these questions by formulating a series of methods or strategies that teachers use as they attempt to advance the moral and intellectual capacities of their students. We encountered six methods used by most or all of the 11 teachers in our study to foster improved intellectual dispositions and enhanced moral relationships. (For reasons explored later, we exclude virtuous conduct by the teacher, which is often categorised as modelling.) The six methods are:

1 construction of the classroom community.
2 didactic instruction.
3 design and execution of academic task structures.
4 calling out for conduct of a particular kind.
5 private conversations.
6 showcasing specific students.

Constructing classroom communities

Nearly all the teachers in our study had a vivid conception of the kind of place they wanted their classrooms to be. Mutual respect, sharing, tolerance, orderliness and productive work were the notions most often mentioned by the teachers when describing their aspirations for their classrooms. To accomplish these aspirations, the teachers set rules and expectations for student conduct. These rules and expectations, they felt, created a classroom that is a normative community, a community that imposes rules and duties upon its members, presumably for their mutual benefit. The sole exception was the physical education teacher at Highlands, who had many fewer degrees of freedom for what took place in his gymnasium. At some times it was a site for physical education, but at other times it served as the cafeteria, the overflow area for school-wide events, and the main assembly point for all students entering or departing the building at the beginning and end of the school day.

All the teachers in our study were adept at the creation of classroom communities, although the teachers at Highlands Academy, the African-centred school, jointly subscribed to the view that their classrooms were sites of what Thomas Green (1999) describes as 'strong normation'. As such, they had no difficulty with the notion that their classrooms reflected their closely held personal and professional beliefs about the importance of education, and about the role their classrooms and their school played in the lives of their students. Moreover, little grace was given for infractions of the rules and expectations. There was a pervasive attitude that is perhaps best captured by the expression 'shape up or ship out'. The teachers at Jordan Elementary were no less desirous of having classrooms that reflected just and caring communities, but their methods of attaining this end differed from those at Highlands.

At Jordan the teachers were more likely to find the authority for constructing community in their personal relationships with each student. Their approach contrasted with the strong ideological commitment to the importance of community that characterised both the mission of Highlands Academy and the personal philosophies of its teachers. The teachers at Jordan were more likely to imply to their students that they needed to behave in a particular way if they were to have a successful relationship with the teacher, or a successful experience in this teacher's classroom. The Highlands teachers, by comparison, were more likely to insist that learning could not go on unless students behaved in a certain way. Thus the rules and norms of classroom conduct were defended on the basis of the point or purpose of the school as social unit. (An offshoot of this difference is that while the Highlands teachers were quite sensitive to what the students thought of them, they gave the impression that they were less concerned with whether students liked or enjoyed a teacher than whether they learned from the teacher.)

An incident at Highlands offers a revealing insight into teachers' sensitivities to the views of the students. A confused communication between the school and the research team led to some members of the Highlands staff, who were not participating in the study, being surprised to discover that team members were interviewing students. Moreover, the researchers were asking them for their impressions of their teachers. Despite the fact that the interview protocol had been jointly constructed with and approved by the teachers participating in the project, some Highlands staff members expressed consternation at students being asked what they thought about their teachers and classrooms. The sense was that students really are not in a position to answer such questions, and that asking them sends the wrong message about what they (the students) are in school to do. Students are not to judge teachers or the school; teachers and the wider school community judge the students.

These observations about constructing community are further expanded in two other articles from this study. Matthew Sanger (2001), in his study of two teachers' views of morality, showed how the meaning of and grounding for the construction of community differed depending on the moral starting points of the teacher. Todd Chow-Hoy (2001) examined the school-level constructs that may lead teachers at the two schools to frame different views about the nature of community. Chow-Hoy described how both schools have mission statements and principals that stress a wide range of moral and intellectual virtues. Given the mission statements and principals of the two schools we studied, it should not surprise the reader that the 11 teachers in the study were quite conversant with talk about fostering virtue and the importance of becoming a morally good person.

Constructing community turns out to involve more than laying down rules and building norms, as became apparent to us when noting the physical differences between the two schools. How the teacher arranges the furniture of the classroom and provides ways for students to gain access to supplies and materials also signals appropriate and inappropriate conduct. At Highlands, the African-centred academy, for example, it was somewhat unusual to see small groups of students working independently. Whole class instruction, with all eyes on the teacher, was the more characteristic mode of instruction – even in the primary grades. Whereas at Jordan student desks were arranged in groups of two, four, or six, and small group or one-to-one teaching was more common than whole class, teacher-centred instruction. These room designs bear prominently on how the teachers construct community. The whole-group setting in Highlands was in some sense made possible by the strong ideological orientation to the need for community. The small-group settings at Jordan were managed by the teacher's tendency to 'ground' the rules and norms in the relationship established between teacher and student. In addition, how a room is arranged affects the use of other methods for conveying the virtues, as noted below.

Didactic instruction

In the context of this study, didactic instruction is teaching that has as one of its primary purposes the direct presentation to the student of what is morally or intellectually desired by the teacher. Perhaps the most obvious example of this method in our study is the Life Skills Curriculum (Kovalik with Olsen, 1994) used at Jordan Elementary. This curriculum is a direct effort to gain student allegiance to and compliance with approximately 16 life skills, including integrity, initiative, humour, patience, friendship, pride, courage and common sense. Jordan teachers in the study regularly discussed these life skills as part of the programme of classroom instruction, and frequently referred to them in the course of teaching other subjects. For example a lesson on sustaining a healthy ecosystem, grounded primarily in general science, could be an occasion for calling on students to see the importance of sharing the earth's resources, and of acting justly with respect to the development and distribution of those resources.

Highlands Academy had a different, but no less direct and didactic approach to the attainment of moral goods. The African-centred curriculum at Highlands placed extensive emphasis on such African-derived values (Asante, 1987) as unity (*Umoja*), collective work and responsibility (*Ujima*), co-operative economics (*Ujamaa*), creativity (*Kuumba*) and faith (*Imani*). In the classrooms of many Highlands teachers, these values were cultivated quite directly through the frequent telling of stories, choral recitations of memorised songs and slogans, and frequent references to these values when commenting on student conduct.

Teachers at both schools provided lessons to the whole class on these ideals. The lessons were frequently grounded in recent actions by students or the teacher, and extended to how the students were to behave later in life. At Highlands in particular, teachers frequently discussed the futures of the students as a planned lesson for the whole class. They referred to scholastic attainment, careers and moral goodness. These didactic lessons appeared to be taken quite seriously by the teachers and the students at both schools, and their effectiveness showed up with remarkable clarity in the interviews we had with the students at each school.

Design and execution of academic task structures

Teachers have a broad range of choices in how they engage their students in the work required to gain mastery of a concept, topic, or lesson. This choice becomes manifest in how they set up the tasks students engage in as they progress through their academic work. Walter Doyle refers to these demands on students as 'academic task structures', and has written incisively on the power of such tasks (Doyle, 1983, 1986). Many of the teachers in our study constructed these tasks so that they could analyse and assess the students' work in ways that extended the students' ability to think more deeply or more imaginatively. They thereby fostered an enhanced range of intellectual virtue. Indeed, some teachers proved to be particularly adept at designing tasks so that they could gain ready access to a student's work and offer extensive commentary on it.

For example, Cheryl taught a seventh-grade English class at Highlands. For a lesson on punctuation, she wrote a number of unpunctuated sentences on the chalkboard, then asked various students to go the board to insert the correct punctuation. After Sheila inserted a semicolon in a particular sentence, Cheryl said to the class, 'Sheila put a semicolon in that sentence. I would like to know who agrees with her?' After a show of hands, Cheryl asked, 'Now who disagrees with her?' Another show of hands, this time far fewer, and Cheryl said that it is not enough to just agree or disagree, you have to have reasons to support your position. Then she turned to Mindy and asked her to go to the board to insert her correction. Mindy did so, substituting a colon for the semicolon.

Cheryl asked her why, and Mindy was able only to say it seemed right. Cheryl turned to Jamal and asked him if he could explain the difference between a colon and semicolon and offer a good reason why one is better in this sentence than the other. Jamal offered an explanation, and Cheryl's speech brightened as she said, 'You're absolutely correct.'

The lesson to be gained here is difficult to miss: Cheryl's interest is in the explanation or argument for the decision about punctuation. Mindy inserted the correct punctuation, but went unpraised by Cheryl for her inability to provide a justifying rationale. What Cheryl did so often and so well is set up academic task structures that engaged the full class in the activity. She was then able to comment publicly on performance, frequently signalling to the entire class what kind of thinking she was seeking and the form she wanted it to take as students responded to her questions. An observer had the sense that tasks were structured to permit an increase in the time provided for didactic instruction, as well as for what we have labelled 'call-outs'. Task structuring of this kind is in marked contrast to providing assessment in private asides with students, or in the grading of individual student assignments.

Calling out for conduct of a particular kind

One of the most frequently observed techniques for cultivating student conduct was what we refer to as the call-out. It is simply the teacher saying something to a student that indicates to this student and all others within earshot how the student ought to behave. Call-outs typically consist of friendly reminders about deportment or outright censure for inappropriate conduct. Margaret, a Jordan Elementary teacher, organised her class so that students worked independently and in small groups. She was assisting a student who had been working alone, when upon looking up and over the full class, she called out across the room, 'Soosun, how does what you are doing now help your team to complete its work?' The question was rhetorical, for the student was aware that he was being disruptive and the call-out refocused him on the task at hand. This call-out signalled the expectation for non-disruptive, co-operative effort, and was, of course, heard by many other students in the class.

In a different Jordan classroom, Hannah convened her class in the form of a circle, with many students sitting on the floor. The topic of discussion was caring for the environment. As she prepared the ground for soliciting students' views on issues explored in a prior assignment, one loudly proclaimed his view. Hannah said, 'Goodness Jason, you're anxious to participate today. But isn't it polite to wait until the person speaking is finished, then raise your hand?' Jason nodded, and sat back on his heels. Hannah followed with, 'It's also a fair way to bring others into the conversation, isn't it?' This comment was addressed not so much to Jason as to the group as whole (Jason did not acknowledge this second comment, and the teacher did not appear to expect him to do so). The message of this call-out to Jason was that we do not get heard by being the quickest or the loudest, but by taking turns, the fair way to have a conversation. A great deal of moral freight seems to have been carried by so modest a move.

Call-outs are frequently reminders to students of the rules and expectations for good deportment in the classroom. They are teacher-to-student communications, conducted within view and earshot of most or all of the class. They serve not only to call the disobedient student to account, but also to refresh everyone else's memory of what is desired in this setting. We found call-outs to be one of the most obvious and frequently used ways that teachers signalled their expectations for student conduct, particularly in moral domains involving co-operation, fairness and regard for others.

On our first pass through the data we almost missed call-outs. Our initial inclination was to view them as demands for order, or quiet, or mere compliance with what some might regard as arbitrary rules. And indeed there are call-outs of this kind. But there are also call-outs directed quite specifically to the cultivation and encouragement of virtuous conduct. At least in the case of the teachers participating in our study, the call-outs were, in the main, far from simple demands for compliance or order. Rather, they were the expression of a very genuine interest in helping the student to become a good person. (This observation is based, in part, on listening to the comments the teachers made as they viewed videotape of their own teaching and shared their reactions with us.)

Private conversations

Didactic instruction and call-outs are public and visible means of cultivating the moral and intellectual dispositions of students. Private conversations are another method of doing so. They typically occur when a teacher takes a student aside for a 'chat'. But they may also occur as students enter the room at the beginning of the day, or at other times when the chance arises for a teacher to direct attention to a single student. And while many private conversations are intended to be corrective (where the teacher is seeking to correct conduct that is harmful to the student, the group, or both), many are highly affirmative and nurturing.

For example, Darlene greeted many students personally as they entered her classroom in the morning, seeking to have a private talk with as many of them as possible. Her purpose, she said, was to help the students make the transition from home to school, particularly in the case of students for whom the home experience was troubling at this time in their lives. Darlene indicated that these exchanges with students were rooted in a profound concern for the welfare of her students. She was especially concerned that her students should get themselves mentally ready for life in the classroom that morning, setting aside worries they might have about matters beyond the school.

Letti, a teacher at Jordan Elementary, was often engaged in private conversations with students throughout the school day. The frequency of private conversations in the classroom may be related to the fact that it adjoined a special education classroom, and students from both rooms frequently intermingled as a means of ensuring inclusion of the students with special educational needs. As a result, Letti was not always able to manage her class as a single large group. Nor was it clear that she would prefer to do so even if the opportunity were more available, as she was a person who made deep, personal connections to her students. As such, she handled initial flare-ups with call-outs, but quickly shifted to private conversation if the matter was not soon resolved. Taking students aside, she tried to reflect their conduct back to them, apparently to make them aware of just what it was they were doing and how it was affecting other class members and the teacher. In almost all instances of such private conversations that we observed, Letti's conversations focused on being co-operative, on respecting the needs of other students, and moderating one's behaviour.

It is clear that teachers have many different kinds of private conversations with their students. Of interest in the context of manner are those directed at altering a student's conduct to make it more closely conform to a moral ideal, either by censure of unacceptable behaviour or extended praise for appropriate conduct, or at eliciting a deeper intellectual engagement in the topics of instruction. We witnessed a fair amount of this kind of private conferencing at Jordan, particularly in the classrooms with a higher concentration of students with special educational needs. The ways that Jordan teachers designed the physical environment made it more conducive to private conferencing, because the other students had independent tasks or small group work to keep them engaged while the teacher was having a private conference. We observed fewer private conferences at Highlands, at least during regularly scheduled class periods. That there are fewer such conferences at Highlands may be due to the more extensive use of teacher-led, whole class instruction, and the greater likelihood that Highlands teachers would discipline, reprimand, or reward their students in a more public way (often by using a call-out). Moreover, it was difficult to have a private conversation during class time because the Highlands classrooms are generally too small to permit a teacher and student to separate themselves physically from the other students. On the other hand, private conversations were not uncommon before classes began for the day, at change-of-class times, and at the day's end.

Showcasing specific students

From a philosophical point of view, what we have termed showcasing may be among the most interesting techniques used by classroom teachers. It is interesting because the teacher is not featuring his or her own virtues, but those of the student. In a sense, the teacher is not modelling virtuous conduct for the students, but placing students in the role of modelling such conduct for their peers. A Jordan teacher asked a question about whether the group liked a lesson being taught by a student teacher. One of the students shook her head from side to side, and the teacher asked why. The student explained, and the teacher said, 'I like how Corinne is being honest. She's giving me an honest answer to my question, even though it may hurt a little bit. Thanks for being honest, Corinne.'

The full group heard this praise for Corinne, and the message it contained about honesty. We believe that what was taking place here is that the teacher was calling other students' attention to a virtue being displayed by one student, and signalling the value of this virtue by showcasing this student. Of course, there was the element of reinforcement for the virtue of honesty that

Corinne displayed, and that was certainly a means for the teacher to encourage honesty in Corinne. Yet we detected in our conversations with the teachers that they had more in mind when publicly praising the good conduct of their students. The teacher was shifting the role-model from himself or herself to a student, saying to other students something like, 'See, you don't have to be grown up like me to be able to act this way. Here's one of your fellow students who is doing it quite well.'

We know from our own experiences in school that there are risks here, for a teacher who praises a student may succeed in having that student identified as a teacher's pet or favourite, thereby reducing the student's impact as a model for other students. Yet we found that the teachers we observed navigated these potential problems with considerable facility. They may indeed have had favourite students, but the technique of showcasing was distributed with apparent even-handedness in the classrooms we observed. For example, Nandi, teaching an English lesson to eighth-grade Highlands students, directed a question at Alfred, whom she knew to be a marginal student. This time Alfred had the right answer. The teacher followed up with another question, and Alfred got it right again. Nandi became effusive in her praise for Alfred, and encouraged the class to commend his strong performance. They whistled and clapped, and Alfred smiled broadly while holding his hands aloft with the victory sign on each hand. When this incident was explored with Nandi, she indicated that Alfred had a difficult time with this material, and she wanted him to feel proud of the progress he was making with it. She also wanted his classmates to honour his accomplishment, a trait she signalled as an important one by showcasing Alfred as she did.

Teachers appear to have multiple reasons for showcasing, ranging from reinforcing student conduct to providing a positive object lesson for all who are in view or earshot. Whatever the reason, showcasing seems a prominent method for signalling praiseworthy conduct, and for informing the group that it is within their grasp to exhibit similar conduct.

One method that is not among these six is modelling on the part of the teacher. Given that it is so often mentioned as a critical feature of how teachers foster the moral development of their own students, it is useful to explore at some length its exclusion from our list of six.

Some problems with modelling

There is a sense in which modelling is manner. That is probably too restrictive a claim, but it is not far off the mark. Manner, for purposes of this paper (and the MITP as a whole), is conduct that expresses highly regarded moral and intellectual traits. Thus when we speak of a person as fair-minded, caring, thoughtful, generous, honest, brave and so on, we are describing the manner of that person. A person's manner could be morally unacceptable, too, as when he or she is described as mean, unfair, cowardly, lying and so forth. However, in the context of our work, we have used the term 'manner' only to pick out conduct that evidences the various human virtues. For us, manner picks out what is good, moral, sound, and defensible about persons, rather than what is bad, immoral, silly or stupid about them. Yet, in a frame larger than ours, manner could point to conduct that is good, bad or both.

The manner of a teacher takes on particular importance insofar as it serves as a model for the students. It would not be likely to concern us if it were not serving as a model: as something the student will see and believe to be proper, or imitate and accept as a standard for how things should be. But it is not quite so clear when manner is modelled. For example, is a teacher modelling some virtue only when she or he intends that it be observed or imitated? Or does modelling occur whenever the teacher displays a virtue, whether or not he or she intends to have it observed or noted by another? If modelling falls into the former category, it might be a kind of method. If it falls into the latter category, it appears to be the case that the teacher is acting without instructional intent or purpose. If there is no intent to have the manner observed with a measure of regard by the student, then it seems inappropriate to think of modelling as a method employed by the teacher.

There is more at issue here than the teacher's instructional purpose or intent. One can try to model, but fail, in the sense that persons nearby pay no attention to the person doing the modelling. If no one pays attention, is the teacher modelling? (A variation on the common riddle, if a tree falls in the woods with no one nearby, is there any sound?) Does one need an attentive listener or viewer in order properly to be said to be modelling? What if the viewer is attentive but fails fully to pick up on what is being modelled? Did the person then model for the viewer? These modest conundrums can be resolved with precise, stipulative definitions, but their existence reveals some of the challenges to clear deployment of the concept of modelling.

Because of this confusion, we think it is wise to give modelling separate standing in the repertoire of ways to cultivate the moral and intellectual virtues in students. We find ourselves undecided on just how tightly linked manner and modelling are, and under what circumstances modelling may be said to be among the methods a teacher might use to foster virtue. We know that modelling takes place, and that most teachers, school administrators and parents consider it important. But our excursions through our data lead us to wonder about its precise status. Consider the intriguing possibility that a teacher whose manner could be viewed as somewhat deficient could employ the six methods described above with considerable finesse. Entertaining this possibility leads us to wonder about the possibility that teachers adopt persona on entering their classrooms, and that these persona may perform in ways that are morally and intellectually more powerful than is the case for the teacher as a person outside the classroom. In other words, who are we looking at when we look at teachers? Are we looking at a person who possesses a manner, which is somehow made manifest in the practice of teaching? Or are we seeing someone in a role, who may perform with considerable moral and intellectual acuity in that role – perhaps because the role demands acuity of this kind – but is less than a paragon of virtue when the teaching mask is off?

Nothing in our experience with the 11 teachers with whom we worked prompts us to ask these questions. That is to say, we have not found some of our teachers to be less moral or less intellectually sophisticated outside their classrooms than they are inside them, thus leading us to wonder whether the role of teacher alters the moral and intellectual character of the one teaching. Rather, this puzzlement about persona and role arises from seeking to frame the analysis of our data in the context of the intriguing philosophical questions about moral agency and moral development. Moral agency is that quality possessed by a person to act morally. Moral development is the bringing about of moral agency in others. Breaking these concepts apart permits us to ask some vexing – but exciting – questions about how fully developed a moral agent must be in order to be good at moral development. Put another way: how morally good does a person need to be in order to engage effectively in methods for moral development? Might a less than morally exemplary teacher employ the methods we describe here effectively to foster the moral agency of his or her students? We have tossed these questions about a good deal in the last few years, wondering about their proper answer. At this point, we are certain only that the data we have do not prompt any particular answers to these fascinating questions.

Conclusion

In our exploration of the concept of teacher manner, we began with an aretaic (Aristotelean) sense that the way students learn virtues is by being in the classroom of a virtuous teacher. Our first puzzle focused on how a teacher exhibits virtuous conduct in the classroom, and how an observer 'sees' virtuous conduct, determines that it is indeed virtuous, and renders an adequate description of it. The second puzzle was how to determine that students pick up on this virtuous conduct, and if they do, how they do so.

However, before arriving at the second puzzle, our study took an important turn. We found that although teachers did indeed exhibit dispositions that represent many of the virtues, their own conduct was not what they appeared to depend on most to gain morally good or appropriate conduct from their students. Rather they depended more on a series of methods or techniques to foster the intellectual and moral virtues in their students. A careful consideration of these six methods led us to question teacher manner as the critical ingredient in fostering moral agency in classrooms. Our scepticism about teacher manner was somewhat reinforced as we sought to understand the role of teacher modelling in the classroom and the degree to which teachers used modelling as a means for fostering moral development. These vexing questions led us to wonder whether a teacher had to be a virtuous person before he or she could nurture virtue in others, or if it is possible for a less than virtuous person to employ the six methods described here to do a good job of fostering virtuous conduct in students.

At an intuitive or 'gut' level we believe that a teacher has to be, in some way, a morally good person before he or she can successfully employ the methods described above. What we do not yet know is whether this moral *person* can become a much more moral *teacher* when adopting that persona. It does appear that in deploying these six methods, teachers can raise expectations for the moral conduct of their students that may well exceed the moral expectations they hold for themselves – a point that several teachers in the study expressed during our interviews with them. While this point seems somewhat surprising at first, it is in fact not very exceptional. One finds parents constantly having expectations for the conduct of their children that exceed the expectations that parents hold for themselves (like telling children that they should never lie). Teachers are not so different in this respect. Indeed, perhaps a distinguishing mark of the educator of children is that she or he holds higher expectations for the children than for herself or himself.

A final point. At both school sites there existed some school-wide programme for the moral development of the students attending the school. At Jordan Elementary, it was the adopted Life Skills Curriculum. At Highlands Academy, it was the African-Centred Curriculum. We found it of more than passing interest that the teachers were less likely to promote these programmes in their classrooms than to use them as 'permission givers' for attending to the moral development of their students. The 11 teachers in our study were quite clear about the constituents of this moral development, usually without reference to either of the school-wide programmes. This finding led us to speculate that perhaps school-wide programmes for such things as character development or pro-social skills might be useful, not so much because they accomplish what they purport to accomplish, but because they signal to teachers what is valued and important in the setting. Such a programme could encourage teachers to construct their own paths and means to the general ends the programme is designed to achieve.

As we hope we have made clear, this modest study taught us a great deal about how these 11 teachers undertook the moral dimensions of teaching. It also raised a number of enticing questions for further study. We would be delighted to have you in the company of scholars pursuing answers to these provocative and important questions.

Acknowledgements

Our research was funded by the Spencer Foundation for three years from July 1997. We would like to express our gratitude for their financial support. The principal investigators in MITP were Gary Fenstermacher and Virginia Richardson. Others who have worked on the project are Todd Chow-Hoy, Catherine Fallona, Alexandra Miletta, Richard Ogusthorpe, Charlotte Ratslaff, Matther Sanger, Jillo Williams and Nicola Williams.

References

Asante, M. (1987) *The Afrocentric Idea*. Philadelphia: Temple University Press.
Ball, D. and Wilson, S. (1996) 'Integrity in teaching: recognising the fusion of the moral and intellectual', *American Educational Research Journal*, 33 (1): 155–92.
Bebeau, M., Rest, J. and Narvaez, D. (1999) 'Beyond promise: a perspective on research in moral education', *Educational Researcher*, 28 (4): 18–26.
Bogdan R. and Biklen, S.K. (1998) *Qualitative Research on Education: An Introduction to Theory and Method*. 2nd edn. Boston: Allyn and Bacon.
Buzzelli, C.A. and Johnston, B. (2002) *The Moral Dimensions of Teaching*. New York: RoutledgeFalmer.

Campbell, E. (2002) 'Moral lessons: the ethical role of teachers', *Educational Research and Evaluation* 9(1): 22–50.

Carr, D. (1991) *Educating the Virtues*. New York: Routledge.

Carr, D. and Struetel, J. (eds) (1999) *Virtue, Ethics and Moral Education*. New York: Routledge.

Chow-Hoy, T. (2001) 'An inquiry into school context and the teaching of the virtues', *Journal of Curriculum Studies*, 33 (6): 655–82.

Crittenden, P. (1990) *Learning to Be Moral*. Atlantic Highlands, NJ: Humanities Press International.

Doyle, W. (1983) 'Academic work', *Review of Educational Research*, 53: 159–99.

Doyle, W. (1986) 'Classroom organization and management', in M. Wittrock (ed), *Handbook of Research on Teaching*. 3rd edn. New York: MacMillan.

Erickson, F. (1986) 'Qualitative methods in research on teaching', in M. Wittrock (ed), *Handbook of Research on Teaching*. 3rd edn. New York: MacMillan.

Fallona, C. (2000) 'Making manner visible: a study in observing and interpreting teachers' moral virtues', *Teaching and Teacher Education*, 16 (7): 681–96.

Fenstermacher, G. (1992) 'The concepts of method and manner in teaching', in A. Oser and J. Paltry (eds), *Effective and Responsible Teaching*. San Francisco, CA: Jossey-Bass.

Fenstermacher, G. (2001) 'On the concept of manner and its visibility in teaching practice', *Journal of Curriculum Inquiry*, 33 (6): 639–53.

Goodlad, J., Soder, R. and Sirotnik, K. (eds) (1990) *The Moral Dimensions of Teaching*. San Francisco: Jossey-Bass.

Green, T. (1999) *Voices: The Educational Formation of Conscience*. Notre Dame, IN: Notre Dame University Press.

Hansen, D. (1993). 'The moral importance of teachers' style', *Journal of Curriculum Studies*, 25 (5): 397–421.

Hansen, D. (2001) 'Teaching as a moral activity', in V. Richardson (ed), *Handbook of Research on Teaching*. 4th edn. Washington: American Educational Research Association.

Hostetler, K.D. (1997) *Ethical Judgement in Teaching*. Boston: Allyn and Bacon.

Jackson, P. (1986) *The Practice of Teaching*. New York: Teachers College Press.

Jackson, P., Boorstrom, R. and Hansen, D. (1993) *The Moral Life of Schools*. San Francisco: Jossey-Bass.

Katz, M.S., Noddings, N. and Strike, K.A. (eds) (1999) *Justice and Caring*. New York: Teachers College Press.

Kovalik, S. with Olsen, K. (1994) *ITI: The Model. Integrated Thematic Instruction*. 3rd edn. Kent, WA: Books for Educators.

Lickona, T. (1991) *Educating for Character*. New York: Bantam Books.

MacIntyre, A. (1984) *After Virtue. A Study in Moral Theory*. 2nd edn. London: Gerald Duckworth and Co.

Oser, F. (1986) 'Moral education and values education: the discourse perspective', in M. Wittrock (ed), *Handbook of Research on Teaching*. 3rd edn. New York: MacMillan.

Rest, J. (1986) *Moral Development: Advances in Research and Theory*. New York: Praeger.

Richardson, V. and Fenstermacher, G. (2001) 'Manner in teaching: the study in four parts', Journal of Curriculum Studies, 33 (6): 631–7.

Ryle, G. (1975) 'Can virtue be taught?', in R.F. Dearden, P. Hirst and R. Peters (eds), *Education and Reason*. London: Routledge and Kegan Paul.

Sanger, M. (2001) 'Inquiring into the moral dimensions of teaching: talking to teachers and looking at practice', *Journal of Curriculum Inquiry*, 33 (6): 683–704.

Sockett, H. (1993) *The Moral Base for Teacher Professionalism*. New York: Teachers College Press.

Solomon, D., Watson, M. and Battistich, V. (2001) 'Teaching and schooling effects on moral/prosocial behavior', in V. Richardson (ed), *Handbook of Research on Teaching*. 4th edn. Washington, DC: American Educational Research Association.

Strike, K. and Soltis, J. (1985) *The Ethics of Teaching*. New York: Teachers College Press.

Tom, A. (1984) *Teaching as a Moral Craft*. New York: Longman.

Wynne, E. and Ryan, K. (1997) *Reclaiming our Schools: A Handbook on Teaching Character, Academics and Discipline*. New York: Merrill.

Chapter 6

Investigating formative classroom assessment

Harry Torrance and John Pryor

The substantive focus of this chapter is formative assessment, and particularly the interactions between teachers and students. Harry Torrance and John Pryor locate their empirical study within the policy context in Britain from the late 1980s onwards, which had led to an increasing emphasis on assessment in primary schools. They carefully justify the need for the research in relation to the generation of research knowledge about formative assessment, as well as that related to policy and practice. Torrance and Pryor highlight an important problem: how assumptions underpinning policy relating to assessment appeared to be at odds with current research and theoretical knowledge about the cognitive and social dimensions of learning.

An interesting feature of this research was that the investigators sought to combine theoretical knowledge from psychology and sociology. They did so in order to understand and conceptualise the process of assessment in early years (infant) classrooms and its relationship with learning and power. The authors argue that using only one of these theoretical perspectives would have limited the explanatory power of their in-depth study.

One important issue they raise is the role of teacher questioning in classroom interaction. Whilst this is considered to be a central element of formative assessment, Torrance and Pryor argue – from close analysis of transcripts – that it can also be problematic. Their data indicate how the intention of teachers underlying the use of extended questioning to gain a fuller understanding of students' thinking may be interpreted differently by students, according to the social norms of the classroom.

The chapter provides detailed examples of analysis of classroom interaction between teachers and students. The authors also explain how they engaged iteratively with the data to produce their interpretation. Their study demonstrates how detailed micro-level analysis of classroom interaction can be connected with wider theoretical and conceptual issues. This is something that masters and doctoral students often find rather challenging.

The authors highlight how they developed a model of two ideal-typical approaches to assessment. It is interesting to compare some of the features of this ideal-typical model with issues raised by Hilda Borko relating to changes in teachers' beliefs and practices about assessment (see Chapter 3).

Introduction

This chapter reports on selected aspects of a funded research project (see Torrance and Pryor, 1998 for a full account). Within the British education system, Key Stage 1 (KS1) of the national curriculum encompasses the reception class (Year R) and Years 1 and 2 (i.e. age 5–7). Key Stage 2 includes Years 3 to 6 (age 7–11); Key Stage 3 includes Years 7–9 (age 11–14) and Key Stage 4 includes Years 10 and 11 (age 14–16).

The project originated in the context of developments in British education policy: specifically, the introduction in 1988 of a national curriculum and national assessment; and the articulation of a proposed system of national assessment developed in the report of the government's Task Group on Assessment and Testing (TGAT, 1988). Various elements of policy development and implementation in Britain seemed to be paying very little attention to relevant research. Moreover, claims were being made about the formative impact of assessment on learning that seemed to take very little account of relevant psychological theory, or of sociological studies of classroom interaction. So while the research reported here arose from a particular juxtaposition of educational policy and theory, the findings are of interest well beyond the initially parochial context of national curriculum assessment in the UK. Our interest is in combining social constructivist perspectives on learning with interactionist perspectives on the sociological accomplishment of classroom life. Our aim has been to produce work that will contribute to wider debates about the complexities of classroom assessment and the way in which learning can be scaffolded through the *process* of assessment. Similarly, although early years (infant) classrooms provided the context for the study, the analysis is equally significant for other age groups and indeed has subsequently been applied in research on schools and further and higher education (e.g. Dann, 2002; Filer and Pollard, 2000; Ecclestone, 2002).

Background to the research: the initial policy context

Teacher assessment involves the evaluation of students' coursework by teachers to contribute towards the final grades that they are awarded in formal public examinations. It has a long history in the UK. Coursework assessment was introduced on a limited scale with the introduction of the Certificate of Secondary Education (CSE) in the 1960s, and spread to the more prestigious General Certificate of Education (GCE or 'O' level) in the 1970s. Both forms of examination were usually taken by students at the age of 16. Subsequently, these procedures were incorporated into the new single system of secondary school examination for students at 16, the General Certificate of Secondary Education (GCSE) introduced in 1986.

This extension of 'teacher assessment' or 'coursework assessment' was largely argued on the grounds of the validity of the examining process and the validity of final results. Curriculum change has involved the use of more practical work in science and technology, more emphasis on oral communication in English and foreign languages, and more local fieldwork studies in history and geography. Consequently assessment of the new skills of planning, carrying out, and writing up extended tasks has come to be conducted by teachers over a period of time within the classroom and the laboratory.

More recently, however, the argument for involving teachers in the assessment of their students' achievements has come to incorporate notions of identifying progress and providing formative feedback to students on their progress. This involves using new methods of assessment to promote learning as well as measuring the outcomes of that learning more validly: assessment *for* learning, as well as assessment of learning.

Claims for formative assessment featured very strongly in the report of the British government's Task Group on Assessment and Testing (TGAT, 1988) which provided the initial blueprint for the emerging system of national curriculum assessment. A key argument within the report was that assessment would provide information on children's strengths and weaknesses in relation to their progression through the national curriculum as a whole, which teachers could use in planning what to do next. Additionally the authors of this report argued that the formative rationale for national assessment would be best realised through extensive use of teacher assessment (TA) with externally devised Standard Assessment Tasks (SATs) being used sparingly to moderate TA and ensure some degree of comparability in the system. They recommended that end-of-Key-Stage grades (levels of attainment) should be produced by combining TA grades with SAT results, though it was not at all clear how TA grades should be generated or how they might relate to routine classroom assessment.

Extensive political intervention has led to considerable modification of the TGAT original recommendations (Black, 1994; Torrance, 2003) but nevertheless claims for the 'formative' role of assessment in the learning process have come to be widely accepted (e.g. Black and Wiliam, 1998; Shepard, 2000).

Theories and evidence of formative assessment

However, claims for the beneficial formative impact of assessment on learning raise important questions about their theoretical justification and empirical realisation. Sadler's excavation and exposition of what one might term the logical implications of formative assessment articulated in great detail the numerous steps that could be involved. His argument was that:

> *for students to be able to improve, they must develop the capacity to monitor the quality of their own work during actual production. This in turn requires that students possess an appreciation of what high quality work is, that they have the evaluative skill necessary for them to compare with some objectivity the quality of what they are producing in relation to the higher standard, and that they develop a store of tactics or moves which can be drawn upon to modify their own work.*
>
> *(Sadler, 1989: 119)*

This conception of formative assessment derives from Sadler's interest in the complexity of learning tasks and outcomes. He argued that most previous work on learning had been 'based on stimulus-response...theories...[] ...While...student development is multidimensional rather than sequential, and prerequisite learnings cannot be conceptualised as neatly packaged units of skills or knowledge' (Sadler, 1989: 123). In making this distinction Sadler identified two very different perspectives on formative assessment that certainly seem to have had an implicit impact on policy and practice in the British context, even if they are rarely acknowledged explicitly.

While developments in the UK seem to have taken place on a fairly ad hoc and pragmatic basis, two underlying perspectives can be discerned. One remains essentially behaviourist in the mastery learning tradition (e.g. Bloom, 1971; Popham, 1978, 1987). Objectives are defined and taught quite specifically, making sure that teachers and students alike know what behaviour is required of them: what counts as achieving the objective. A corollary of such an approach can be a very mechanical and hierarchical view of learning. The assumption is that students learn the basics, the nuts-and-bolts, before they move on to more complicated material. This certainly appears to be the policy makers' view behind the incremental organisation of the national curriculum into four Key Stages and specific levels of achievement through which students should progress during their period of compulsory schooling (ages 5–16).

The other perspective derives from the social constructivist position in cognitive psychology. It entails a far more ambitious approach to assessment. Teacher-student interaction is conceptualised in terms that reach beyond the provision of test results and additional or remedial instruction. The teacher has a role in assisting students to engage with and comprehend new ideas and problems. The process of assessment is seen as having an impact on the student as well as the product, the result. The argument, deriving from Vygotsky (1978, 1986), is that one should identify not just what students have achieved, but what they might achieve with the help of an adult or, in some circumstances, a collaborating peer (the 'zone of proximal development', Vygotsky, 1978: 86). Learning should therefore be 'scaffolded' (Bruner, 1985) by children being set appropriate tasks and provided with appropriate support. The purpose of assessment and its focus is to identify what children could achieve next.

Such an interpretation of formative assessment takes us into much more dynamic and challenging territory, and has the merit of identifying an integrated role for assessment in the learning process itself. Yet exactly what formative classroom assessment looks like in practice, and indeed what observable differences there might be between a behaviourist and a constructivist approach to formative assessment, are still far from clear. It must also be recognised that such empirical evidence as exists on constructivist approaches to learning and assessment derives from very small-scale studies, often of non-formal educational settings. Thus Cole (1985), reviewing the concept of the zone of proximal development with respect to the relationship between material context and individual cognition, notes that it makes most explanatory sense in studies of parent–child interaction or relatively informal educational situations such as apprenticeships. Here the implied level of adult or tutor support exceeds that which one could reasonably expect to find in ordinary classrooms. Forman and Cazden (1985) likewise note the detailed level of teacher–student interaction implicit in the idea of 'scaffolding' and explore peer collaboration as a way of overcoming some of the logistical problems of the traditional classroom. Brown and Ferrara (1985) report an explicit attempt to develop instruments to measure the zone of proximal development, precisely in order to use assessment formatively. But they were working in experimental settings with individual children. Their concern was to develop a more sensitive and meaningful instrument than the traditional intelligence test.

The exploration of the social context and indeed the social construction of individual cognition by Newman et al. (1989) raises further issues. They draw attention to the differences between what they characterise as research-oriented 'dynamic assessment' (similar to Brown and Ferrara cited above) and the 'assessment while teaching' in which teachers routinely engage. 'Assessment while teaching' necessarily subordinates assessment to instruction because of the imperatives of classroom life, and particularly to the periodic reinforcement of learning – irrespective of whether or not individual students require such reinforcement (Newman et al., 1989: 80–7). This work also raises some interesting questions with respect to teachers identifying evidence of *individual* achievement and capacity to achieve more. Their attention is usually geared towards groups of students, if not the whole class, and so 'the process of cognitive change is as much a social as an individual process' (Newman et al., 1989: 1).

Motivation and attribution

Given the claims for formative assessment, it is also rather surprising that more attention has not been given to the extensive psychological literature on achievement, motivation and attribution: to studies of what makes a difference to student motivation, and to what factors students attribute their academic success and failure. Where might formative assessment fit into this work?

A key issue with respect to the impact of feedback on motivation and learning is the way in which 'reinforcement' is understood and applied. In particular, a narrowly behaviourist view is unlikely to have the desired effect. Researchers such as Ames (1984), Dweck (1989) and Weiner (1984) have established that many practices routinely adopted by teachers as 'positive reinforcement' to maintain attention and enhance motivation may actually result in children avoiding intellectual tasks. They may approach these tasks with limited confidence and not persist in the face of difficulties. Dweck (1989: 88–9) makes a distinction between two kinds of achievement goals:

▶ *learning goals* in which individuals strive to increase their competence, to understand or master something new;
▶ *performance goals*, in which individuals strive either to document, or gain favourable judgments of, their competence or to avoid negative judgments of their competence.

What is being identified here is whether students see schoolwork as an intrinsic intellectual challenge or as a performance for teachers, for which they receive extrinsic instrumental rewards (or punishments) such as high (or low) grades. Similarly Weiner (1984) explores to what extent students attribute success and failure to stable or unstable factors which they think they can (or cannot) control. Clearly, feedback that does not contribute to students' sense of self-efficacy is unlikely to have a positive impact (see also Dweck, 2000 for a more recent review of these issues).

Classroom interaction and the language of teaching

The extensive literature on teacher-student interaction in the classroom, and on the role of language in constructing and realising the teaching and learning process in action, are equally important for a well-founded understanding of the problems and possibilities of teacher involvement in formative classroom assessment. Claims for formative assessment often seem to assume that the assessment process is entirely transparent, with teachers being able to ask precise questions and elicit clear responses from individual students in an unambiguous manner. A good deal of research suggests that this is not the case, especially with respect to younger children. Considerable work has been done investigating how and why young children can make apparently simple 'errors' when being questioned, with the role of context and language being shown to be particularly important in children's perceptions of the task. It is not necessarily the case that they didn't 'know the answer', or couldn't 'answer the question'. They may have thought they were being asked something else, or thought they had to answer the *implicit* question deriving from the context of questioning, rather than the explicit question, and so forth (e.g. Donaldson, 1978; Beveridge, 1982). Similarly, studies such as that of Cicourel et al. (1974) have demonstrated how students may interpret even apparently straightforward standardised test questions in different ways and produce misleading results. More recent work by Cooper (1994; Cooper and Dunne, 2000) has shown that even when test items attempt to introduce elements of contextualisation, scope for misinterpretation remains and in some respects is increased as students struggle to come to terms with new forms of task presentation.

Perhaps more important still, with respect to routine classroom assessment, is research evidence demonstrating that teachers' questions and students' responses carry meaning about the structure of classroom interaction as well as its content. Teacher–student interaction has been shown (Sinclair and Coulthard, 1975) to incorporate a basic three-part sequence of *initiation* by the teacher, *response* by the student, and *feedback/evaluation* by the teacher (IRF). This sequence can be extended if the *response* is not considered appropriate by the teacher, so that questioning continues until what is considered to be an appropriate response is elicited and 'closure' of the interactive sequence can occur. A number of studies have demonstrated the role that teacher questioning plays in establishing and continually confirming teachers' control of the classroom environment, and in constructing and sequencing the very definition of a 'lesson' (e.g. Edwards and Furlong, 1978; Edwards and Westgate, 1987; Mehan 1979). Teachers' questions are as much to do with managing and accomplishing the lesson – making it happen as a piece of social interaction – as they are to do with eliciting particular information from particular students.

Given the almost universal endorsement of teacher questioning as a primary strategy in formative assessment it is salutory to note the key observation of Edwards and Mercer (1987: 45) that, in the context of routine teacher–student interaction 'repeated questions [by the teacher] imply wrong answers'. Precisely that which is being recommended for gathering in-depth 'information' about student achievements could actually interfere with students' taken-for-granted assumptions about the teaching process, and thus interrupt the learning process. Edwards' and Mercer's statement derives from observations of teacher–student interaction in the context of an individual lesson, rather than, for example, repeated questioning over a sequence of lessons. Nevertheless it is interesting to speculate on whether teachers' felt need to explore, confirm and reconfirm that students do indeed 'know' or 'understand' something might be interpreted by students as *not* knowing it.

Teachers' questions and students' responses will always be serving a number of different purposes and accomplishing a number of different functions at the same time. In particular, students constantly strive to interpret teachers' questions and 'make sense' of what is being asked of them in the context of this interactive process, over and above what might be taken to be the 'obvious' meaning of a particular question. Now this does not mean that all attempts at formative assessment will necessarily founder. But it does mean that the process of accomplishing formative assessment is likely to be much more complicated than presently acknowledged. Certainly significant questions are begged about the sort of shared knowledge that exists between teachers and students; about the purpose and process of routine classroom assessment; and in what ways teachers and students – particularly very young students – can construct common understandings of the criteria by which school work is assessed.

In designing and carrying out the research our contention was, therefore, that claims for the positive effects of formative assessment on learning were both overstated in terms of empirical evidence and under-theorised in terms of how learning actually takes place in social contexts – particularly early-years classrooms. Teacher questions and student responses are in no sense a straightforward and transparent medium whereby information about student progress is transmitted unproblematically to teachers, and back again to students. Linguistic interaction in the classroom is much more complex, communicating through its pattern and structure implicit messages beyond the immediate spoken word. This process realises in action both the social relationships of schooling and the social construction of knowledge. On the other hand, the assessment tasks that children undertake and the assessment 'conversations' which they have with teachers and with other students can provide rich contexts in which learning is 'scaffolded' through focused questioning and spoken articulations of perceptions and emergent understandings.

The 'Teacher Assessment at Key Stage 1' Research Project

These are the sorts of issues that the 'Teacher Assessment at Key Stage 1' Project addressed. In particular the project sought:

1 To identify and describe how assessment is practised in infant classrooms (i.e. ages 5–7).
2 To focus on particular assessment 'events' or 'incidents', explore to what extent teachers and students share a common understanding of the nature and purpose of such events, and consider to what extent these events might be said to constitute 'formative' assessment.

Classroom assessment was an under-researched field, with 'teacher assessment' being very much an emergent activity when the study was undertaken (and in many respects it still is). For this reason the research approach was exploratory and qualitative. A key theoretical interest was to explore the social construction of assessment and learning *in action*, in ordinary classroom settings. In addition, the theoretical conceptualisation of assessment and learning as socially situated acts led to a focus on the interactive 'assessment incident' as the unit of analysis: the inter-psychological 'space' or 'moment' wherein learning is collaboratively constructed (Newman et al., 1989). Data was gathered by a combination of interviews (of teachers and students) and, particularly, extensive classroom observation, recorded on audio and videotape. To begin with, the research adopted the approach of multi-site case study (Stenhouse, 1982) in order to identify a reasonable range of practice while allowing for fairly detailed investigation in each case. As the research developed and issues were identified for more in-depth study, a much more focused programme of observation was mounted in a small number of classrooms. Nine schools were initially involved in fieldwork, from two different Local Education Authorities (LEAs or school districts). They were selected on the principles of 'theoretical sampling' (Glaser and Strauss, 1967). Different sizes, organisational structures and socio-economic contexts of KS1 schooling were represented (e.g. infant schools (5–7 years), primary schools (5–11 years), rural or urban location, small or large intake of students each year), along with some contrast of LEA in-service training support. 'Progressive focusing' (Parlett and Hamilton, 1972) was then employed to select the small number of classrooms from which most observational data was collected. The transcribed observational data presented here derive from over 100 hours of videotape-recordings made in the infant classrooms of a small village primary school, an inner city primary school and two suburban primary schools (see Torrance and Pryor, 1998 for a fuller account).

In order to illustrate our methods and findings we present below two short extracts from the many incidents we identified and analysed in detail (Tables 6.1 and 6.2). The data are presented in two parallel columns. The left hand column contains a transcription of dialogue and non-verbal interaction derived from the video and audiotape-recordings. The non-verbal interaction, which we term 'stage directions', is in italics. In the right hand column is a running commentary on and initial analysis of the transcription.

Creating these written accounts was very labour intensive. The video camera was placed in a convenient corner of the classrooms under study and was able to 'zoom in' on aspects of interaction. However, once focused, for example on a small group at work, the researcher generally left it to record while observing interaction more informally, taking field-notes to complement the electronic recordings. The audio recording on the videotape was picked up via a radio microphone usually attached to the teacher. In addition an audio-tape recorder was often placed in the centre of the group of students under study. Particularly interesting incidents (including both of these presented below) were usually followed up by interviews with students and teachers. Where possible these interviews took the form of 'stimulated video recall' whereby the actors were asked to pause the tape whenever they wished to comment. During this initial playback the researcher's prompts were simply to maintain the focus (e.g. 'what was going on here? what were you thinking just then?'). Other viewings then followed with more searching interview questions ('what did you expect them to say? why did you do that?'). For some of the younger children – the youngest were only just 4 years old – we found it helpful to provide further prompts in the form of cards that could be sorted (see Pryor, 1995).

We gathered a great deal of data for each of the short incidents. From the many hours of classroom observation that took place, every incident that might be termed an assessment event was transcribed. Following initial reading and analysis of the transcripts, we then selected some of the more interesting incidents and reviewed the videotape-recording once again. Working together, we then set about constructing the detailed 'stage directions' for these extracts. This formed a focus for discussion of the interaction and we began to construct the commentary. Thus, on the left hand side we had a description at a low level of inference, which was then 'thickened' by our first interpretation on the right. Some of these incidents were discussed further with colleagues and postgraduate students.

The two-column text is not just a convenient way of presenting data to the reader, but also a key methodological device that has helped to channel our own discussion and interpretation. We do not claim objectivity for either left or right hand text, since both are our own constructions. But they are grounded in a considerable wealth of data from several different perspectives. Both the exploratory nature of our research and our theoretical positioning of formative assessment as problematic guided our approach. We intend the simultaneous provision of both columns to facilitate the reader's own understandings of the data, with the gap between the two texts permitting alternative interpretations of our interpretation. To paraphrase Stronach and Maclure (1997: 57), we present accounts that offer the reader the possibility of occupying different ground from the authors.

The first transcript (Table 6.1) is of part of a lesson in a reception class. The teacher is working with a group of three boys: Jimmy, Simon and Seb, whilst a classroom assistant supervises the rest of the class. A re-telling of the story of the 'The Three Bears' forms the context for assessment of early mathematics (though the teacher initially defines the activity as making 'our own story' about bears). The teacher has brought to the group three different sized teddy bears which are in front of the teacher, leaning against the wall. As the event starts she places three large cardboard tiles with numbers on them behind the teddy bears.

Table 6.1 *Re-telling the story of the three bears*

T right – now then – we're going to make our own story – you're going to help me to make a book – about bears – and I've got a very famous story here – and there's a clue –	T initially defines the activity as making a 'story' and a 'book' about bears.
	A clue to what? Holding up the book and rearranging the bears is presumably meant to draw attention to these objects. But what might the word clue signify for these 4/5 year olds?
T holds up a book and rearranges three teddies on the table. Jimmy looks across room. Only Seb looks at the bears.	
T >what story do you think this is about...	
Simon is making marks on his paper.	
T Simon – >would you like to look< at the bears –	This utterance appears to be designed to bring Simon back on task: it is an instruction, not a question.
T opens book as she addresses him.	
T do you know a story =	
Simon >= no<	
Jimmy > yeah (**)<	
T about that number of bears what number what number's that -	T grasps the tile whilst still talking about the bears (three of them) but without a pause starts to ask a question about the number on the tile. 'That' is used to stand both for the quantity three and immediately afterwards for the symbol for one. The question seems to be addressed to the group in general rather than Simon in particular. There is no acknowledgement of the children's correct answer; 'would you put your pencils down', again, is an instruction, not a question, aimed at reasserting teacher control. The pencils seem to be distracting the children from the task in hand. The declared purpose of this task is to encourage emergent writing – 'to make our own story' – but it has quickly developed into a maths lesson. This shift is further emphasised by the use of the word 'game'. What expectations might this arouse in the children?
T holds up large tile with number one on it.	
Cs one	
T now you have the one	
Hands tile to Jimmy revealing the number two.	
T and would you put your pencils down for a minute because we're going to play a game...what number's >that one<	
Simon >umm<	
T looks at Seb and puts her finger to her mouth when Simon says 'umm'.	
T >do you (*know what that is)<	An answer is clearly expected and Simon gives one. It is not correct; has he been influenced by the original enquiry about the bears? Would he expect to be shown the number three? Does he think the question refers to the bears?
Simon um – three	
T it's a three you think -	
T looks back at Seb	
T what number do you think it is Seb?	
Seb um – two	
T two –	
T looks back at Simon	T is correcting Simon's mistake, presumably assuming that he cannot recognise the numbers two and three.
T it's a two –	
T looks back at Seb	
T so you have the two	
T gives number two tile to Seb; number three tile is revealed.	

T closes Three Bears Book and places it behind her.	This appears to be some sort of unconscious symbolic closure. The lesson is no longer a language activity – the book has been replaced by the number tiles.
T turns to face Simon directly across the table.	
T what number's that one Simon?	
Simon er – (*four)	T uses the word 'one' in her question while holding up the symbol for three; and, although the recording is unclear, T seems certain that Simon has said a wrong number.
T it's a – three	
Simon three =	
T that one's a three	The confusion of one and three is compounded.
T hands tile to Simon.	
Jimmy you don't know all your numbers	Two errors are generalised to 'all your numbers' (note personalising possessive).
T sorry – Jimmy – could you say that again – I didn't quite hear.	Either T really did not hear or this is another question where locutionary force is different from ostensible purpose, possibly an example of T attempting to protect Simon from a harsh peer assessment.
Jimmy he dun't know about (*all of) his numbers	
T he doesn't know about all the numbers – well we can help him, can't we, if we play a game.	

Key: * Word difficult to interpret
      = Rapid change of speaker

In this sequence, Jimmy is privileged by being handed the 'number 1' tile. Later he was also given the biggest bear, which the teacher obviously had in mind all along to associate with the 'number 1' tile. Subsequently Jimmy's annunciation of himself as 'daddy bear' allowed him to be interpreted as answering a question about relative size correctly. Seb appeared content to acquiesce to the schooled conventions of the interaction without really engaging with the task, while Simon was continually frustrated in his attempts to intervene and receive the teacher's attention. He was given the 'number 3' tile and relegated to being third out of three in the group's social dynamics. He remained unable to move out of this deficit position as long as the text of the interaction stayed tightly controlled by the teacher and he was construed as being unable to count to three. However, much later, he spontaneously indicated his capacity to count by observing and commenting on how few children remain in the classroom (Table 6.2):

Table 6.2 *Simon demonstrates what he knows*

The door squeaks – Seb, Jimmy and T look round.	Someone has left the room. Simon notices there are only five people in the classroom (the fifth is the researcher). In a 'naturalistic' context he has demonstrated his knowledge and understanding of number up to five. Moreover he has a notion of that being a relatively small number in the context of the whole class ('that's all').
Simon (*) how many've we got there – one two three four five – that's all.	
Simon turns around and looks at the rest of the classroom. He points to each person in the classroom in turn.	
T there's lots isn't there right – so you've done your bit of writing teddy bear and he eats honey and he puts it behind his back – right Simon – would you do me a picture –	T responds to Simon's comment in desultory fashion. Her agenda has moved on and she doesn't 'hear' him counting. She is more focused now on the writing of the story.
The lesson continues	

A sociological analysis

The teacher said that in this activity she was being opportunistic, trying to assess as much as possible in order to plan future activities. She had been successful making many notes about the children's attainment. However, what is an opportunistic use of a holistic activity for an adult may be very perplexing for young children. Far from providing them with a flexible and responsive context in which to demonstrate what they know, understand and can do, it may well confuse and constrain them, actively contributing to the social construction of their failure. This incident was one of a number where the text of the interaction was ostensibly enabling the teacher to gain a good idea of what the children could do or understand. Yet the incident seemed on closer inspection to interact with the social context, contributing to the mis-assessment of the children involved.

Even in this short extract, the multifaceted nature of teacher questioning comes to the fore, as does the struggle of the students to comprehend both the nature of the task and the specific cognitive demands of each question. We see the social construction and accomplishment of assessment judgements captured in action. The teacher is using her control of the discourse, as the person who both initiates exchanges with a question and finishes them off with an evaluative feedback move, to steer the text of the lesson in the direction that will accomplish a legitimate encounter. At a linguistic level the potential for confusion is great. The word 'one' is used as an ordinal (the first bear), a cardinal (a single bear), and a pronoun. The second sense seems to have been the major focus of the teacher's attention. In an interview later she stated that she wanted to know 'if they actually, any of them, knew their numbers one to four.' The purpose of the activity is stated as assessment. However, this cognitive agenda is necessarily situated within and overtaken by the social agendas of both teacher and students, where issues of cultural acuity and gender come to the fore.

Simon seems to suffer from the gendered competition for attention which the activity promotes among the three boys. Within the interaction the teacher appears to interpret his utterances as evidence of lack of understanding, a judgement she later confirmed at interview. Yet Simon is able to count up to five when he notices that the rest of the class have left the classroom. Since this observation was not part of the teacher's 'official' assessment agenda, it did not appear to attract her attention. Detailed analysis of the transcript enables us to highlight the sociologically implicated nature of both the teacher's judgement and the student's accomplishment. But this analysis should not be taken as criticism of the teacher. We were not attempting to evaluate teaching but to illuminate complex issues, and we had the benefit of the audio and video record.

Simon's position as number three later led to him receiving the smallest bear, and his subsequent engagement with the assessment process seems to have been completely coloured by this. The teacher's agenda was to engage each child in turn. Simon received the smallest bear and hence each time had to wait his turn until last. He wasn't prepared to do this, possibly because he genuinely didn't appreciate the differing size of the bears, or understand counting in relation to taking turns. More probably it was because he didn't comprehend the teacher's implicit agenda (the social rules of the classroom 'game'). So he constantly made bids for attention and in so doing got the answers to the questions 'wrong'. This problem was compounded because all three boys were new to schooling and were bidding against each other for the attention of a female teacher, a surrogate mother.

A further complication was provided by the power struggle between the boys. Not only was Simon given the smallest bear, but in the course of the interaction it was defined as the 'baby' and, by association, so was he. His attempts to reposition himself socially in this hierarchy were misinterpreted by the teacher as a lack of understanding of the cognitive issue.

The point we are seeking to emphasise is that policy and practice guidelines tend to assume a socially decontextualised cognitive agenda, yet we would argue that competence cannot be disentangled from the social context of performance. Avoiding obvious pitfalls such as the characterisation of one participant in an assessment task as the 'baby' of the group ought to improve the overall validity of the inferences drawn. Nevertheless, the data demonstrate that Simon's inability to read or take power in one social situation fails to elicit a legitimate performance and so positions him as incompetent in one context. He displays competence in another context – one of his own spontaneous choosing which makes sense to him – but one that is overlooked by the teacher.

In other work we have made more explicit the relationship between this micro-level analysis and more general sociological dimensions such as social class and gender (see especially Pryor and Torrance, 2000). Having highlighted some of the sociological issues at stake, we now look briefly at another incident and the way in which a psychological analysis grounded in the literature on motivation can act as a springboard for a continuing theorisation of classroom assessment.

The context this time is a full, busy classroom and involves slightly older (7 year old) children. At the end of each week, the students have a lesson time for finishing off incomplete work and the teacher is reviewing their work on an individual basis. A small queue gathers as the teacher reviews their work in turn (Table 6.3).

Table 6.3 *Reviewing Mario's work*

T – come on Mario – you should have that already – come and stand here. *T points to left hand side. Mario moves round. T touches Mario on arm.*	T says this with some annoyance. Mario has been standing in the queue for some time and yet does not have all the necessary documentation.
11:18	
T right did you find this a bit tricky by the looks of it.	T has been able to look at the book while Mario was away. He seems to have decided that it is not very good. T's first comment assigns this to the difficulty of the material, using the word 'tricky'.
Jason who is behind Mario in the line repositions himself slightly so that he can see Mario's book	Throughout Mario's assessment Jason looks at his book and at T, moving slightly when his vision is obscured by Mario's back.
Mario mmm	
T mmm – seventeen – nineteen – twenty – two oh OK – what did you find the hardest thing about it –	These are the words that Mario has had to write. T is asking about the *process* of writing, potentially a fruitful way of exploring what it was about the handwriting that Mario found
Mario hardest thing – was that one. *Mario points to the book*	difficult. However instead of focusing on process Mario concentrates on the most difficult item.

T	was it – is it – is it cos the words are quite long –
Mario	mmm

T does not receive the answer he requires and therefore uses a 'reformulator' (French and Maclure, 1983) which has the effect of moving from an open question 'what did you find ...' to a closed one 'is it cos...?' In this way he has taken control of the discourse.

T	and you find (*that they) keep going – and you want to s/ =

T is prompting again about the process but in a rather closed and directive fashion ('you find', 'you want').

Mario	= yeah and you get yer finger aching.
T	yeah – OK.

Mario responds but it is difficult to say whether the sore finger affected the quality of the handwriting or was merely a consequence of the difficulty. T does not probe further.

Mario holds up his hand and waves his finger. T writes in book.
At this point another T enters and engages T in a conversation about the whereabouts of a member of the school support staff. T continues to write whilst she talks to him. (Not transcribed 29 seconds). As the other T is still talking but has retreated towards the door, Mario says loudly

T seems at first to be annoyed by the intrusion but prolongs it by asking 'How's it going?' and prompting a further narrative from T2.

Mario	(*) that's the best I've done in my book.

Mario appears annoyed that his time has been interrupted and speaks across T2.

11:19

T	- just a (*moment then) Mario.

Meanwhile other T continues to speak (not transcribed 10 seconds) before leaving

The tone of this utterance suggests that it is not to be construed as an admonishment, T is just asking Mario to be patient.

T	sorry Mario – what did you say?
Mario	that's the best piece of writing.
T	well I was going to say that – yes – I mean I mean – sometimes it's looked a bit neater, but – I think as you've tried so hard I think I'm going to give you a team point =

...[ ]...

T shuts Mario's book and taps it with his finger

This apology is said much more animatedly in sharp contrast to the previous statement. T appears to have returned to annoyance with the intrusion and to be affirming that Mario's irritation was justified. Significantly Mario's interruption marks a shift in the way the piece of work is viewed. Mario's suggestion appears to have had an effect. T appears to have been persuaded that the work is more meritorious than he did to begin with. Mario has been determinedly ipsative in his view. Indeed he appears to have applied very sophisticated success criteria to the work persuading T to weigh the difficulty against the neatness. Though this juxtaposition is not articulated overtly, it seems to be the socially constructed outcome of the interaction, with T agreeing that he was 'going to say that' although in the past Mario's work has 'looked a bit neater'.

T	right Mario well done – team point – put that away – look in your basket for what you've got to do next.

Mario turns and begins to go

Mario	(*) I'll do that.

T seals the change with a team point. Is this necessary? Lepper's work (Lepper and Hodell, 1989) would suggest that this is precisely the wrong moment to introduce an extrinsic reward as the student's intrinsic pleasure with the results might be deduced from his judgement of the work as 'the best'.

Key:	* Word difficult to interpret
	= Rapid change of speaker

A psychological analysis

We chose to use this seemingly insignificant incident as an exemplar of one of the myriad routine interactions that lay down the 'sediment' of student identity and self-esteem. At first sight, it might be seen as a purely cognitive issue about this child's individual achievement and development (or, more specifically, a psychomotor problem since it is to do with handwriting). Yet below the surface, complex social and affective issues are being played out. The interaction here is concerned not only with issues of success and failure but also with the explanations that the actors put forward for their judgements.

The literature on attribution and goal theory would suggest that three main issues are at stake:

1 Is this piece of work to be viewed as a success or a failure?
2 To what is performance attributed?
3 How is achievement rewarded or punished?

Our analysis of these issues is summarised in Table 6.4. Interview data suggested that the teacher saw Mario as a confident child with, in Dweck's (1989) terms, learning goals. What is of most interest here though is not that he already had this orientation, but that it appeared to be amplified by the interaction. This outcome occurred not so much through the action of the teacher as through Mario's own assertiveness in seizing the opportunity presented by the interruption to take charge of the assessment situation. The teacher appeared to be judging the work negatively, but Mario's own intervention shifted the agreed understanding from failure to success. The *task difficulty* attribution was accepted, but less as an excuse for failure than a reinforcement of success.

Crucially, the theory states that attributions of high effort act as a 'double-edged sword' (Covington, 1984). If, in the context of failure, students have tried very hard yet still do not succeed, they are liable to conclude that they lack the necessary intelligence. This experience contributes to a negative view of themselves. However, in the context of success, effort is a positive characteristic. Since Mario says he has tried very hard, the positioning of the work as success can now contribute to Mario's positive self-image. As he later stated when interviewed, he saw continued effort as a way of enhancing his learning and ability. Interestingly, subsequent work by Dweck (2000) has emphasised the importance of learners adopting this kind of attitude, which she describes as an incremental – as opposed to an entity – theory of intelligence.

Table 6.4 *A psychological analysis of social and affective issues for Mario*

Social and affective issue for Mario	Analysis
Success/failure	
T right did you find this a bit tricky by the looks of it	failure
Mario (*) that's the best I've done in my book	success
Mario that's the best piece of writing	success
T well I was going to say that - yes - I mean I mean - sometimes it's looked a bit neater	success/ failure
Attribution	
T right did you find this a bit tricky by the looks of it	ability/ task difficulty
T was it - is it - is it cos the words are quite long –	task difficulty
T I think as you've tried so hard I think I'm going to give you a team point =	effort
Rewards	
Mario (*) that's the best I've done in my book	intrinsic
Mario that's the best piece of writing	intrinsic
T I think as you've tried so hard I think I'm going to give you a team point =	extrinsic
T right Mario well done – team point	extrinsic

Key: * Word difficult to interpret
         = Rapid change of speaker

The use of an extrinsic reward is problematic. To some extent Mario's evident intrinsic pleasure at progress makes the reward redundant, and it may therefore undermine intrinsic motivation (Lepper and Hodell, 1989). On the other hand, because Mario is already pleased with himself, the team point becomes a 'bonus not a bribe' (Lepper and Hodell, 1989: 70) which should not harm intrinsic motivation.

Attribution, goal theory and the notions of intrinsic and extrinsic reward provided us with a useful analytic framework, but we wished to go further. The differences that we noted between the possible effects of the interactions on Simon, Mario and their classmates could have been ascribed to the individual personality features of the children. But looking more closely at the social context and structure of the interactions presented more interesting explanations.

Combining sociological and psychological insights

The children's different access to power in both our examples is striking. Power in schools is inscribed in knowledge, but recursively realised through interaction. The confidence of Mario is not only a static feature that he brings to the lesson, but is also being constantly invoked and reworked by the interactions in which he takes part. As we see in this incident, his voice is heard and in this way the power relationship between him and his teacher becomes more even. Simon, on the other hand, is placed in a subservient role in the earlier extract. He is positioned as powerless in the interaction and remains so. He is defeated not so much by his lack of content knowledge as by his inability to access the 'rules of the game'. So he remains unheard and so is mis-assessed.

In developing these ideas we have made use of Kreisberg's distinction between coercive *power over*, based on domination, and *power with*, 'charac-terised by collaboration, sharing and mutuality' (1992: 61), which he claims is 'manifest in relationships of co-agency' (1992: 85) and is the 'power that empowers' (1992: 175). Here it is the negotiation and contestation evident in Mario's intervention that causes the relationship with the teacher to evolve from the 'power over' position at the start into the 'power with' category. Mario has identified an area where he can have an impact on the socially con-structed outcome of the interaction and he moves to realise it.

This teacher is powerful and dominant because of his position in organising and managing the class and in assessing children's work, but he also has an ideo-logical commitment to a child-centred approach that involves him in 'making a big effort to be nice and considerate' (tape recorded interview). Mario is assertive enough to make his case, but we encountered others in the class who were not. To a certain extent we see this also with the other event, where Jimmy is able to access power whilst Simon is not. The important point to note is that neither classroom structures nor individual students' psychological make-up determine the outcomes. Rather, they emerge through the interaction in which they are manifest. We would argue that the constant replaying of this kind of routine incident leads to the creation of patterns which become ever more marked in those who participate in them. Moreover, the injection into any exchange of judgements about schoolwork or about students (i.e. an assessment event) raises the stakes for the students and amplifies the effect.

The situation is further complicated by the fact that macro issues such as gender and social class are implicated in the way that the micro-level interac-tion is played out (Pryor and Torrance, 2000; Torrance and Pryor, 1998; compare also Filer and Pollard, 2000 for similar exploration of such issues). Nevertheless, this complexity does not mean that classroom assessment is so intricate as to be beyond teachers' scope to seek improvement. There are many ideas that we have been able to take forward in later collaboration with teach-ers (Torrance and Pryor, 2001).

Developing formative assessment

We suggest that if teachers wish to encourage autonomy and boost confidence through formative feedback, a critical analysis of motivational issues, contex-tualised in the micropolitics of the classroom, is necessary. We would argue that the power relationships required for effective formative assessment mirror the ideal of Kreisberg's 'power with'. The teacher remains in a privileged posi-tion and takes the prime responsibility for providing feedback on performance, but the aim is to foster self-monitoring in the student. Being sen-sitised to the potential of assessment dialogue to shape attributions and either reinforce or subvert performance or learning goals is also helpful. So is a criti-cal awareness of the way the structures of classroom discourse can impinge on power relations. The key issue is that teachers recognise and are cautious about the implications of cueing 'right answers' through routine, taken-for-granted teacher-student interaction.

In our research we identified two 'ideal-typical' approaches to formative assessment, which we termed 'convergent' and 'divergent' (see Table 6.5). These ideal types seemed to be associated with teachers' differing views of learning and of the relationship of assessment to the process of intervening to support learning, and might be said to represent a continuum of possibilities for classroom teachers. In *convergent assessment*, the important thing is to find out *if* the learner knows, understands or can do a predetermined thing. It is characterised by detailed planning, and is generally accomplished by closed or pseudo-open questioning and tasks. Here the interaction of the learner with the curriculum is seen from the point of view of the curriculum. The theoretical origins of such an approach would appear at least implicitly to be behaviourist, deriving from mastery-learning models and involving assessment *of* the learner by the teacher. *Divergent assessment*, on the other hand, emphasises the learner's understanding rather than the agenda of the assessor. Here the important thing is to discover *what* the learner knows, understands and can do. It is characterised by less detailed planning, where open questioning and tasks are of more relevance. The implications of divergent teacher assessment are that a constructivist view of learning is adopted, with an intention to teach in the zone of proximal development (Vygotsky, 1986). As a result, assessment is seen as accomplished jointly by the teacher and the student, and oriented more to future development rather than measurement of past or current achievement.

Table 6.5 *Contrasting convergent and divergent assessment*

CONVERGENT ASSESSMENT	DIVERGENT ASSESSMENT
Assessment which aims to discover *if* the learner knows, understands or can do a predetermined thing. This is characterised by:	Assessment which aims to discover *what* the learner knows, understands or can do. This is characterised by:
Practical Implications a. precise planning by the teacher and an intention to stick to it; b. recording via check lists and can-do statements; c. closed or pseudo-open teacher questioning and tasks; d. a focus on contrasting errors with correct responses; e. authoritative judgmental or quantitative feedback, f. feedback focused on the successful completion of the task in hand; g. involvement of the learner as recipient of assessments.	**Practical Implications** a. flexible planning or complex planning which incorporates alternatives; b. open forms of recording (narrative, quotations etc.); c. primarily open tasks with questioning by teachers and students directed at 'helping' rather than testing; d. a focus on miscues – aspects of learner's work which yield insights into their current understanding – and on prompting metacognition; e. exploratory, provisional or provocative descriptive feedback aimed at prompting further engagement from the student; f. discussion prompting reflection on the task and its context with a view to constructing understanding of future situations in which new knowledge might be applied; g. involvement of the student as initiator of assessments as well as recipient.

Theoretical Implications	**Theoretical Implications**
h. an analysis of the interaction of the learner and the curriculum from the point of view of the curriculum;	h. an analysis of the interaction of the learner and the curriculum from the point of view both of the learner and of the curriculum;
i. a behaviourist view of learning;	i a constructivist or socio-cultural view of education and an acknowledgement of the importance of the context for the assessment;
j. an intention to teach or assess the next predetermined thing in a linear progression;	j. an intention to teach in the zone of proximal development;
k. an interaction embedded within a restricted Initiation-Response-Feedback (IRF) sequence;	k. part of an on-going dialogue between and amongst learners and teachers where learners initiate as well as respond, ask questions as well as reply;
l. a view of assessment as accomplished by the teacher.	l. a view of assessment as a collaboration between and amongst teachers and students.
This view of assessment might be seen less as formative assessment, rather as repeated summative assessment or continuous assessment.	This view of assessment could be said to attend more closely to contemporary theories of learning and accept the complexity of formative assessment.

Developed and adapted from Torrance and Pryor, 1998: 153

In our subsequent work with teachers we found that convergent and divergent assessment was a useful heuristic device which helped them to reconceptualise their approaches to formative classroom assessment (Torrance and Pryor, 2001). They investigated divergent approaches more closely, because these approaches seemed potentially more powerful in fostering the social and intellectual conditions in the classroom that would lead to enhanced learning. Nevertheless, the teachers still argued that convergent approaches were important, and indeed inevitable given the convergence of the curriculum and constraints on teacher time. Indeed, coming to understand that they could develop and use a 'repertoire' of assessment strategies and practices was important in allowing them to feel more secure in their explorations. Rather than having to implement something completely new, the concept of divergent assessment became a sort of *aide-mémoire*, as they sought to expand the boundaries of their classroom practice.

Conclusion

To sum up, our research identified the importance of combining sociological and psychological perspectives on classroom assessment and of studying routine classroom assessment in situ, under 'naturally occurring conditions' in the classroom. Other recent work has recognised the importance of such an orientation (Gipps, 1999; Pellegrino et al., 1999) but we highlight the dynamic and interactive significance of linguistic and social context, demonstrating the social construction of cognition in action. Our work has sought to emphasise that assessment is not an activity that can be *done to* children, but is accomplished by means of social interaction in which the practices of the participants have a critical effect on the outcome. The outcomes of assessment are actively produced rather than revealed and displayed by the assessment process. Further, each participant brings understandings not only of the cognitive agenda to the event but also of the kinds of social relations and practices that are legitimate in the circumstances. These understandings are then subject to change as a result of the inferences that are made during the interaction. By failing to recognise the issue as important, assessment policies and classroom practices are likely to reinforce and perpetuate the poor performance of many school students.

We would claim therefore that raising the quality of classroom assessment is an extremely difficult but worthwhile enterprise. The first step would involve teachers becoming aware of the importance and possibilities of the social context of assessment and holding it as continuously problematic. The next stage would involve opening up the discourse to the children and at suitable, strategic moments, making the students more aware of the meta-cognitive and crucially also the meta-social agenda.

Acknowledgement

This chapter is based on findings from the research project 'Teacher Assessment at Key Stage 1: Accomplishing Assessment in the Classroom' funded by the Economic and Social Research Council from1993–96 (award number R000234668).

References

Ames, C. (1984) 'Competitive, co-operative and individualistic goal structures: a motivational analysis', in R. Ames and C. Ames (eds), *Research on Motivation in Education* (Volume 1). Orlando, FL: Academic Press. pp. 177–207.

Beveridge, M. (ed) (1982) *Children Thinking through Language*. London: Edward Arnold.

Black, P. (1994) 'Performance assessment and accountability: the experience in England and Wales', *Educational Evaluation and Policy Analysis*, 16 (2): 191–203.

Black, P. and Wiliam, D. (1998) 'Assessment and classroom learning', *Assessment in Education*, 5 (1): 7–74.

Bloom, B. (1971) 'Mastery learning', in J. H. Block (ed), *Mastery Learning: Theory and Practice*. New York: Holt, Rinehart and Winston.

Brown, A. and Ferrara, R. (1985) 'Diagnosing zones of proximal development', in J. Wertsch (ed) *Culture, Communication and Cognition: Vygotskian Perspectives*. Cambridge: Cambridge University Press.

Bruner, J. (1985) 'Vygotsky: a historical and conceptual perspective' in J. Wertsch (ed) *Culture, Communication and Cognition: Vygotskian Perspectives*. Cambridge: Cambridge University Press.

Cicourel, A., Jennings, K.W., Jennings, S.H.M., Leiter, K.C.W., Mackay, R., Mehan, H. and Roth, D.R. (eds), (1974) *Language Use and School Performance*. New York: Academic Press.

Cole, M. (1985) 'The zone of proximal development: where culture and cognition create each other', in Wertsch J. (ed), *Culture, Communication and Cognition: Vygotskian Perspectives*. Cambridge: Cambridge University Press.

Cooper, B. (1994) 'Authentic testing in mathematics? The boundary between everyday and mathematical knowledge in national curriculum testing in English schools', *Assessment in Education*, 1 (2): 143–66.

Cooper, B. and Dunne, M. (2000) *Assessing Children's Mathematical Knowledge: Social Class, Sex and Problem-solving*. Buckingham: Open University Press.

Covington, M. (1984) 'The motive for self-worth', in R. Ames and C. Ames (eds), *Research on Motivation in Education* (Volume 1). Orlando, FL: Academic Press.

Dann, R. (2002) *Promoting Assessment as Learning*. London: RoutledgeFalmer.

Donaldson, M. (1978) *Children's Minds*. London: Fontana.

Dweck, C. (1989) 'Motivation', in A. Lesgold and R. Glaser (eds), *Foundations for a Psychology of Education*. Hillsdale, NJ: Erlbaum.

Dweck, C. (2000) *Self-Theories: Their Role in Motivation, Personality, and Development*. Hove: Psychology Press.

Ecclestone, K. (2002) *Learning Autonomy in Post-16 Education*. London: RoutledgeFalmer.

Edwards, A. and Furlong, V. (1978) *The Language of Teaching*. London: Heinemann.

Edwards, D. and Mercer, N. (1987) *Common Knowledge: The Development of Understanding in the Classroom*. London: Methuen.

Edwards, A. and Westgate, D. (1987) *Investigating Classroom Talk*. London: Falmer Press.

Filer, A. and Pollard, A. (2000) *The Social World of Student Assessment*. London: Continuum.

Forman, E. and Cazden, C. (1985) 'Exploring Vygotskian perspectives in education: the cognitive value of peer interaction', in J. Wertsch. (ed), *Culture, Communication and Cognition: Vygotskian Perspectives*. Cambridge: Cambridge University Press.

French, P. and Maclure, M. (1983) 'Teachers' questions, students' answers: an investigation of questions and answers in the infant classroom', in M. Stubbs and H. Hillier (eds), *Readings on Language, Schools and Classrooms*. London: Methuen.

Gipps, C. (1999) 'Socio-cultural aspects of assessment', *Review of Research in Education*, 24: 355–92.

Glaser, B. and Strauss, A. (1967) *The Discovery of Grounded Theory*. Chicago: Aldine.

Kreisberg, S. (1992) *Transforming Power: Domination, Empowerment and Education*. New York: State University of New York Press.

Lepper, M. R. and Hodell, M. (1989) 'Intrinsic motivation in the classroom', in C. Ames and R. Ames (eds) *Research on Motivation in Education* (Volume 3). San Diego, CAL: Academic Press.

Mehan, H. (1979) *Learning Lessons: Social Organisation in the Classroom*. Cambridge, MA: Harvard University Press.

Newman, D., Griffin, P. and Cole, M. (1989) *The Construction Zone: Working for Cognitive Change in School*. Cambridge: Cambridge University Press.

Parlett, M. and Hamilton, D. (1972) 'Evaluation as illumination', reprinted in R. Murphy and H. Torrance (eds), (1987) *Evaluating Education: Issues and Methods*. London: Paul Chapman Publishing.

Pellegrino, J., Baxter, G. and Glaser, R. (1999) 'Addressing the 'two disciplines' problem: linking theories of cognition and learning with assessment and instructional practice', *Review of Research in Education*, 24: 307–53.

Popham, J. (1978) *Criterion-referenced measurement*. Englewood Cliffs, NJ: Prentice-Hall.

Popham, J. (1987) 'The merits of measurement-driven instruction', *Phi Delta Kappan*, 68: 679–82.

Pryor, J. (1995) 'Hearing the voice of young children: problems and possibilities', paper presented at the European Educational Research Association annual conference, University of Bath.

Pryor, J. and Torrance, H. (2000) 'Questioning the three bears: the social construction of assessment in the classroom', in A. Filer (ed), *Assessment: Social Product and Social Practice*. London: RoutledgeFalmer.

Sadler, R. (1989) 'Formative assessment and the design of instructional systems', *Instructional Science*, 18: 119–44.

Shepard, L. (2000) 'The role of assessment in a learning culture', *Educational Researcher*, 29 (7): 4–14.

Sinclair, J. and Coulthard, R. (1975) *Towards an Analysis of Discourse*. Oxford: Oxford University Press.

Stenhouse, L. (1982) 'The conduct, analysis and reporting of case study in educational research and evaluation', reprinted in R. Murphy and H. Torrance (eds), (1987) *Evaluating Education: Issues and Methods*. London: Paul Chapman Publishing.

Stronach, I. and MacLure, M. (1997) *Educational Research Undone: The Postmodernist Embrace*. Buckingham: Open University Press.

Task Group on Assessment and Testing (1988) *A Report*. London: Department of Education and Science.

Torrance, H. (2003) 'Assessment of the national curriculum in England', in T. Kellaghan and D. Stufflebeam (eds), *International Handbook of Educational Evaluation*. Dordrecht: Kluwer.

Torrance, H. and Pryor, J. (1998) *Investigating Formative Assessment: Teaching, Learning and Assessment in the Classroom*. Buckingham: Open University Press.

Torrance, H. and Pryor, J. (2001) 'Developing formative assessment in the classroom: using action research to explore and modify theory', *British Educational Research Journal* 27 (5): 615–31.

Vygotsky, L. (1978) *Mind in Society*. Cambridge, MA: Harvard University Press.

Vygotsky, L. (1986) *Thought and Language*. Cambridge, MA: MIT Press.

Weiner, B. (1984) 'Principles for a theory of motivation and their application within an attributional framework', In R. Ames and C. Ames (eds), *Research on Motivation in Education*. Orlando, FL: Academic Press.

Chapter 7

Participation and control in learning: a pedagogic democratic right?

Diane Reay and Madeleine Arnot

Student voice in the process of consultation about learning is the substantive focus of this chapter. Diane Reay and Madeleine Arnot examine critically the notion of the autonomous or independent learner. They explore the ways in which students' control over their learning is regulated through the social hierarchies of classroom life, which in turn reflect wider patterns of social stratification. Reay and Arnot outline how they used Basil Bernstein's social theory to inform an empirical study of the social dynamics and influences on participation in learning in British schools. They point out that their research was explicitly informed at all stages by a particular theoretical stance, unlike many qualitative studies that work in a more grounded way. This approach enabled them to make connections between micro-analyses of social processes in classrooms and the wider theoretical issues about ways in which social hierarchies are enacted through the organisation of the curriculum and forms of pedagogy.

A particularly interesting methodological feature of this research was the use of focus group interviews with secondary school students, along with individual interviews and classroom observations. Reay and Arnot explain that the reason for using focus group interviews was that they wanted to find out whether students felt they belonged, as individuals and groups, within the school community. The researchers point out that most work on student consultation has tended to focus on individuals or whole class discussion. In this project, the group and individual interviews generated different perspectives on the same issues. The former provided insight into social processes and dynamics. The latter illuminated particular students' understanding and experiences of teaching and learning. Reay and Arnot argue that these two types of interview, together with the observation data, allowed them to *triangulate* evidence from three sources.

The authors reflect on the limitations of their study, the compromises that were made, and the constraints and tensions they experienced in conducting the research. Two important constraints were the restricted amount of time that could be spent in the schools, and difficulties for teachers undertaking action research. Reay and Arnot are also reflexive about their own position as researchers in the school sites, and the issue of researcher subjectivity. They highlight how they had to negotiate their intentions, as researchers, with the preoccupations of the young people who participated in the study. A particular ethical dilemma they experienced was dealing with students' (often uncomfortable or hostile) disclosures about teachers. As they began to see the school and learning through students' eyes, the researchers suggest that this experience inevitably affected their perceptions of, and relationships with, the teachers. They argue that there is often a fine dividing line between researcher subjectivity and partiality.

Introduction

This chapter reports on a small-scale qualitative research project: 'Consulting Students about Teaching and Learning'. Our investigation focused on the control of learning in secondary school classrooms. But it was also linked to a larger project with a much broader brief: to consider the transformative potential of student consultation at both primary and secondary school levels, and the constraints associated with using such potential from a sociological point of view. In turn, this larger project was part of a programme (The Teaching and Learning Research Programme, Phase 1) funded by the Economic and Social Research Council in the UK.

   We know a good deal about the social dynamics of schools, the relations between peer cultures and teacher–student relations. Paradoxically, however, we know very little about how student voice is heard within social relations of class, ethnicity and gender in the classroom, and about what different groups of students might say about their experience of learning. The aims of our particular project were twofold:

▶ To explore the potential of student consultation, and to get behind 'the mythological discourses of schooling' (Bernstein, 2000: xxv) in order to reveal the social principles embedded within the learning process. We were interested in exploring the social diversity of student voice through consultative processes, and to discover what students from a range of backgrounds and different school contexts might tell us about the social conditions and values which shape their learning.
▶ To explore the potential of using student consultation in the classroom to increase students' control of their learning and the social conditions which shape it.

This chapter focuses on a very specific aspect of the project: what students can tell us about the social dynamics and influences on participation in learning at secondary school level, and who they think controls the speed, the level and the nature of what they learn. The concept of an autonomous or independent learner is one that is celebrated within our educational ideals, but is not, as the students in our study reveal, offered or experienced equally by all students. Rather, as we found, students' control over their learning was regulated through the social hierarchies and dynamics of classroom life.

Our focus on control and student autonomy related directly to a central concern with contextualising the notion of student consultation within the relations of power and control in schools. From our perspective, student consultation needs to be located within what Bernstein (2000: xxv) called the 'intrinsic stratification features' of schools. It cannot, therefore, be dissociated from the constraints and grip of class regulated realities, nor indeed within such realities those of ethnicity and gender in the educational system. Student consultation is a form of pedagogic communication in schools which, as Bernstein argued, has become more important today than at any other period.

We have drawn on Bernstein's theory of pedagogic transmission and operationalised it in the analysis of data, in order to grasp both the significance of this form of pedagogic communication and its contribution to understanding the everyday processes of learning. Unlike many small-scale qualitative studies which work in a grounded way with data (Strauss, 1998), Bernstein's theoretical insights and concepts guided our project: from the initial ideas for research questions through to data analysis. At the planning stage, we brought together student voice and Bernstein's social theory of pedagogy to identify our research questions and the research tools necessary to answer them. In the sections below we describe those aspects of Bernstein's work that we employed in the research design and data analysis, and illustrate the power of such a framework in eliciting students' often silent or unheard perspectives on the social organisation of their learning.

The theoretical orientation of the study

Bernstein (2000: 7) suggests that projections of a hierarchy of class values shape the visual and temporal organisation of the school and the different forms of knowledge transmitted to different groups, creating inequalities of value, potential and power. Such values may be found in the inequalities of effective support for students' learning needs, as well as deep within the processes of knowledge acquisition. Schools distance themselves from the internal hierarchy of success, and also from external social class hierarchies, by creating 'a mythological discourse in which all groups are seen as sharing their communality and interdependence' (Bernstein 2000: xxv). The concept of 'the learner' or 'student' as an assumed common identity can thus be used to hide the reality of social class values, differentiations and hierarchies. The mechanisms by which schools attempt to create the notion of the student – rather than admit to creating and maintaining socially differentiated groups – are likely to be not just complex, but also mystifying.

These insights challenge current perspectives on student consultation, especially if the establishment of consultative mechanisms might itself be one such mythologising discourse. They suggest that we need to engage critically with what it would mean, in practice, to extend democracy in schools through student consultation. For example, should student consultation not take into account the class regulated realities that shape schooling? In this context, students will be understood to have neither neutral nor independent voices within the structures that shape their pedagogic identities. Their voices, arguably, are constructed by the same class values used to structure the transmission and acquisition of knowledge: principles that mobilise and demobilise particular social identities; that evoke some and ignore other student voices; and that exclude and include certain social groups.

Describing the school as a metaphorical mirror of society, creating both positive and negative images of it, Bernstein lists a set of key empirical questions for those committed to notions of student consultation. He asks (2000: xxi): 'who recognises themselves as of value? what other images are excluded by the dominant image of value so that some students are unable to recognise themselves?' And in relation to the 'acoustic of the school' he asks:

- Whose voice is heard?
- Who is speaking?
- Who is hailed by this voice?
- For whom is it familiar?

He argues that these questions about the structure of social communication within the pedagogical relationship should be of central concern to sociologists. We have used them to frame both the research design and our analysis of the data we collected.

Research design

In designing the project we also bore in mind the central premise of student consultation: that it should involve the promotion of a more genuinely democratic participatory environment. Whilst student consultation suggested greater student participation in the formation of school principles, policies and practices, it did not necessarily entail consulting students about the extent to which such a democratic environment was promoted in schools. Bernstein (1996: 6), in rather brief notes, identified what might constitute the conditions for effective democracy. One such condition he argued must be that people have a stake in society, in the sense of both giving and receiving. They must have 'confidence that the political arrangements they create will realise this stake.' These conditions can only be realised in a school if it could ensure what he called, the three *pedagogic democratic rights* (Table 7.1).

Table 7.1 *Bernstein's typology of pedagogic democratic rights*

Rights	Conditions	Levels
enhancement	confidence	individual
inclusion	communitas	social
participation	civic discourse	political

Enhancement offers critical understanding and sense of possibility, conventionally associated with critical pedagogies. Bernstein (ibid) argues that where this right is not met, students may not develop the individual confidence to act. The second condition for effective democracy, *inclusion*, is the right to be included: whether socially, intellectually, culturally or personally. The third democratic right, *participation*, operates more at the political level and represents the right to participate in the construction, maintenance and transformation of order. For example, students would need to be party to decisions about the organisation of teaching and learning, the grouping of students, and the principles which govern the expressive and moral order of the school.

The concept of *framing* is particularly relevant to the third democratic right of participation, as it refers to the degree of control teachers and students possess over the selection, organisation, pacing and timing of the knowledge transmitted and received in the pedagogic relationship. Framing directly influences students' ability to participate. The purposes of such distinctions for Bernstein are clear. They can be used to assess whether all students receive and enjoy such rights, or whether there is an unequal distribution of such rights within schools.

The design of our research project was based on some key principles, informed by the concept of pedagogic democratic rights. First, we would ensure through our choice of methods that collective as well as individual voices were heard, especially voices which may not always have been elicited, listened to or preferred. Our chosen methods of investigation would, therefore, involve discussions with socially significant groupings of students, individual observations and interviews. Secondly, we decided that the key questions to ask students were whether they felt that they had the confidence to act; whether they felt they belonged, as individuals and as groups, within the school community; and whether they felt they had the power to influence the procedures and practices which shaped their learning. Our theoretical and methodological principles were successfully combined by using the three themes of *enhancement*, *inclusion* and *participation*, derived from Bernstein's pedagogic democratic rights (outlined above), to design focus group discussions, observations of mathematics and English lessons, and debriefing interviews with students. The three themes were converted into several research questions as the basis for interview and observation schedules:

Theme 1 (enhancement) - pedagogic identities

▶ What constitutes the good learner?
▶ How do students recognise themselves as learners?
▶ What are the criteria for success as a learner?

Theme 2 (inclusion) - inclusive learning

▶ What are the (spatial/social) conditions for getting teaching attention?
▶ Is there social equality (treatment and participation) in the classroom?

Theme 3 (participation) - participation in learning

▶ Who controls learning?
▶ How much can students control teaching (pacing, sequencing, evaluation criteria)?

This chapter presents the analysis of data and findings relating to the third theme dealing with *participation in learning*. As we will demonstrate later, one of the tensions we faced was that whilst our pre-specified analytic frame proved particularly valuable in eliciting student perspectives, flexibility to allow unpredicted issues to emerge was equally important – especially in a project on student consultation. This flexibility was more successful in contexts where students were sufficiently motivated to feed their strong concerns into the interviews. In other contexts, students went along with, rather than challenged, the agenda of the project. More studies would be needed to determine whether such differential flexibility in qualitative research is a result, for example, of student or school culture, the relationship of the research team to the teachers, or the differential impact on youth of suburban and inner city cultural and political contexts.

Framing: a key concept informing data analysis

Analysing the data on students' perspectives on participation in learning required further theoretical work. Of particular relevance to our analysis of the participation in learning theme was Bernstein's much-neglected concept of *framing*. Through this concept, Bernstein was able to distinguish and discriminate between *what* is transmitted and *how* it is transmitted. Whilst the shape of the curriculum indicates to students the rules that govern the social structure, the framing of teacher–student relations in the context of learning is central to students' understanding of social control. As shall be seen in our data, these experiences of social control are vivid in students' accounts of their classroom learning experiences.

Framing refers to the specific pedagogic relationship of teacher and taught in the context in which knowledge is being transmitted. Framing refers not to the content of pedagogy, but to the forms of realisation by students (Bernstein, 1977: 143) and the range of options available to them to control how knowledge is transmitted and acquired. As Bernstein (1977: 89) described it: '...frame refers to the degree of control teacher and student possess over the selection, organisation, pacing and timing of the knowledge transmitted and received in the pedagogical relationship.'

As far as the students are concerned, strong framing reduces their power over what, when and how they receive knowledge and it increases the teachers' power in the pedagogical relationship. Student consultation over learning is likely to be formal, objective and circumscribed by the control of the teacher. If students experience weak or relaxed framing, they are more likely to feel they are in control over their own learning – especially the pacing and sequencing of learning. According to Bernstein, relaxed framing may not only change the nature of the authority relationship by increasing the rights of the taught but also weaken or blur the boundary between what may or may not be taught. And so more of the teacher and taught is likely to enter this pedagogic frame. In a context of weak framing, Bernstein speculates that in order to protect themselves from the intrusive nature of socialisation which could, in these contexts, be intensive and penetrating, students' informal age group affiliations become the source of identity, relation and organisation. In the 1970s,

Bernstein speculated that when the framing was relaxed to include everyday realities, this weakening was for the purposes of social control of deviancy. He argued that the weakening of framing occurs usually with the less able children whom we have given up educating.

Where framing refers to the extent of student control, Bernstein's (1977) twin concept of *classification* draws attention to the way the curriculum is organised. Strong classification implies that the curriculum is divided into discrete areas of knowledge with clear boundaries, as in the subjects of the national curriculum in England and Wales. Weak classification implies that the curriculum may be more thematic, and so less bounded by distinctions between areas of knowledge.

Our research data involved very different contexts from those which Bernstein analysed in the 1970s. The project involved working closely with two English secondary schools and two of their 'feeder' primary schools (whose oldest students transferred to the secondary schools). Access was aided by approaching some of the schools where we had already conducted research, and consequently institutions in which we had already established credibility as researchers.

We chose schools that differed not just in terms of locale and student catchment area, but also in relation to ideological ethos and student organisation. While both secondary schools taught the national curriculum, in effect the framing of the learning experience was considerably different (although becoming less so). What differentiated the two secondary schools was not the curriculum, but rather the relative strength of the framing of educational knowledge (Bernstein, 1977). In the predominantly white middle-class city school, which we called Greenfield, students in Year 8 (students aged 12–13) were grouped into sets according to attainment. Many working-class students found themselves in the lowest sets, whilst the middle-class students dominated the upper sets. Despite such firm structuring, students were nevertheless encouraged to value individual and personal achievement and autonomy. In this school, students identified clearly with the concept of the good learner and, across social class, seemed to be able to articulate a highly individualised notion of learning and motivation. The delivery of the national curriculum, whilst not easy, was likely to be less problematic for a school in which grammar school traditions (selective schools with a highly academic orientation) were part of its history. The presence of professional middle-class students meant that successful educational results could be achieved.

In contrast, the teaching of a strongly segmented curriculum in a predominantly working-class and multi-racial secondary school, which we called Mandela, was highly disruptive of its ethos. Whilst it is beyond the brief of this study to map all these changes empirically, what was evident was that students in the latter school (no less than the teaching staff) had to manage the continuing dissonance between the institutional habitus of the school (Reay, 1998; Reay et al. 2001) – which had evolved out of an earlier commitment to weak framing and weak classification – and the externally-imposed status quo. The school had had the reputation of being 'laid back', popular with the new middle-classes, but also with a large working-class and multi-ethnic intake. Teaching and learning in the school downplayed competition (part of the legacy of moves to make inner city schools comprehensive and accept, without selection, pupils of all academic abilities and from a range of social and cultural backgrounds). The staff at this school were vocal in their commitment to the kinds of values once typified by the now defunct Inner London Education Authority, which used to have responsibility for educational provision throughout the whole of the greater London area. This was reflected in discourses of equality and in a defence of a broad humanistic curriculum. Teaching was still mainly in mixed achievement groups. In this inner city school, students encountered a curious mixture of strong egalitarianism, mixed attainment teaching and a desire to be inclusive, trapped within the delivery of a strongly classified and bounded, traditionally defined, national curriculum. In a school where it had become normative for students to expect, and be given, a degree of control in relation to the curriculum, they now had virtually none.

Methods of data collection

In these schools, we designed an in-depth qualitative study, adopting a multi-method approach to collecting data. With the help of Year 8 teachers in each school, we created focus groups of male and female students from different ethnic and class backgrounds. Information on both ethnicity and class position came from two sources: a brief questionnaire on parental occupations and educational credentials that students filled in; plus knowledge the teachers had about tutor groups within Year 8. Using these two sources of information meant we could clarify and substantiate information that may have proved more ambiguous had it came just from one source. However, we had not anticipated that teachers in both schools would suggest that the best criterion for deciding on the composition of the focus groups was attainment level, as measured in national and school-based tests. This made more sense in Greenfield, where the students were set in most subjects, but was unexpected in Mandela where Year 8 students were taught in mixed attainment classes. However, we started the research with the premise that within the arena of student consultation confident, 'higher attaining' students would be able to articulate 'a speaking voice'. We were more concerned about working-class groupings who were seen to be 'lower attaining', and their possibilities for being heard in the schooling context. So the teachers' suggestions helped us resolve the difficult issue of grouping. As a consequence the perceived achievement of students, together, in Greenfield, with the set in which they were placed, became a salient part of the research. It informed our analysis of differentiated responses to participation and control in the classroom. At the same time we were, and are, wary of treating test results as certain indicators of ability. This was an issue we never successfully resolved, hence we have referred to attainment or achievement throughout, rather than to ability.

Our choice of focus group interviews as a research method was decided from the outset of the project. We wanted to find out, following Bernstein, whether students felt that they belonged as individuals, and as groups, within the school community. Focus group interviews were clearly an appropriate research method for attempting to access group voice (Morgan, 1997). Traditionally, most student consultation has focused on individual interviews with students and class discussions. We wanted to hear what student voice sounded like in the focus group context in order to find out if focus groups were a useful way of hearing student voice. Past research experience of utilising focus groups (Reay and Lucey, 2003) had convinced us that they were an effective research tool for eliciting commonalities and differences of opinion among young people (Lewis, 1992). In this project, also, they proved useful in revealing consensus among students and providing a forum for contestation and for challenging opposing viewpoints about participation in the classroom. There were many such moments of contestation of which the extract below is just one example. Here, a group of low to medium attaining and mainly middle-class girls talk about who controls what they learn at school. Kelly opens the discussion with the view that students themselves control what they learn by co-operating, or not, with the school agenda. The reality of the system used for setting pupils according to perceived attainment (strong framing) is juxtaposed with her belief in the principle of choice:

> *Kelly: I think the government has a little tiny inch but we have that much to decide what we do. If we want to be naughty and do nothing...if we really know what we're doing if we concentrated and really tried our hardest we could be in top set...and if we're in top set and you think I really don't like this you could just be naughty, start not doing the work even though you're capable of it and then you go down.*

Jemima, on the other hand, sees students' lack of power:

> *Jemima: No offence to Kelly or anything, but I disagree. I think the teachers, like, the teachers and government decide our education so we don't go to our teachers and say: 'Can we have drama for all six periods?'...And go the next day: 'Oh do we have to do maths today? Can we have drama again?'*

So whilst exploring dominant, collective discourses, we were also careful to address perceptions, experiences and opinions that dissented from the group as well as noticeable silences and gaps. Although one or two students in both schools remained silent in the focus group context, overall, we felt that we effectively constructed a collective voice through the focus group method.

At a later point in the fieldwork we observed Year 8 students in English and mathematics classes and then interviewed them individually. The focus group interviews and individual interviews generated different perspectives on the same issues. The focus groups provided valuable insights into social processes and dynamics, whilst the individual interviews provided insights into particular students' understanding and experience of teaching and learning in the classroom. The two different types of interview, together with participant observation of lessons, allowed for a process of triangulation. We could look for reinforcement of findings as well as contradictory evidence across all three sources of data. Reports summarising findings from the focus group interviews were fed back to both the teachers and students in the two schools. At this stage, planning meetings were organised with the year tutors and English and mathematics teachers in both Greenfield and Mandela in order to design an intervention which worked with the concerns of the students in both schools.

One of the main limitations of the research related to lack of time. As in many qualitative research projects, there seemed to be insufficient time to develop trust and rapport. Although we spent as much time as possible in the secondary school setting during break and lunchtimes with students, it was still not sufficient. Working with a tightly prescribed interview schedule was also problematic at times. In a number of the focus groups, there was a dissonance between the areas we wanted to explore, as academic researchers attempting to operationalise Bernstein's theory within the context of focus group interviews, and the preoccupations and concerns of the young people themselves. Particularly in Mandela, the sense of urgency and passion with which they communicated the issues they considered important meant that, ethically, we felt compelled to follow up on the matters that they raised. But on a number of occasions this entailed diverging from our own pre-specified research agenda.

Also, whilst the quality of the interview data was very high, that of the observational data was more patchy. This was again due mainly to pressure on time. Ideally, both structured and unstructured observation requires a preliminary period of familiarisation before data collection begins (what Becker (1996) calls immersion in the field). Within our limited time span this was impossible and the quality of the data suffered as a consequence. Less tangible, but still powerfully emotive, was the whole issue of researcher subjectivity: it became evident that relations between teachers and a significant minority of students were adversarial in Mandela, and to a lesser extent in Greenfield. In such circumstances it is difficult to deal adequately with researcher subjectivity in the field and, for us, a natural inclination to side with 'the underdog' (Steier, 1991). There was a lot of uncomfortable disclosure about and, at times, manifest hostility expressed towards, a number of teachers. We began to see the secondary school through the students' eyes and this inevitably compromised relationships with teachers. There is a very thin dividing line between research subjectivity and partiality. At times, despite our best intentions, being aware of our subjectivity as researchers and reflecting on it was not enough to avoid crossing the line.

Finally, it is important to highlight the wider contextual constraints that impinge on researchers as well as teachers. We have already discussed constraints imposed by lack of time. However, the dominant discourses of performance in the UK shape the role of the researcher just as much as that of the teacher. If student learning is strongly framed in the new performative market culture so, increasingly, is the work of both teaching and research. The government agenda in Britain, with its focus on quantifiable outcomes, audit and target setting, is reflected in the way the research councils powerfully shape what researchers can do. In the obsession with results and measurement, depth is often sacrificed for breadth and even qualitative research tends to operate at the surface, failing to engage sufficiently with the complex messiness underneath that constitutes classroom life. We both would have preferred to spend far more time in the field than was possible. Also, we had hoped to institute a programme of action research, something both of us had been heavily involved in during the 1980s, when teachers and researchers had been weakly framed (Arnot, 1993; Reay, 2003). We soon discovered that teachers' area of discretion in terms of time, space and outcome is now far more severely restricted. We had to adapt to, and operate within, this restricted context, and what was to be action research had to be scaled down into a smaller micro-level intervention.

What do students have to say about participation and control in the classroom?

Analysing student voice collected through focus group interviews involved thinking clearly about the social context in which such voices were produced. One of our first tasks was to analyse students' experiences of social control within the two schools, both of which had a strongly classified national curriculum with sharp subject boundaries, delivered through hierarchical and performance based school systems. The ways in which the national curriculum was delivered (transmitted), however, was different in the two schools. In one school (Greenfield), with its formalised setting procedures, both classification of students and framing appeared strong. Whereas in the other (Mandela), with its history of teaching in mixed attainment groups and strong egalitarian ethos, the classification principles for student organisation and framing were weaker. (Strong classification with strong framing at Greenfield versus strong classification with weak framing at Mandela.) As the data unravelled, we began to see that whilst the formal curriculum remained the same, the formal and informal pedagogical relationships took different forms. It became apparent that similarly differentiated groups of students experienced the strong and weak framing of knowledge *within* each school.

However, there were also similarities of experience across these institutional contexts. Preliminary analysis of the data suggested that social class positioning, coupled with the social consequences of ethnicity and gender, together shaped groups of students' experience of control and their degree of participation in it. Where and when these different experiences of control over learning work within the classroom is what our research is about. Indeed as Bernstein himself commented (1977: 112): 'It should be quite clear that the specific application of the concepts of classification and framing requires at every point empirical evidence. We have for example little first hand knowledge which bears upon aspects of framing.'

Let us now turn to our data. We begin by considering the data from Mandela (the mixed attainment teaching context in a multi-racial city school) and then the data collected by consulting students in the more strongly framed context of learning in Greenfield. We focused particularly in each case on the ways in which students reported levels of control over their own learning, especially over the pacing and sequencing of educational knowledge.

Mixed attainment teaching and social differentiation in Mandela

In Mandela, control over the experience of learning and, in particular, the pedagogical practices appeared to be heavily shaped by the social relationships of the classroom. At the one extreme, higher attaining girls seemed to be operating with weaker framing than the other groups in the class, hoping and trying to sustain individual control over their learning. At the other extreme, they appeared to feel robbed of control by the behavioural tactics of a group of working-class lower attaining boys who experienced and responded to the lack of control over their own learning by contesting teachers' demands and resisting conformity to classroom rules.

Some groups of students appeared to have greater levels of opportunity for manoeuvre. But the increasingly strong framing of learning created by a centralised curriculum and a dominant performance ethic led to a sense of lack of control among all groups. For example, while the higher attaining girls were the only group to talk in terms of being in control of their learning, they also made continual complaints about being held back by 'slower' students in the class. The pace of working was perceived to be too slow and with insufficient challenge. Throughout these girls' texts there were constant references to intelligence, and implicit within them was a sense of their own high intelligence colliding with too low a level of work.

The notion of an individualised relationship to knowledge was constantly destabilised in the girls' commentary. It was 'the social' in the form of 'other people' who disrupted, got in the way of, and undermined the possibilities of challenge, the 'right' level of pacing and more positive relationships to knowledge. These girls held boys, not just teachers, as instrumental in maintaining the pacing and challenge at too low a level. Control by boys of the pacing of learning was also referred to by Kylie, one of two girls in the class receiving special educational needs support: 'It's the boys who slow everything down. If the teacher goes through it a hundred times then they'll get it and then they'll do it. But, like, they wait for the teacher to spell it out to them.'

Although middle and higher attaining girls talked frequently about the negative impact the boys had on their own experience of learning, they seemed to feel that it was impossible to get the boys to change. Nor did they suggest any sort of stronger framing by teachers of the learning process. In fact, Carlene suggested that the only solution would be for girls to adapt better to the boys' disruptive behaviour. However, the three middle-class girls identified a mechanism for increasing motivation and improving their learning which was, in effect, to provide stronger framing for their learning. Emily, for example, turned to grouping students according to achievement, reminding the other girls of the value of such groups in primary school:

> *Emily: They should teach everyone, like tell the whole class what they are doing and then put us on a group table with some of the boys that are clever, and then just come over to us and tell us something else because we know that's easy.*

> *Fiona: Like in primary school they put you in groups of cleverness.*

> *Emily: The red group, blue group, orange group or whatever. And each group would be the cleverer one, the next cleverest and then the people who find it more difficult. And that would be so much better.*

These girls were torn between the social integrative values of the school (weaker framing) and the need to strengthen the frames and keep the children of different levels of attainment apart. In the meantime, they appeared to have a degree of control over the pace at which they worked: 'Sometimes we zoom and sometimes we just take our time' (Fiona). At times they could claim a positive active relationship to knowledge. Positive experiences of learning should incorporate opportunities for initiative and autonomy: 'They should let you work it out for yourself instead of telling you the answer all the time' (Fiona).

This confidence in terms of the pacing of learning, the enjoyment of learn-ing and the desire for independent thinking contrasts sharply with the views of Carlene and Candice, both of whom found it difficult and uncomfortable to ask teachers for help if they were stuck, and found work too hard or the pace too fast. They implied that they could only voice their concerns within parental or familial relations.

> *Candice: I'm not really comfortable asking for help from the teacher. I don't know why. But it's because they don't listen to you. I just prefer to talk to my mum and dad and my brother.*

> *Carlene: With your parents, because with your parents you've got a special bond. You can tell them stuff. With the teacher you don't have anything. You can't exactly tell them how you feel, that you're stuck on something, can't actually speak to them.*

It would be interesting to speculate on the extent to which these two girls' positioning as Afro-Caribbean and working-class influenced their sense of dis-tance from a predominantly white middle-class staff; and their lack of control over their own learning. The gendering of concepts of autonomy, dependency and the control of learning came up for these girls in the context of boys' learning behaviour. For them, boys' attempts to control their learning, and the pace of learning for others verged on the manipulative. They employed strate-gies of disaffection, indifference, or illness. As Carlene described, all boys have to do is 'just sit back in their chairs and the teachers will write it down for them – so they don't ever make any effort'. When boys made learning demands, girls again felt despair. The boys asked for more grammar 'verbs and stuff' which they had already covered in primary school. Candice and Carlene described the disruption this represented to the sequencing rules. As they pointed out, the class was meant to have moved on long ago.

> *Candice: That's what you are meant to learn in the first year. I can understand them teaching us in the first year, Year 7, but going on to Year 8 we are still learning it, but you know them already.*

> *Carlene: Things that we've never learnt about before, then we'd be interested to learn about it, but things that we already know, its boring.*

The sense of boredom was also to some extent shared by high attaining boys in Mandela. Though on the whole they had little to say about the pacing of learning apart from 'it is fine' and would not be drawn. Yet, like the high attaining girls, these boys were also aware of the overly slow pace of some teaching and this experience was linked to a sense of boredom. Yet all were adamant that if any of the teachers were going either too fast or too slow, they would be able to tell them. Their sense of control may have been greater than that of girls who relied more on teachers changing their tactics, especially with boys, or using organisational strategies such as differentiation, extension work or setting procedures.

In stark contrast with girls' views of boys' capacity to manipulate and control their own pace of learning and that of the class, the majority of the male working-class students seemed to be learning that knowledge was something beyond, rather than within, their control. In particular, the low attaining working-class boys experienced strong framing over the pacing of work in the classroom:

Stuart: Some teachers, they write it on the board and then they say it really fast. Teachers, like, they should explain it more clearly, more slowly.

Paul: When you're just on the last line he rubs it off quick.

Stuart: Before you've managed to write it all down!

Paul: Teacher should wait. Write it down for you.

While a few of the working-class boys certainly gave the impression that they were able to have the teacher adjust the pace of lessons to fit their needs, not all boys were so successful. Getting stuck, particularly in English and mathematics, and being unable to get sufficient support brought learning to a halt. Central to these boys' assumptions was that their learning required additional teacher support. There was also a clearly articulated degree of resentment that girls broke all the rules and still received more help.

There is a very thin line for teachers to tread because, coming back to issues of exposure and 'being shown up', the boys had a strong sense of antipathy when work was too difficult. At the same time, work that was too easy could also be a problem. Although easy work allowed these boys to be educationally productive, something they normally struggled to achieve, it also generated ambivalence.

Bernie: You sometimes get much too easy work in maths and it's below your level, and you ain't learning nothing.

Robin. Because you already know it.

Bernie. And that's not good.

Most of the time they seemed to be putting lots of energy into avoidance strategies not because the work was too hard but because they 'just can't be bothered'. They engaged in tactics, as the girls had noticed, to ensure the work was not too challenging – despite protestations that challenge was what they 'really' want. Yet there was also a sense that when they managed to get away with making less effort than they were capable of, they were in effect letting themselves down. The contradictions of weaker framing were vividly illustrated by a desire to control but not necessarily to value the consequences. In the context of the desire to strengthen the framing of transmission and acquisition, the working-class boys' attempts to control pacing had negative consequences both in terms of their identity and their achievement.

To sum up, the students in this school talked of not being in complete control over their learning. Teachers and disruptive students dented any aspirations to control events. But it is clear that some middle-class higher attaining students, nevertheless, were able to experience a certain degree of autonomy. Speed and the use of time in the learning process played a critical part in these students' conceptualisations of learning.

Setting by attainment and students' control of their learning at Greenfield

At Greenfield, the concept of students' control over their own learning in the context of setting by attainment was to some extent contradictory. Teachers had already determined with whom students would learn; the speed at which they were able to learn; and the appropriate dissemination of information, competencies, skills and identities. The organisational structure of learning was not only explicit but also strongly based on a concept of ability, of which the students at Greenfield were consciously aware. For them, the concern was less about controlling the events of classroom life and more about coping with the decisions that had already been made for them, and about them, in relation to their learning capacity. Paradoxically, students in this school appeared to be putting forward a notion of their own individualised responsibility for learning rather than ascribing the responsibility to the teacher to cater for their different needs. Therefore, they colluded to some extent with the mythological discourse of the 'independent learner'.

In Greenfield classrooms the problem was reported to be less that of one group of students seizing control of the pace of learning and of slowing it down, more that of adjusting the pace of learning to the expected learning speeds for different sets. In this context of a strongly classified structure, students were clearly aware that they had relatively little control over the selection, pacing and sequencing of knowledge. They were also aware that their approaches to teachers, especially in the context of negotiating the learning experience, were shaped more by the teachers' character and amenability than by desires for more teacher-control over classroom management, more intervention on the part of the teacher, or more active engagement on their part. In Greenfield, as in Mandela, student strategies for dealing with the differential pace of learning were diverse.

According to most students, opportunities to comment on the pace, in the context of setting by attainment, were fraught with difficulty. Students could be laughed at, shouted at, but even more significantly they thought they might be dropped a set if shown to be unable to 'keep up' (no student in our study considered the possibility of being raised a set). In a context of strong classificatory principles, students' sphere of agency (capacity to choose their course of action) in controlling the pace of learning was minimal, especially for those who had already been defined as having the most difficulty in learning.

As we shall see, the strongest contrasts were found between girls (not those in the top sets) and lower attaining working-class boys. For most of the girls, any sense of agency came through finding ways of communicating better, or more subtly, with the teacher. They were prepared to think through strategies that might work to overcome their own powerlessness and the sensitivities of the teaching profession. Agency, for these girls, was described as a communication problem. For most of the lower attaining working-class boys, such skills were not central. Instead there was repeated concern for the possibility of public embarrassment (being seen again as a slow learner) and of not having enough control over the teacher to feel effective in making a difference.

The majority of girls in Greenfield were not confident that they could tell the teacher they were going too fast or slow. Some, particularly the higher attaining girls, felt they could not intervene lest their intervention challenged their positioning in the hierarchy of learning. These were girls who held positions as the 'boffs' (those perceived as clever and studious) in the class – a position they encouraged if it signalled high achievement, but rejected if it implied negative personality attributes. All the girls across sets were happy at keeping the lesson too slow (this made it easy), but worried about slowing down a lesson in case they were felt to be not bright enough. Alice expressed this dilemma well:

> Alice: If they're going too fast then you're then thinking 'Owww! They're going to think I'm really dumb!' But if they go too slow, you don't want to criticise them because you know, if they're going too slow it's quite good sometimes...

These girls' feelings of frustration and lack of control were expressed by Abby:

> In German, you haven't even been back to school for about a week, since half term or six weeks holiday or something – they, like, haven't taught you anything, then they, like, spring a test on you. It's, like: 'Whoooo!'

Girls in the lower attainment sets experienced even stronger control over their learning than those such as Alice and Abby in higher attainment sets, and their solution was to attempt to reshape the pedagogic relationship rather than their own relationship to learning. However, even in the lower sets, some girls saw the value in speaking to the teacher and could begin to see how it could be done. These girls engaged in a discussion about what would be an appropriate style of communication:

> Carrie: I might say 'Sir' or it maybe 'Miss'. 'If you don't mind me saying could you speed up a bit cos I feel like I'm a...'

> Jemima: Snail.

> Kelly: Coming back to what Jemima said, I think if someone's going really slow (laughter) I'd feel like saying: 'God, Sir, I'm not a dunce.' Cos they sort of treat us like it – cos you're thinking 'God, I'm not dumb, Sir! We can take it going a bit faster.' It's like you feel dumb. You say...'Sir, please can you go a bit faster, please?' Being polite.

At other times, Carrie needed to find a way of slowing the teacher down, fearing that otherwise she would miss out on her education:

You can get a really good education otherwise cos, like, they say, 'Copy this into your books and then you can revise it for a test.' Then you're still writing it and they're rubbing it off and writing something else. And then before you've even wrote that they're rubbing it off again, so I think you should be able to tell them.

The fact that these girls saw the value in saying something to the teacher demonstrated a desire at least to relax the teachers' control over their learning.

As in Mandela school, gender differences were also strong in Greenfield, with many themes resonating across the two schools despite their structural and cultural differences. Here too lower attaining working-class boys appeared to have the least control over the pace of learning, despite the high levels of reported disruption and 'mucking about'. The anger of the lower attaining working-class boys about the pace of learning, or what they considered irrelevant knowledge or pointless activities, was clearly in evidence. Members of the group were adamant that whilst teachers wanted students to learn, this desire was placed in the context of their pay packet, or their desire not to have to repeat themselves. These boys reported that they had little control over what they learnt, the choice of what they did in class and the speed of learning.

Even if they were offered more opportunities to control the pace of their learning, they were unlikely to take them. As Craig admitted: 'Sometimes the teacher will say "Tell me if I am going too fast," or something' but for most of these boys the opportunity was not real. On the one hand, there was the danger that 'people laugh at you'. On the other hand, the culture of resistance was so ingrained that it could not easily be broken. As Sean pointed out, when teachers asked you to do something, these boys did the 'opposite': 'If they say, "Don't muck around!" you will muck around. So you muck around because you kind of don't agree with the teacher ever.' With this level of opposition, in a relationship of non co-operation, there was little space for communication or consultation. If the boys were offered more opportunities to control the pace of their learning, they were unlikely to take them.

An element of suspicion between boys and teachers and a failure to communicate were found not only amongst working-class boys. Higher attaining middle-class boys at Greenfield also believed not only that teachers were in charge of the pace of their learning, but also that student strategies for getting more help and slowing down the lesson were not necessarily effective. Whilst some teachers were helpful, others ignored requests for help and were prone to anger or annoyance. When asked if they could tell the teacher whether he or she was going too fast or slow, members of the group of higher attaining boys replied that while some teachers would stop (or slow down or speed up), others would not.

At Greenfield, both teachers and students were affected by the strong classificatory principle underlying the national curriculum. Some students (mainly girls) were critically reflective about the constraints on teachers themselves (strong framing by government). But most students thought the source of authority rested with teachers themselves. The experience of strong framing over the selection of knowledge and the pace of learning by students, however, did not necessarily generate similar or identical responses from different groups. Academic achievement, social class, gender and ethnicity worked in complex ways in shaping the strategies students used to relate to what was seen as the teachers' transmission project.

Paradoxically, it appeared that the majority of girls seemed to be operating, at least in their minds, with weaker framing even though they were aware of the pressures on teachers from government. They perceived that although the control of learning was in the teachers' hands, if they had not got anything planned for the lesson they might offer students choice over activities. Yet these choices (moments of weaker framing) are illusory since, as the girls noticed, teachers set the knowledge terrain and the choices were proscribed by external structures. As Claire commented: 'If we have to choose A, B or C we don't have a choice obviously in the work, it's just A, B and C.' As in Mandela, most of the girls and boys did not think that teachers listened to students about how they learnt. However, in contrast to Mandela, it was teachers, rather than a combination of teachers and other students, who were seen to be in control of student learning.

Discussion

We have so far examined a small part of our research on the nature of *participation in learning* (the third of Bernstein's pedagogic democratic rights). What we have attempted to show is the considerable social variation within the same school or classroom setting. The evidence we have collected suggests that participation in learning is experienced differentially. Working-class students – especially working-class boys – experience pacing as a form of overt control and a mechanism which ensures their disengagement from learning. Bernstein's concept of framing offered a language of description for the control of students' learning that was useful in comparing the two school sites. Without such a concept, the notion of participation in school decision-making becomes blurred. His concept focused our attention on the extent to which students felt in control over the pacing and sequencing of the knowledge they were being taught (Arnot and Reay, 2001). In the small slice of data presented here, it is possible to see the power of this concept as a heuristic device (or probe), which linked what students said to more theoretical issues of social control inside classrooms. Student consultation, in this case through our focus groups, threw light on the differential experiences of control within and between the different forms of student organisation. The implicit forms of strong framing found within Greenfield's individualising ethos, and the explicit forms of weak framing found in Mandela's egalitarian ethos, were experienced differentially by particular social groups.

In Mandela, we saw that higher attaining middle-class girls were able to employ both strong and weakened framing. At one moment they were able to work with concepts of individual property, strong sequencing and pacing norms, and at another moment they suggested a desire for more control over their learning (more relaxed framing). They worked with notions of individual choice over when to co-operate, when to slow down, speed up (or zoom) through their work. They could work independently but they could also make considerable demands on the teacher to deal with their need for extension activities.

The threat to these girls' academic control of their learning was, on the one hand, teachers who failed to cope with their needs. But just as important was their need to cope in a mixed attainment, mixed sex environment with the demands of boys, especially working-class lower attaining boys. This threat came through male power of manipulation using disaffection, endless demands for attention, disruption of the rules, requests to repeat work from earlier stages and teachers' acquiescence. Perceiving the expression of male power as a threat, the middle-class girls suggested setting by attainment. By contrast the black working-class girls suggested a change in their own attitudes to try to understand the boys, and the rest of the girls expressed frustration.

In both these latter groupings, there was far less sense of control over their learning generally. For the working-class boys, controlling situations where they might not be able to perform well publicly, or might be ridiculed by the teacher, appeared to be made possible by breaking behaviour rules. At the same time, there was concern that their own work was highly controlled by teachers. It was either too easy or too difficult. Despite girls' view of male power as capable of controlling the learning of others, boys themselves appeared to experience strong framing, with teachers taking control over their seating, their learning and their demands. In the context of this inner city multi-racial school, despite the earlier commitment to student autonomy and control, the working-class students appeared to consider their learning as largely the responsibility of others – namely teachers.

In Greenfield, the strong classificatory principles underlying the national curriculum were supported by the differentiation of learners in Year 8 according to attainment in particular subjects. The setting structure sent strong messages to students about how their learning was to be controlled and how it reflected their abilities, at least in principle. Teachers had the power to shape learning experiences, the content of learning and students' trajectory through the school structure. In this context, student control of their own learning was strongly circumscribed by structures rather than the social dynamics of the classroom.

Of interest to students, however, was how such structures could be mediated: first, through better communication with the teacher and by responding to teacher moods and atmosphere; second, by a range of oppositional strategies. Girls, on the whole, talked more about the former. Boys – particularly working-class boys – talked more about the latter. Ability, gender and social class worked in complex ways to shape the response of students to the perception that they were not in control of their learning. The higher attaining white middle-class boys and girls found small discretionary spheres in terms of co-operation, working with their own interests and being successful within the set structure. Lower attaining students discussed strategies to gain more control of the pace and sequencing of learning, the boys through disruption and non co-operation unless teachers were felt to respect and listen to them, the girls through trying to talk to the teacher about the pace. Although individual responsibility for learning was part of the students' dialogue, teacher control of student learning was ingrained in their school experience. The question for them was whether the teacher could still respect their individual needs. Within this school context, weaker framing was only experienced by those who had internalised motivation and control over their progress and learning.

Conclusion

Bernstein suggested that there is an unequal distribution of images, knowledge, possibilities and resources, which will affect the rights of participation, inclusion and individual enhancement of groups of students. He argued that it is highly likely that the students who do not receive these rights in the school come from social groups who do not receive these rights in society (1996: xxii). Our analysis suggests the importance of exploring, through student consultation, how such inequalities work in practice. One of the major elements of student consultation is the implied shift in the mode of pedagogic communication and by implication, the democratising of the social order in the school. A range of different assumptions are made that by so doing, not only could there be a greater or more effective knowledge acquisition on the part of students, but that young people would be better prepared for a democratic social order. Our data suggests that student voice is socially constructed through the distribution of power and control within schools. It is a specifically pedagogic voice, which speaks about the way in which knowledge is transmitted through schools as much as it describes the social relations of schooling. It is the product of specific modes of communication already constructed by the school and as such reflects the constraints and possibilities of the change within it.

If student voice through consultative mechanisms is used to explore the relations of power and control within such settings, there is a possibility that it will contribute to the enhancement of pedagogic democratic rights. If it is used to support the mythologising discourses of schooling which mask relations of power and control, then it will fail to advance both learning and social cohesion. The right to participate in pedagogical contexts, fully implies, as Bernstein (1996, xxii) argued: 'The right to participate in procedures whereby order is constructed, maintained and changed. It is the right to participate in the construction, maintenance and transformation of order.'

The methods employed yielded rich insights into our key research question concerning students' perspectives on who controls the speed, level and nature of what they learn. Attempting to operationalise Bernstein's concept of framing in the analysis of our data revealed the class assumptions lying behind notions of pedagogic voice. However, in relation to our overarching concern with the transformative potential of student consultation and associated constraints, our findings raise as many questions as answers. A major finding relates to the social inequalities of existing practices. But, in the face of evidence of very unequal participation in learning, we need to ask to what extent is a positive pedagogic identity achievable, particularly for working-class boys? Bernstein (1975: 250) writes about how socialisation within schooling can be deeply wounding, either for those who wish for, but do not achieve a pedagogic identity, or for the majority for whom the pursuit of an identity is early made irrelevant. He asserts that an increase in the strength of framing often means that the images, voices and practices that the school reflects makes it difficult for working-class children to recognise themselves in schooling. This consequence clearly has profound consequences for the establishment of positive pedagogic identities for working-class students.

Our findings also challenge assumptions surrounding student consultation. The social conditions of school life are too important to overlook. Student consultation needs to work with identity, recognising group memberships and allegiances rather than, as is the current tendency, treating students as if they are operating in a vacuum. Our research also reveals the risks of student consultation that is not sensitive to differential methods of voicing, different strategies for sustaining control and complex social dynamics of the classroom. There are losses as well as gains for students in articulating how they feel about participation in learning. A further related challenge for effective student consultation clearly indicated by our data is that there is no homogeneous student voice, but rather a cacophony of competing voices. Both schools were microcosms of the wider social world, full of competing groups and characterised by myriad bids for attention and status. Currently, social inclusion for some groups comes at a cost of the social exclusion of others. One of the most important questions we need to ask, and one our research does not come near to answering, is how to develop forms of student consultation that would include the entire student body.

Acknowledgements

We are grateful to the Economic and Social Research Council for funding this project, and to the students and teachers who participated in the study.

References

Arnot, M. (1993) 'The challenge of equal opportunities: personal and professional development for secondary teachers', in P. Woods (ed), *Working for Teacher Development*. Norfolk: Martin Francis.

Arnot, M. and Reay, D. (2001) 'Participation and control in learning: a pedagogic democratic right?' Paper presented at the University of Bath, 6th February.

Becker, H. S. (1996) 'The epistemology of qualitative research', in R. Jessor, A. Colby and R. Shweder (eds), *Ethnography and Human Development: Context and Meaning in Social Inquiry*. Chicago: University of Chicago Press.

Bernstein, B. (1975) *Class, Codes and Control (Volume 2)*. 2nd edn. London: Routledge and Kegan Paul.

Bernstein, B. (1977) *Class, Codes and Control (Volume 3)*. London: Routledge and Kegan Paul.

Bernstein, B. (1996) *Pedagogy, Symbolic Control and Identity: Theory, Research, Critique*. London: Rowman and Littlefield.

Bernstein, B. (2000) *Pedagogy, Symbolic Control and Identity: Theory, Research, Critique*. 2nd edn. London: Taylor and Francis.

Lewis, A. (1992) 'Group child interviews as a research tool', *British Educational Research Journal*, 18 (4): 413–21.

Morgan, D. (1997) *Focus Groups as Qualitative Research*. London: Sage.

Reay, D. (1998) '"Always knowing" and "never being sure": institutional and familial habituses and higher education choice', *Journal of Education Policy*, 13 (4): 519–29.

Reay, D (2003) '"Troubling, troubled and troublesome": working with boys in the primary classroom', in C. Skelton and B. Francis (eds), *Boys and Girls in Primary Classrooms*. Buckingham: Open University Press.

Reay, D., Ball.,S.J. and David, M. (2001) 'Making a difference?: institutional habituses and higher education choice', *Sociological Research Online,* 5 (4): U126–U142.

Reay, D. and Lucey, H. (2003) 'The limits of choice: children and inner city schooling', *Sociology,* 37 (1): 117–38.

Steier, F. (1991) *Research and Reflexivity.* London: Sage.

Strauss, A. (1998) *Qualitative Data Analysis for Social Scientists.* Cambridge: Cambridge University Press.

Chapter 8

Primary school teachers' theoretical beliefs about literacy: an exploratory study

Louise Poulson and Elias Avramidis

Poulson and Avramidis outline research on primary (elementary) school teachers' theoretical beliefs about literacy and how to teach it. The research represents a small part of a much larger project and it would be within the scope of single researcher undertaking masters or doctoral work. Unlike other research reports in this volume, this chapter presents quantitative analysis of survey data. It can be compared and contrasted with the research in Chapter 3, which addressed a similar substantive topic but using a different methodological approach. Here the authors ground their work within a brief critical review of literature on teachers' beliefs and their relationship to practice, highlighting some of the substantive, theoretical and methodological problems of researching this topic.

Whilst acknowledging the limitations of their approach, the authors justify the use of a self-report instrument within a questionnaire survey in relation to the wider aims of the research. Poulson and Avramidis outline how the instrument was devised and the compromises made in its design. They explain how an existing instrument was adapted and acknowledge the trade-off that was made between weakening the construct validity of the original instrument and strengthening the instrument's focus on literacy (as opposed to a focus solely on reading). The authors also discuss how they identified a suitable population of effective teachers of literacy and a smaller comparison group in the absence of any obvious sampling frame. They highlight how they sought evidence of teachers' effectiveness from a number of sources, both from pupil outcome data and external inspection reports, and from professional sources that might be considered more subjective.

Poulson and Avramidis make explicit the various stages in the process of data analysis. They justify their choice of multivariate statistical techniques in relation to the aims of the study, and discuss how and why a doctoral student – or any researcher doing a small-scale investigation – might make use of multivariate rather than univariate analysis. An important point is that whilst this form of analysis may require more secure knowledge of statistical techniques, it enables the exploration of complex relationships between variables. Multivariate analysis also avoids a fairly common problem in theses and dissertations: the repetition of numerous univariate tests (e.g. ANOVA or t-tests), bringing a greater likelihood of what are known as 'type 1' errors (erroneously rejecting the null hypothesis and identifying significant relationships between variables).

In discussing their findings Poulson and Avramidis suggest alternative explanations, for example in relation to the finding that teachers with the most experience were less inclined towards a phonic theoretical orientation, and that those with least experience were more inclined towards this orientation. The point was made in Chapters 1 and 2 that researchers should maintain a critical and sceptical stance towards their own findings and consider the possibility of alternative interpretations.

Introduction

This research represents a small part of a substantial funded study investigating the knowledge, beliefs, practices and professional learning of 225 class teachers in English primary sector schools who were identified as effective in teaching literacy. The study also compared them with a smaller group of 71 class teachers representing the full range of effectiveness. The larger study was conducted in the mid to late 1990s, employing a mixed research methodology that included a questionnaire survey with several sections (including both closed and open-ended questions), interviews with teachers, observation of lessons, and tasks completed by teachers. A full account of the study can be found in Wray et al. (2002).

Primary sector schools in England are largely based on a 'generalist' system where each teacher is responsible for teaching most or all areas of the curriculum to her or his class of children. Most experienced teachers also have an advisory role in co-ordinating the teaching of a particular area of the curriculum in which they have specialist expertise. So effective teachers of literacy will be generalist class teachers, who might or might not also be responsible for co-ordinating this area of the curriculum across the school.

The aspect of the larger study to be discussed in this chapter involves a comparison between effective teachers of literacy and a variably effective group consisting of teachers with specialist responsibility for co-ordinating school-wide teaching of mathematics. It should be noted that these teachers with particular mathematics expertise were also generalist teachers, responsible for teaching literacy to their own class. (Just as the effective teachers of literacy were also generalist teachers responsible for teaching mathematics to their own class.)

Here we focus on a section of a questionnaire survey in the larger study where we examined theoretical beliefs about the teaching of literacy. The first section of this chapter locates our research within the wider literature on teachers' beliefs. Our methodology and specific methods for sampling, data collection and analysis are outlined. We present our findings, discuss them in relation to the literature, then briefly consider their policy implications.

Research on teachers' beliefs

A growing body of research on teachers' thinking and knowledge suggests that it is not only cognitive and behavioural factors in teaching that influence student learning, but also the affective dimensions, including teachers' beliefs, values and implicit theories guiding their actions. As beliefs and values and their relationship to classroom action have come to be regarded as an important aspect of understanding teaching, research in the area has come to reflect a considerable diversity of approach. Part of the problem has been that beliefs and their relationship to knowledge have been defined in different ways by educational researchers. (See Fenstermacher, 1994 for a more detailed discussion. Alexander et al. (1991) also discuss the wide range of different terms used in the literature on teachers' knowledge and thinking.)

Some researchers, usually working within a psychological perspective (e.g. Kagan, 1990), assume beliefs and knowledge to be the same. Whereas others with an orientation towards philosophy and epistemology (e.g. Fenstermacher, 1994) have drawn a distinction between beliefs and knowledge. A further challenge has been the fact that teachers' beliefs and values are often implicit and not easy for researchers to access directly. The relationship between beliefs and practice is complex: it appears to be dialectical rather than unilateral, in that practice does not always follow directly from beliefs. Sometimes changes in belief may come after, or result from, a change in practice.

In an overview of research on the relationship between teachers' beliefs and practice, Fang (1996: 52) identifies the 'consistency thesis' as dominating much of this work. He points out that researchers have reached varied conclusions about the degree to which teachers' beliefs and practice are consistent. Fang shows that in research on reading a substantial number of studies support the notion that teachers possess theoretical beliefs about reading which tend to shape the nature of their teaching (e.g. Harste and Burke, 1977; De Ford, 1985; Richardson et al., 1991). However, other studies (e.g. Bennett et. al., 1984; Desforges and Cockburn, 1987) highlight apparent inconsistency between teachers' stated beliefs and intentions and their observed classroom practice. Duffy and Anderson (1984) suggest that although there may be some congruence between practice and beliefs, the relationship is not strong.

Pajares (1992: 326) warns that regarding teachers' educational beliefs as detached from, and unconnected to, broader belief systems and values is 'ill-advised and probably unproductive'. Drawing on the work of Munby (1982: 216), he suggests that when teachers' beliefs about a particular subject are inconsistent with their practice in that area, the cause may be different and weightier beliefs. Pajares argues that it is important to think of connections among beliefs instead of beliefs as independent sub-systems. Apparently inconsistent findings can become clearer and more meaningful when educational beliefs are carefully conceptualised and their implications seen against the background of a broader belief system.

It is also important to bear in mind that teachers' beliefs and values are not only individual and personal. They also have a socio-historical dimension and are shaped, in part, by time, context and circumstance. Duffy and Anderson (1984) argue that whilst teachers might be able to articulate their beliefs outside the classroom, their actual practices are often governed by the nature of teaching and classroom life. Fang's review (1996: 54) also demonstrates that a range of research (e.g. Davis et al., 1993) has shown how differences in the degree of consistency between beliefs and practice also stem from the diverse contexts in which teachers work, and from the constraints which these impose: for example school climate, or the need to follow national, state and local district policies and mandates.

Fullan and Hargreaves (1994) outline a number of contextual factors that help to shape teachers' beliefs and values. These factors include the period when they train and enter the profession, and the dominant values of that time; the particular stage of their career; and their degree of confidence in their own teaching. A further factor highlighted by Alexander (1992) is that people may be reluctant to express unpopular beliefs that seem to be counter to current thinking and official policy, and especially where career progress is perceived to be associated with allegiance to particular beliefs. Pajares (1992) maintains that overall, despite the theoretical and methodological diversity in studies of teachers' beliefs, the research literature does suggest that teachers' educational and pedagogical beliefs and values influence their classroom practice and teaching decisions. But he also cautions that researchers need to examine and make explicit their assumptions about and operational definitions of teachers' beliefs in order to make clearer what has been considered to be a 'messy construct' (Pajares, 1992: 329).

Methodological issues

The complexity of teachers' beliefs has also led to methodological diversity in their study. Pajares (1992: 327) has argued that if reasonable inferences about beliefs require assessments of what individuals say, intend and do, then teachers' verbal expressions, predisposition to action, and teaching behaviour must all be included in the investigation. Although Munby earlier (1984) suggested that qualitative methodologies are especially appropriate to the study of beliefs, the choice of qualitative or quantitative approaches ultimately depends on what researchers wish to know.

Reviewing research on teacher cognition, Kagan (1990: 420) contended that many studies of teacher beliefs were strongly embedded in a specific context; and whilst they had a high degree of internal validity, they were small in scale (usually between one and 12 subjects) and often appeared 'to be so context or teacher-specific that generalisation seems risky.' Wideen et al. (1998: 144) also pointed out that a difficulty in reaching a cohesive picture of the role of teachers' beliefs lies in their situated nature. These authors remarked that whilst a high degree of contextualisation in terms of methodology and reporting contributed to the validity of such studies, it made comparisons and cross-generalisations problematic. In other words, internal validity may be achieved at the expense of external validity.

By contrast, quantitative studies employ large samples, so allowing the identification of patterns of orientation towards theoretical assumptions and associated practices that could not be obtained in small scale, qualitative studies. Moreover, the utilisation of more sophisticated statistical techniques for analysing numerical data, such as multivariate statistics (Tabachnick and Fidell, 2001), allows the researcher to explore complex inter-relationships between the variables of interest – in our case theoretical beliefs about teaching. Also the growing popularity of multivariate statistical techniques has paralleled the greater complexity of contemporary research.

However, the sole application of a quantitative research design on the study of teachers' beliefs is far from unproblematic. Three substantial reviews of literature on teachers' beliefs (Kagan, 1990; Pajares, 1992; Fang, 1996) have highlighted the inadequacies of even the most carefully constructed self-report instruments. Pajares (1992: 327), although accepting that the use of belief inventories can help to detect inconsistencies and areas that merit attention, strongly advocates the inclusion of additional measures such as interviews, responses to dilemmas or vignettes, and observation of behaviour to allow richer and more accurate inferences to be made. What agreement there is on ways of studying teachers' beliefs suggests the desirability of multi-method approaches, using a range of tasks and instruments to elicit teachers' beliefs, and the triangulation (cross-checking) of data from these multiple sources.

We took account of the issues discussed above in our investigation of teachers' beliefs and their relationship to classroom practice and educational outcomes in English primary sector schools. Rather than investigating the range and diversity of individual teachers' beliefs in the survey, we wanted to examine whether there were any clear patterns of orientation to dominant philosophies of, and approaches to, literacy teaching. We also wondered whether there was any variation between different groups of respondents. Harste and Burke (1977) defined theoretical orientation in reading as particular knowledge and belief systems held about reading: the philosophical principles that guide teachers in their decision-making. (Individuals' beliefs and values, and the relationship between beliefs and practice, were examined at a later stage through observation, interview and the completion of tasks.)

We devised an extensive questionnaire, covering a range of personal and situational variables. It explored teachers' theoretical beliefs about literacy teaching and learning, conceptualised as their theoretical orientation. The part of the questionnaire survey addressing theoretical orientation sought answers to the following research questions:

1 What were the theoretical orientations of the effective primary school sector teachers of literacy and mathematics co-ordinator groups, as measured by a self-report instrument, and what were the differences, if any, between the two groups?
2 Were there any differences in theoretical orientation within the sample of identified effective primary school sector teachers of literacy according to years' teaching experience, level of academic qualifications, or type of degree course or training?

In designing this section of the questionnaire, we drew on existing research on teachers' theoretical orientation. De Ford (1985) had already constructed a theoretical orientation to reading profile (TORP), which was validated through a multi-method process of analysis. This instrument had also been used extensively by other researchers in North America (e.g. Richards et al., 1987; Levande, 1990; Mergendoller and Sacks, 1994; Ketner et al., 1997).

De Ford (1985) identified three clusters of theoretical orientation to teaching reading which reflected differing degrees of emphasis on three levels of language or discourse: sub-word, word and sentence, and text level features. First, the *phonic orientation* was bottom-up, focusing on sub-word and word-level units first, and then working up to text-level features. Then, once the foundation in sound-letter correspondence had been established, teaching activities increasingly centred on comprehension and fluency.

Second, the *skills orientation* emphasised building up an adequate sight vocabulary in reading and skill in recognising whole words. New items were introduced in context. Whilst sound-letter correspondence was evident, it tended to concentrate on initial and ending consonants. Word attack skills, such as breaking down and building up words, were also emphasised (e.g. affixes, compound words, use of context cues). The quality of reading material improved with increases in vocabulary.

Third, the *whole language orientation* was top-down. It focused on the provision of good quality literature from the outset, with an initial emphasis on developing a sense of story and text as a framework for dealing with smaller units of language such as words and segments of words. Such an orientation placed emphasis on students' own writing and the experience of shared reading. De Ford's instrument consisted of a total of 28 statements, divided more or less evenly between the three orientations. Teachers whose practice appeared to be consistent with one of these orientations would be more likely to agree with statements related to that position.

For the purposes of our study, the De Ford TORP appeared to offer a useful initial way of exploring teachers' theoretical orientations to literacy within the questionnaire survey. Since we began this research, other instruments have been developed to measure teachers' beliefs about literacy and their relationship to practice. They include the Teachers' Beliefs About Literacy Questionnaire reported by Westwood et al., (1997) and Lenski et al.'s (1998) Literacy Orientation Survey. The original instrument was modified, since the examination of teachers' theoretical orientation formed only one section of a lengthy questionnaire. Its purpose was to identify any general patterns within a fairly large group of teachers which were to be further explored through interview, observation and the completion of literacy-related tasks. From the original TORP statements, six items relating to beliefs were chosen. A further six statements were selected, or rewritten, to represent the practical action a teacher would be likely to take if he or she had a particular orientation, and these statements were presented separately. Some items from the TORP were re-worded using terminology more familiar to British teachers.

As the TORP had investigated only theoretical orientations towards teaching reading, a parallel set of three pairs of statements related to teaching writing was devised which reflected the three identified theoretical orientations. In devising these statements, we examined research and professional literature on writing development and instruction, and drew on statements generated by teachers during in-service training courses.

First, what we termed the *presentation orientation* was concerned with word-level and presentational features in writing, such as spelling and handwriting. Second, the *process orientation* prioritised understanding of writing as communication, engagement in the writing process and whole text composition. Third, the *forms orientation* reflected a concern with vocabulary choice, sentence organisation and the importance of learning the relationship between purpose, form and structure in writing. For each of these hypothesised orientations, two teaching activities were suggested which would be consistent with each orientation.

So overall the instrument contained:

 ▶ twelve statements relating to theoretical orientation consisting of six statements about teaching reading (with two statements for each of the three theoretical orientations) and six equivalent statements about teaching writing;
 ▶ twelve teaching activities relating to the theoretical orientations consisting of six connected with teaching reading (with two teaching activities for each of the three theoretical orientations) and six equivalent activities connected with teaching writing.

Strength of agreement or disagreement with each of the 12 items for both reading and writing was measured using a Likert scale which offered the following choices: Strongly agree (1), Agree (2), Neutral (3), Disagree (4), Strongly disagree (5).

Modifications to the original De Ford TORP had already been used in a previous study investigating changes in student teachers' beliefs about the teaching of reading (Wray and Medwell, 1993). The modified instrument was also piloted with a smaller number of teachers who were interviewed and their classroom practices observed. On both occasions, the instrument provided reliable scores.

While it could be argued that changes to the original instrument had weakened the construct validity of the TORP, we felt that these changes reflected the focus on literacy (as opposed to reading) in our study. Further, we were not using the instrument to predict or make firm claims about the sample's classroom practice. We were employing it to explore the patterns of theoretical orientation within a relatively large population of effective teachers of literacy and to compare them with a comparison group of teachers in similar primary schools. The patterns emerging from the questionnaire data would then provide a basis for further exploration through interview and observation.

As already mentioned, the theoretical orientation profile was only one section in a much longer questionnaire, and we did not wish to discourage respondents from completing all the items. Indeed, the return rate for the questionnaire turned out to be relatively good for a postal survey (59 per cent of effective teachers of literacy, and 47 per cent of the comparison group). And, most important, there were few missing values within the TORP item data. (The items included in the modified TORP can be found – although not in the same order – in Table 8.4.)

Procedures for sampling, data collection and data analysis

As there was no obvious sampling frame from which to choose effective teachers of literacy in England, we used a three-stage process to identify an appropriate sample. The first step was to ask for nominations from local education authority (district) advisers or inspectors in 14 localities. They included a range of geographical areas (the study was limited to teachers in England) including the north, the south, the Midlands, the west and Greater London. We considered areas with different demographic patterns – urban, suburban, rural – and school types, including small and large primary schools (for children aged 4–11) and separate infant (4–7) and junior (7–11) schools. Through this process, we drew up a list of over 600 teachers recommended as effective.

Aware of the limitations of selecting a sample based only on personal recommendation, we also checked available external data sources on the recommended teachers and schools for evidence of effective literacy teaching. These sources included external inspection reports, national curriculum assessment results, 'value-added' data on pupil learning outcomes from previous research, and databases of the Office for Standards in Education, the national government inspection agency, and local education authority databases. Only those teachers were retained for whom there was adequate evidence of effectiveness from a range of sources.

The next step was to contact the schools in which these teachers worked, and ask the headteacher (principal) whether she or he agreed that the teacher in question was effective at teaching literacy, and whether there was objective evidence to support the headteacher's opinion. The key issue was whether headteachers could supply additional evidence of above average pupil learning gains in the classes taught by these teachers, such as standardised test scores for at least two years. Satisfactory answers to the two questions led to inclusion in the final number of some 382 effective teachers of literacy, to whom the questionnaire survey was sent. In some cases there was more than one effective teacher of literacy in the same school.

In addition, we identified a comparison group of teachers that included the full range of effectiveness. For ethical and practical reasons, we decided not to identify a group of ineffective or less effective teachers. The sampling frame we used was mathematics co-ordinators in the same schools as the effective teachers of literacy, or similar schools in the same localities. In this way, 150 mathematics co-ordinators were selected. The purpose of the comparison group was to check whether characteristics identified among the effective teachers of literacy might also be found among teachers who represented the whole range of effectiveness. We chose the mathematics co-ordinators because they were less likely to be subject specialists in English or literacy. However, it is worth noting that many of the mathematics co-ordinators worked in the same schools as the effective teachers of literacy. So it is possible that this factor had an effect on the overall quality of the comparison group's literacy teaching.

Completed questionnaires were returned by 225 of the effective teachers of literacy group which represented a return rate of 59 per cent, and by 71 of the mathematics co-ordinators, a return rate of 47 per cent. Background details of the two groups of teachers are outlined in Table 8.1.

Table 8.1 *Gender, age and teaching experience of the respondents*

	Effective teachers of literacy		Comparison group	
	Frequency	Percent	Frequency	Percent
Gender:				
Male	11	4.9	16	22.5
Female	210	93.3	54	76.1
Missing values	4	1.8	1	1.4
Total	225	100.0	71	100.0
Age:				
23–29	23	10.2	11	15.5
30–39	39	17.3	11	15.5
40–49	121	53.8	38	53.5
49+	40	17.8	11	15.5
Missing values	2	0.9		
Total	225	100.0	71	100.0
Teaching experience:				
1–5 years	28	12.4	12	16.9
6–10 years	36	16.0	11	15.5
10+ years	159	70.7	48	67.6
Missing values	2	0.9		
Total	225	100.0	71	100.0

Analysis of the data was conducted in three stages, using both descriptive and inferential statistical tests. In the first stage, correlations were calculated between items representing the three theoretical orientations (phonic, skills, whole language) towards teaching reading, and the three theoretical orientations (presentation, forms, process) towards teaching writing. This analysis, conducted on both sets of teachers, served the purpose of confirming the hypothetical structure of the modified TORP instrument by identifying similar patterns of response for each of the theoretical orientations.

The second stage entailed a series of analyses. First, a descriptive estimation of all six theoretical orientations (three for reading and three for writing) was calculated separately for the effective teachers and for the comparison group. Although these descriptive statistics offered a picture of the preferred orientations for both populations, in order to compare the two groups statistically, two one-way MANOVA (multiple analysis of variance) were computed, in which group membership was the independent variable in both analyses, and the respective theoretical orientations to reading and writing were the dependent variables.

This stage also involved the generation of descriptive statistics for the 12 teaching activities included in the questionnaire that were designed to correspond with the six theoretical orientations. To investigate whether teachers' responses to the statements about suggested teaching activities were consistent with their reported theoretical orientations to literacy teaching (including reading and writing), correlations were calculated between their scores on the items measuring the six theoretical orientations and their scores on the items measuring the 12 corresponding teaching activities.

Finally, the third stage aimed to identify possible differences within the theoretical orientations to literacy amongst the effective teachers of literacy only.

This analysis involved a series of comparisons between different groups of effective teachers of literacy determined in terms of the number of years' teaching experience, type of teacher training course experienced, the level of professional qualification, and responsibility for co-ordinating English teaching. Four one-way MANOVA were calculated.

Our use of multivariate statistical techniques stemmed from a desire to address comprehensively the complexity of teachers' beliefs, since there was no expectation that any of the six theoretical orientations represented by the modified TORP instrument would be mutually exclusive. Although multivariate statistical analysis might require more advanced knowledge, beyond the scope of many masters dissertations, it is something which could be undertaken within a doctoral study provided the investigator had a good grounding in statistics. An advantage of multivariate analysis is that it enables exploration of the relationships among variables that may more closely resemble the complexity of the real world (or of classroom life). This form of analysis helps to avoid over-simplification of the relationships between multiple variables, and gets around the problem of conducting a series of univariate tests (e.g. t-tests or ANOVAs), which may lead to type 1 errors (rejecting the null hypothesis).

Findings

Teachers' theoretical orientation

Stage 1: *correlational analysis.* As indicated earlier, the modified TORP instrument used in the study comprised six Likert-type statements. Each of the three theoretical orientations towards the teaching of reading was represented by two statements, and the three theoretical orientations towards the teaching of writing were each represented by another two statements (a total of 12 statements). It was important to examine at the outset whether there were similar patterns of response for each of the six orientations. For this purpose, correlations between the pairs of statements representing particular theoretical orientations were calculated for the whole population of teachers. The full correlation matrices for both the reading and writing orientations are given in Tables 8.2 and 8.3:

Table 8.2 *Correlations between items designed to represent theoretical orientations towards teaching reading*

	Phonic 1	Phonic 2	Skills 1	Skills 2	Whole language 1	Whole language 2
Phonic 1	1.00	.54**	.28**	.34**	−.18**	−.17**
Phonic 2		1.00	.30**	.28**	−.16**	−.19**
Skills 1			1.00	.29**	−.08*	−.11
Skills 2				1.00	−.10	−.13*
Whole language 1					1.00	.31**
Whole language 2						1.00

Note: * Correlation is significant at the 0.05 level (2-tailed)
　　　** Correlation is significant at the 0.01 level (2-tailed)

Table 8.3 *Correlations between items designed to represent theoretical orientations towards teaching writing*

	Presentation 1	Presentation 2	Process 1	Process 2	Forms 1	Forms 2
Presentation 1	1.00	.34**	−.15*	−.22**	−.12*	−.19**
Presentation 2		1.00	−.13*	−.19**	−.01	−.14*
Process 1			1.00	.24**	.17**	.22**
Process 2				1.00	.23**	.21**
Forms 1					1.00	.39**
Forms 2						1.00

Note: * Correlation is significant at the 0.05 level (2-tailed)
       ** Correlation is significant at the 0.01 level (2-tailed)

As indicated in the tables, all items reflecting similar theoretical orientations were statistically significant at the 0.01 level of confidence. That is, a similar pattern of response was given to each of the statements designed to investigate a particular theoretical orientation. It should be noted that one of the items designed to reflect the skills theoretical orientation was found to be also associated with an item reflecting the phonics theoretical orientation. However, there was no expectation that any of the six theoretical orientations represented by the modified TORP instrument would be mutually exclusive. Given that these two items were taken from the original TORP instrument, we decided that they could also be taken together as a pair both for the presentation of the respondents' responses, and for the subsequent analysis.

Stage 2: descriptive statistics. The mean responses of both groups to each of the statements are given in Table 8.4. The two statements designed to reflect each theoretical orientation were grouped together, and the first column of the table gives their details. Low mean responses represent agreement with the statement and high mean responses represent disagreement.

Table 8.4 indicates that the effective teachers of literacy appeared to be inclined towards a whole language theoretical orientation to the teaching of reading. Their responses indicated that they tended to give emphasis to students making sense of texts, and that they believed authentic texts should be used as the principal reading material rather than decontextualised sentences or words (see their responses in the items representing the whole language theoretical orientation). The effective teachers of literacy placed less emphasis than the comparison group on the importance of children's use of sound-symbol correspondences in decoding new words (see their responses to the items representing the phonic theoretical orientation).

Table 8.4 *Mean responses of both teacher groups to each statement*

Theoretical orientation	Statements representing theoretical orientation	Effective teachers of literacy			Comparison group		
		No.	Mean	SD	No.	Mean	SD
Reading:							
Phonic	When children do not know a word they should be instructed to sound out its parts.	203	2.67	1.18	68	2.01	.89
	Phonic analysis (that is breaking a word into its sounds) is the most important form of analysis used when meeting new words.	215	3.24	1.18	70	2.49	1.11
Skills	It is necessary to introduce new words before they appear in a child's reading book.	212	3.67	1.21	71	3.44	1.08
	It is important for a word to be repeated a number of times after it has been introduced to ensure that it will become part of a child's sight vocabulary.	217	1.87	1.19	71	1.46	.67
Whole language	When coming to a word that is unknown, the reader should be encouraged to guess a meaning and carry on.	212	2.03	.94	70	2.44	1.10
	If a child says 'house' for the written word 'home', the response should be left uncorrected.	212	2.46	1.11	70	2.90	1.33
Writing:							
Presentation	It is important to correct children's spellings as they write.	206	3.47	1.12	68	3.10	1.12
	Fluent, accurate handwriting is a very high priority in early writing teaching.	218	3.93	1.06	70	3.17	1.32
Process	If children have spelt a word wrongly but their attempt is clearly logically based it should usually be left uncorrected.	200	2.63	1.10	66	2.83	1.17
	In the early stages, getting children to be confident in writing is a higher priority than making sure they are accurate.	220	1.38	.74	71	1.39	.57
Forms	Most children's writing should be for audiences other than the teacher.	213	2.11	.97	71	2.13	.92
	Young writers should choose their own reasons for writing.	211	2.56	.99	70	2.57	1.00

Note: SD = standard deviation

Both groups tended to disagree with the statement that young readers should be introduced to new words before meeting them in context in a book. But effective teachers of literacy and mathematics co-ordinators agreed that repetition of words was important in early reading. Indeed this item had the highest level of agreement of all the items, with the comparison group appearing to agree more strongly than the effective teachers of literacy. This finding suggests a strong emphasis on building up young readers' sight vocabulary (see the responses of both groups in the items representing the skills theoretical orientation).

With regard to the respondents' theoretical orientations towards the teaching of writing, the effective teachers of literacy appeared to disagree with prioritising presentation features in the teaching of writing, whereas the validation group (mathematics co-ordinators) appeared to be neutral about this (see their responses in the items representing the presentation theoretical orientation). Interestingly, similar patterns of response were given by both groups to the items representing the process and forms theoretical orientations to writing.

As we have noted already, there was no expectation that any of the six theoretical orientations represented by the modified TORP instrument would be mutually exclusive. Nevertheless, the patterns of responses presented in the descriptive Table 8.4 require further scrutiny and it is to the statistical analysis of these that we turn next.

Stage 2.2: multivariate analysis of variance (MANOVA). To make statistical comparisons between the two populations (effective teachers of literacy–comparison group of mathematics co-ordinators), items reflecting the same theoretical orientation were grouped together, resulting in six composite scores (six dependent variables). A one-way MANOVA was performed to test for differences between effective teachers of literacy and the comparison group in the three theoretical orientations to the teaching of reading (phonic, skills, whole language). Another one-way MANOVA was performed for the remaining three orientations related to the teaching of writing (presentation, process, forms). Analysis of the three theoretical orientations relating to reading held by the effective teachers of literacy and the comparison group indicated a multivariate effect $F_{(3,252)} = 10.87$, p.< .001. Univariate analysis revealed that the multivariate difference was due to differences between the effective teachers of literacy and the comparison group in all three theoretical orientations. In the phonic theoretical orientation ($F_{(1,265)} = 27.84$, p.< .001; in the skills theoretical orientation $F_{(1,278)} = 6.8$, p.< .01; and in the whole language theoretical orientation $F_{(1,274)} = 10.04$, p.< .001 (see Table 8.5).

Table 8.5 *Mean scores of the effective teachers of literacy and the comparison group on theoretical orientations to teaching reading*

	No.	Theoretical orientation to teaching reading		
		Phonic	Skills	Whole language
Effective teachers of literacy	225	2.94 (N = 200)	2.77 (N = 209)	2.23 (N = 206)
Comparison group	71	2.21 (N = 67)	2.45 (N = 71)	2.67 (N = 70)

Examination of the mean scores in Table 8.5 indicates that the comparison group appeared to agree with statements which reflect a phonic and a skills theoretical orientation. By contrast, the effective teachers of literacy appeared to be neutral towards these two theoretical orientations. However, it should also be noted that Table 8.4 showed how the effective teachers were positive about the item relating to building up sight vocabulary, but negative towards the item relating to introducing any new words before children encountered them in reading books. When the two scores were combined in Table 8.5, it had the effect of creating an apparently neutral stance towards the skills orientation. The potential effect of combining scores in this way is something to be aware of in analysing and interpreting quantitative data. Analysis of differences between the effective teachers and the comparison group in the three theoretical orientations relating to writing also indicated a multivariate effect F (3,247) = 6.88, p. < .001. Univariate analysis revealed that the multivariate difference was due to differences between the effective teachers of literacy and the comparison group in the presentation theoretical orientation (F (1,271) = 19.30, p.< .001 (see Table 8.6).

Table 8.6 *Mean scores of the effective teachers of literacy and the comparison group on theoretical orientations to teaching writing*

	No.	Theoretical orientation to teaching writing		
		Presentation	Process	Forms
Effective teachers of literacy	225	3.70 (N = 206)	2.00 (N = 199)	2.34 (N = 207)
Comparison group	71	3.14 (N = 67)	2.12 (N = 66)	2.35 (N = 70)

Examination of the mean scores in Table 8.6 indicates that both the effective teachers of literacy and the comparison group agreed with the process and forms theoretical orientations towards the teaching of writing. However, in relation to the presentation theoretical orientation, whilst the validation group could be characterised as neutral (M = 3.14), the effective teachers of literacy group appeared to disagree (M = 3.70).

Teaching activities

Stage 2.3: descriptive statistics. We have noted how the questionnaire included a list of 12 teaching activities connected with the three theoretical positions relating to the teaching of reading and the three theoretical positions relating to the teaching of writing. The respondents were asked to rate each teaching activity on a five point Likert scale according to their views about its likely usefulness in teaching reading or writing, as appropriate. Low mean responses represent agreement with the usefulness of the activity and high mean responses disagreement with its usefulness. The mean responses of both groups to each of the teaching activities are given in Table 8.7.

This table shows how the effective teachers of literacy rated favourably teaching activities that focused upon communication and composition. For example, although they agreed with the activity which involved students sounding out the parts of an unknown word, they did not rate favourably the activity 'Children completing phonic worksheets and exercises'. The comparison group rated this activity more favourably (see the responses of both groups to the items representing the phonic theoretical orientation). Their rating of the activity is consistent with their reported beliefs, presented in Table 8.4. Moreover, the comparison group appeared to be more positive towards the teaching activities reflecting a skills orientation than the effective teachers of literacy group who were, in turn, very positive towards teaching activities associated with a whole language theoretical orientation. Again, these tendencies appeared to be consistent with the respondents' reported beliefs in Table 8.4.

Table 8.7 *Mean responses of both teacher groups to each teaching strategy*

Theoretical orientation	Teaching strategy	Effective teachers of literacy			Comparison group		
		No.	Mean	SD	No.	Mean	SD
Reading:							
Phonic	Teaching letter sounds as a way of helping children build up words.	221	1.64	.73	71	1.61	.76
	Children completing phonic worksheets and exercises.	220	3.03	1.29	69	2.51	1.05
Skills	Using flashcards to teach children to read words by sight.	220	2.70	1.24	68	2.31	.95
	Using graded reading schemes to structure children's introduction to reading.	215	2.42	1.20	70	2.11	.93
Whole language	Children listening to tape-recorded versions of stories while following the text in a book.	222	1.64	.65	70	1.83	.68
	Using big books with a group of children to model and share reading.	221	1.30	.53	70	1.73	.74
Writing:							
Presentation	Children copying or tracing over an adult's writing.	219	2.98	1.27	68	2.71	1.07
	Regular spelling tests using published spelling lists.	220	3.40	1.24	69	2.75	1.16
Process	Children using the 'magic line' when writing: that is, when they reach a word they cannot spell, writing its initial sound followed by a line and then checking the correct spelling afterwards.	219	2.05	1.01	67	2.19	.80
	Asking children to comment upon and help revise each other's writing.	220	1.55	.72	71	1.93	1.05
Forms	Getting children to write to other children in other schools or areas of the country.	218	1.96	.79	69	1.94	.66
	Using worksheets or frames to guide children's writing in particular forms.	215	2.28	1.07	70	2.39	.91

Note: SD = standard deviation

Finally, in relation to the teaching of writing, the effective teachers of literacy did not rate favourably the teaching of spelling by means of spelling lists. Consistent with their tendency to emphasise communication over presentation, they were more likely to place higher value on children helping each other to revise their writing.

Stage 2.4: correlational analysis. To investigate whether respondents' responses to the statements about teaching activities showed a similar pattern to their responses to statements about theoretical orientations towards teaching reading and teaching writing, we computed correlations between each composite score representing a theoretical orientation and each of the two teaching activities designed to reflect this theoretical orientation. The correlations for the effective teachers of literacy are shown for reading in Table 8.8 and for writing in Table 8.9. The equivalent results for the comparison group are depicted for reading in Table 8.10 and for writing in Table 8.11.

Table 8.8 *Correlations between theoretical orientations to the teaching of reading (total scores) and statements about teaching activities – effective teachers of literacy*

Theoretical orientation (reading)	Statement about teaching activity					
	Phonic 1	Phonic 2	Skills 1	Skills 2	Whole language 1	Whole language 2
Phonic	.34**	.35**	.31**	.30**	−.09	−.13
Skills	.17*	.34**	.33**	.34**	.13	−.11
Whole language	−.05	−.27**	−.18*	−.16*	.16*	.28**

Note: * Correlation is significant at the 0.05 level (2-tailed)
           ** Correlation is significant at the 0.01 level (2-tailed)

Table 8.9 *Correlations between theoretical orientations to the teaching of writing (total scores) and statements about teaching activities – effective teachers of literacy*

Theoretical orientation (writing)	Statement about teaching activity					
	Presentation 1	Presentation 2	Process 1	Process 2	Forms 1	Forms 2
Presentation	.21**	.36**	−.14*	−.15*	−.15*	.14*
Process	−.21**	−.19**	.05	.15*	.18*	−.10
Forms	−.24**	−.18**	.12	.30**	.25**	.03

Note: * Correlation is significant at the 0.05 level (2-tailed)
           ** Correlation is significant at the 0.01 level (2-tailed)

Table 8.10 *Correlations between theoretical orientations to the teaching of reading (total scores) and statements about teaching activities – comparison group*

Theoretical orientation (reading)	Statement about teaching activity					
	Phonic 1	Phonic 2	Skills 1	Skills 2	Whole language 1	Whole language 2
Phonic	.21	.16	.25*	.25*	.03	−.26*
Skills	.24*	.36**	.43**	.51**	.14	−.01
Whole language	.078	.02	−.15	−.28*	.15	.21

Note: * Correlation is significant at the 0.05 level (2-tailed)
           ** Correlation is significant at the 0.01 level (2-tailed)

Table 8.11 *Correlations between theoretical orientations to the teaching of writing (total scores) and statements about teaching activities – comparison group*

Theoretical orientation (writing)	Statement about teaching activity					
	Presentation 1	Presentation 2	Process 1	Process 2	Forms 1	Forms 2
Presentation	.37**	.34**	−.04	−.16	.15	.24*
Process	−.53	−.05	.05	.16	.07	0.7
Forms	.05	−.26*	.08	.25*	.22	.07

Note: * Correlation is significant at the 0.05 level (2-tailed)
      ** Correlation is significant at the 0.01 level (2-tailed)

As seen in Table 8.8 and Table 8.9, of the 12 relevant correlations in the analysis (i.e. each theoretical orientation matched with the two items designed to reflect teaching activities matching that theoretical orientation), significant levels of agreement were shown by ten (with eight of these at the 0.01 level of confidence). This finding suggests a level of consistency between the reported beliefs of the effective teachers of literacy and their views about particular teaching activities.

By contrast, a similar level of agreement could not be established between the reported beliefs of the comparison group and their views about particular teaching activities, where only four of the 12 relevant correlations were significant (see Table 8.10 and Table 8.11). However, caution should be exercised in interpreting the degree of consistency between beliefs and practice indicated by the correlational analysis alone. This was an exploratory study, and we did not set out specifically to test hypotheses about consistency between beliefs and practice through this instrument. Other more ecological methods would be required to do this as outlined earlier in the review of relevant literature.

Theoretical orientations of effective teachers about teaching reading and writing

Stage 3: multivariate analysis of variance (MANOVA). As well as comparing the responses of effective teachers of literacy to the TORP items with those of a comparison group, we also wanted to examine whether there were any differences in response *within* the group of effective teachers of literacy. For this purpose, four one-way MANOVA were calculated to test for differences in theoretical orientation to the teaching of reading and to the teaching of writing within the effective teacher sample. We focused on four variables:

1 The number of years' teaching experience.
2 The type of teacher training course experienced.
3 The level of professional qualification acquired.
4 Whether a responsibility post was held for co-ordinating English or literacy within the school.

The first variable 'years of teaching experience' comprised three groups:

- one–five years (N = 28);
- six–ten years (N = 36);
- more than ten years (N = 159).

The second variable 'type of teacher training course' comprised three groups:

- either a four-year BEd (Bachelor of Education) degree or BA/BSc (Bachelor of Arts/Bachelor of Science) degree with Qualified Teacher Status (N = 58);
- a bachelors degree plus Postgraduate Certificate in Education (PGCE) (N = 28);
- a two-or three-year Certificate in Education (N = 133).

It is notable that a number of respondents had initially trained as teachers by taking Certificate in Education courses, but had later upgraded their qualifications by taking in-service training courses to attain a Bachelor's degree.

The third variable 'highest level of professional qualification' comprised three groups:

- a Certificate in Education (N = 96);
- a bachelors degree (N = 114);
- a masters degree (N = 15).

The fourth variable 'responsibility for co-ordinating English' comprised two groups:

- the respondents who held a responsibility post for co-ordinating English or literacy in their school (N = 130);
- those who did not (N = 93).

Theoretical orientations relating to the teaching of reading. Analysis of the relationship between the number of years' teaching experience and effective teachers' theoretical orientations to the teaching of reading indicated a multivariate effect (F (6,368) = 3.88, p.< .001. Univariate analysis revealed that the multivariate difference was due to difference in the phonic theoretical orientation (F (2,195) = 3.12, p.< .05. The post-hoc test (Tukey) revealed that the univariate effect was due to a difference between respondents with 1–5 years of experience and those with more than ten years (see Table 8.12).

Table 8.12 *Mean scores of effective teachers of literacy with different lengths of teaching experience for theoretical orientations towards teaching reading*

Length of teaching experience	No.	Theoretical orientation towards teaching reading		
		Phonic	Skills	Whole language
1–5 years	28	2.48 (N = 25)	3.07 (N = 27)	2.50 (N = 27)
6–10 years	36	3.08 (N = 31)	2.98 (N = 34)	2.25 (N = 32)
More than 10 years	159	3.00 (N = 142)	2.67 (N = 146)	2.17 (N = 145)

Examination of data presented in Table 8.12 indicates that teachers in the younger age-range appeared to be more in agreement with a phonic theoretical orientation to the teaching of reading, whereas the other two groups were neutral towards this theoretical orientation. By contrast, all three age-ranges appeared to agree with the effectiveness of the whole language theoretical orientation.

Analysis of the relationship between type of teacher training course taken and theoretical orientation to the teaching of reading indicated a multivariate effect (F (6,362) = 1.11, p.< .001. Univariate analysis revealed that the multivariate difference was due to difference in the skills theoretical orientation (F (2,201) = 3.15, p.< .05. Although the post-hoc test (Tukey) conducted failed to reveal significant differences, in Table 8.13 a tendency can be detected for respondents with a BEd, BA or BSc degree, or with a degree plus PGCE, to be neutral towards the skills theoretical orientation, whereas those with a Certificate in Education appeared to be in agreement with it.

Table 8.13 *Mean scores of effective teachers of literacy with different types of teacher training course experience for theoretical orientations towards teaching reading*

Type of teacher training course	No.	Theoretical orientation towards teaching reading		
		Phonic	Skills	Whole language
Four year BEd or BA/BSc with Qualified Teacher Status	58	2.89 (N = 54)	2.97 (N = 55)	2.24 (N = 54)
Bachelors degree + PGCE	28	2.93 (N = 21)	2.96 (N = 27)	2.32 (N = 25)
Two or three year Certificate in Education	133	2.86 (N = 120)	2.62 (N = 122)	2.22 (N = 122)

Analysis of the theoretical orientations of effective teachers of literacy, determined according to the level of professional qualification, indicated a multivariate effect (F (6,372) = 3.36, p.< .01. Univariate analysis revealed that the multivariate difference was due to difference in the phonic theoretical orientation F (2,197) = 5.72, p.< .01. The post-hoc test (Tukey) revealed that the univariate effect was due to differences both between respondents with a Certificate of Education qualification and those with a masters degree, and also between the respondents with a bachelors degree and those with a masters degree (Table 8.14).

Table 8.14 *Mean scores of groups of effective teachers of literacy with different levels of qualification for theoretical orientations towards teaching reading*

Highest level qualification	No.	Theoretical orientation towards teaching reading		
		Phonic	Skills	Whole language
Certificate in Education	96	2.98 (N = 86)	2.58 (N = 89)	2.21 (N = 90)
Bachelors degree	114	2.81 (N = 102)	2.89 (N = 106)	2.27 (N = 104)
Masters degree	15	3.83 (N = 12)	3.03 (N = 14)	2.00 (N = 12)

Examination of Table 8.14 indicates that the effective teachers who had acquired the highest level of qualification appeared to be negative towards the phonic theoretical orientation, neutral towards the skills theoretical orientation and very positive towards the whole language orientation. It is worth stressing here that all the groups of effective teachers of literacy can be seen as being very positive towards this orientation.

The one-way MANOVA to test for differences among the effective teachers of literacy according to whether they held a responsibility post for co-ordinating English or literacy within their school (English or literacy co-ordinators; and those without any responsibility), did not reveal significant differences in relation to the three theoretical orientations.

In relation to the variance within the effective teacher population, the proportion of teachers within each of the groups identified by the variables needs to be borne in mind. The largest number of teachers had more than ten years' teaching experience (N=159); a large number had originally trained by taking a two-or three-year Certificate in Education course in a teacher training college; and the most frequently held level of qualification was a bachelors degree. (As noted earlier, some teachers who originally trained by taking a Certificate in Education course had since followed courses to upgrade their qualification to bachelors degree level.) Nonetheless, the analysis does identify interesting variations in orientation to literacy among the effective teachers.

Theoretical orientations relating to the teaching of writing. Four one-way MANOVA, determined again in terms of years' teaching experience, type of teacher training course, highest level of professional qualification, and responsibility for co-ordinating English or literacy, were calculated to test for differences among the effective teachers to the three theoretical orientations to the teaching of writing. The analyses revealed no significant differences in relation to any of the three theoretical orientations.

Discussion

Analysis of responses to the modified TORP items indicated that there were differences in the theoretical beliefs about reading and writing held by the effective teachers of literacy according to the number of years' teaching experience they had, the type of training they had experienced, and the level of qualification they held. But there was no difference in theoretical orientation between those who held a responsibility post within their school for English or literacy and those who did not. There were differences in theoretical orientation between the effective teachers and those held by a comparison group of primary school mathematics co-ordinators. The effective teachers of literacy showed a greater degree of consistency between responses relating to a particular theoretical orientation and the hypothetical teaching activities which would accompany such an orientation.

We have emphasised already that theoretical orientations were not mutually exclusive categories. In fact, teachers in both groups could probably be situated along continua of orientations, as suggested by other researchers in this area (e.g. Richardson et al., 1991; Westwood et al., 1997). Overall, the effective teachers of literacy showed a higher level of consistency between their theoretical beliefs and choice of teaching activities than did the comparison group. They were more positively orientated to whole language theoretical positions which promoted the creation of meaning in reading and writing through:

- a strong emphasis on helping learners to understand text;
- the use of authentic texts and activities in teaching reading;
- a focus on process in writing;
- developing children's understanding of a range of text forms and structures and their ability to write for a range of purposes.

The effective teachers of literacy were negatively orientated to theoretical positions emphasising presentational features in writing, and teaching strategies and focusing on achieving technical accuracy at the expense of meaning. Overall, the theoretical orientation of effective teachers of literacy appeared, in many respects, to be constructivist: prioritising pupils' ability to make sense of, and produce, written texts in a range of contexts and for authentic purposes.

While they were more negatively orientated to theoretical positions and teaching activities which emphasised grapho-phonic decoding, that did not mean they were against the teaching of phonics as such. Apparently contradictory responses to the two items representing a phonic theoretical orientation suggest that the effective teachers of literacy were positive about teaching letter-sound correspondences to help children build up words, but were more negative towards using phonic analysis as the main strategy in decoding unfamiliar words. (See Table 8.4 for the effective teachers' contradictory responses to items representing the phonic theoretical orientation.) Tentatively, this suggests that the effective teachers of literacy supported practices which are consistent with some aspects of what has been termed a 'synthetic phonic' approach (Adams, 1990). However, it may be that the relatively recent developments in research on the role of phonological awareness and analytic phonics has yet to make a strong impact on teachers' beliefs about literacy and how it should be taught.

Analysis of theoretical orientation within the effective teacher of literacy population according to number of years' teaching experience, type of teacher training course, level of qualification, and responsibility for co-ordinating English or literacy yielded some interesting results. In relation to number of years' teaching experience, those who had only one to five years' experience appeared to be more positive towards a phonic theoretical orientation, more neutral towards whole language theories, and more negative towards a skills approach, than effective teachers with six to ten, or more than ten, years' experience. Teachers with six to ten, and more than ten, years' experience were more neutral towards the phonic theoretical orientation. However, all three groups of effective teachers of literacy were positively orientated towards a whole language theoretical perspective.

The more positive orientation towards phonic theoretical perspectives found among effective teachers with the least experience can be interpreted in two ways. First, that greater experience leads to a less positive orientation towards phonic theories – an interpretation which appears to be supported by similar findings in other research (e.g. Pesce, 1990; Troyer and Yopp, 1990). Alternatively, that the teachers with one to five years' experience had qualified more recently, and had experienced courses which reflected more recent approaches to the use of phonics in teaching young children to read. The latter is plausible, in that courses of initial teacher training have probably reflected more recent research developments relating to the teaching and learning of reading.

Adams (1990) has highlighted the impact of recent research in cognitive psychology on our understanding of how successful readers process text. Her review of research on the teaching of reading also indicates strong evidence for the success of approaches which combine systematic teaching of phonics with the use of authentic texts in reading instruction, and a focus on text comprehension and structure. Work on phonological awareness and phonic and syllabic analysis of words, such as that of Goswami and Bryant (1990) may also have been reflected in teacher training courses in the UK in the past decade. Further longitudinal study would be necessary to make any firm claims about changes in teachers' theoretical orientation as they gained more experience in the classroom. However, Pajares (1992) suggests that teachers' beliefs tend to remain relatively unchanged over time.

Our data showed that teachers who had trained by taking a two- or three-year Certificate in Education course – phased out in the UK over 20 years ago – were more positively orientated towards word recognition approaches to reading. They were the only group who appeared to approve of a skills theoretical orientation. It is possible that approaches to reading which emphasised whole word recognition and the development of sight vocabulary were more likely to have been influential in primary school teacher training courses in the 1960s and early 1970s, when those who had taken Certificate courses would have trained.

Differences between the effective teachers of literacy in terms of the highest level of qualification held indicated that those who held masters qualifications were more negative towards a phonic theoretical orientation and very positively orientated towards whole language theories (although it is worth emphasising that all three groups were positive towards a whole language orientation to reading). This finding needs to be interpreted cautiously. Whilst a masters qualification might indicate greater familiarity with theoretical issues in the teaching and learning of literacy, and more opportunities to construct a robust personal philosophy of the teaching of reading, the masters-level qualifications were not necessarily gained in the area of reading or literacy.

However, this finding is generally consistent with other research on teachers' theoretical orientations to literacy, which suggests that teachers favouring a whole language approach were also likely to have the highest level of training (e.g. Pesce, 1990; Troyer and Yopp, 1990). One study by Ketner et al. (1997) of teachers in the USA indicated a much higher proportion who had masters level qualifications than in England (although this was a smaller sample than ours, and all the teachers came from only one school district).

Our data indicated that there was no significant difference in theoretical orientation according to whether or not the effective teachers of literacy held responsibility posts for co-ordinating English or literacy within their schools. Furthermore, in relation to theoretical orientation towards the teaching of writing, there were no significant differences within the effective teachers of literacy according to the four variables already described. This result may suggest that differences in theoretical approaches to the teaching of writing may have had less impact on the teachers in this study, or that they have had much less prominence in initial training and in-service training courses. It is certainly true that until very recently, public and media debate about the teaching and learning of literacy has tended to focus on the teaching of reading – particularly on fears that reading standards may be falling – whereas writing has often been overlooked in these debates.

Conclusion

This exploratory study of primary school sector teachers' theoretical beliefs about the teaching of literacy raises a number of issues for further investigation, and has some implications for policy relating to professional development. An important one is that the differences in theoretical orientation which this exploratory investigation revealed may lead not only to differences in practice, but also to differences in ways of interpreting and making sense of policy requirements relating to literacy. This possibility is particularly significant where ambitious national or state-wide programmes are being implemented. Programme innovations of this nature usually make some provision for in-service training of teachers. However, such provision is often either localised and fragmented – left to staff in individual schools or districts to take 'ownership' of the programme or reform – or, conversely, highly centralised with prescribed content and forms of delivery. In England, and probably in other parts of the world too, preparation to implement new programmes appears to have taken little account of the historical and socio-cultural contexts in which teachers' theoretical beliefs are formed. Rarely has provision for in-service training been differentiated to take account of teachers' levels of expertise, experience, professional qualifications, or theoretical perspective. Educational reforms often fail to provide ways of helping teachers to accommodate or adjust to innovations by relating them to their existing theoretical belief structures.

To sum up, this exploratory study revealed significant differences in teachers' theoretical orientation to literacy, and consistency between theoretical beliefs and reported choice of teaching activities. But as we have already pointed out, we make no claims about the relationship between those beliefs and teachers' actual classroom practice on the basis of their responses to a modified theoretical orientation profile. Research on teachers' thought processes has tended to focus on the extent to which their teaching is consistent with their theoretical beliefs. But, as Fang (1996: 58) points out, less attention has been paid to a more important practical concern: how teachers can apply their theoretical beliefs within the constraints imposed by the complexities of classroom life.

Acknowledgements

The content of this chapter is based on an article published in the academic journal *Research Papers in Education,* 16 (3): 271–92. (htttp://www.tandf.co.uk). We are grateful to Taylor & Francis for permission to reproduce parts of the original article. We would like to acknowledge the contribution of David Wray, Jane Medwell and Richard Fox to the work reported here.

References

Adams, M. J. (1990) *Beginning to Read: Thinking and Learning about Print.* Cambridge, MA: MIT Press.

Alexander, R. (1992) *Policy and Practice in Primary Education.* London: Routledge.

Alexander, P. A., Schallert, D. L. and Hare, V.C. (1991) 'Coming to terms: how researchers in learning and literacy talk about knowledge', *Review of Educational Research,* 61 (3): 315–43.

Bennett, N., Desforges, C., Cockburn, A. and Wilkinson, B. (1984) *The Quality of Pupils' Learning Experiences.* London: Lawrence Erlbaum Associates.

Davis, M. M., Konopak, B. C. and Readence, J. E. (1993) 'An investigation of two chapter 1 teachers' beliefs about reading and instructional practices', *Reading Research and Instruction,* 33 (2): 105–33.

Duffy, G. and Anderson, L. (1984) 'Teachers' theoretical orientations and the real classroom', *Reading Psychology,* 5 (1–2): 97–104.

De Ford, D. (1985) 'Validating the construct of theoretical orientation in reading instruction', *Reading Research Quarterly,* 20 (3): 351–68.

Desforges, C. and Cockburn, A. (1987) *Understanding the Mathematics Teacher: A Study of Practice in First Schools.* London: Falmer.

Fang, Z. F. (1996) 'A review of research on teacher beliefs and practices', *Educational Research,* 38 (1): 47–65.

Fenstermacher, G. D. (1994) 'The knower and the known in teacher-knowledge research', in L. Darling-Hammond (ed), *Review of Research in Education 20*, Washington DC: American Education Research Association.

Fullan, M. and Hargreaves, A. (1994) 'The teacher as a person', in A. Pollard and J. Bourne, (eds), *Teaching and Learning in the Primary School.* London: Routledge.

Goswami, U. and Bryant, P. (1990) *Phonological Skills and Learning to Read.* Hove: Lawrence Earlbaum.

Harste, J. C. and Burke, C. L. (1977) 'A new hypothesis for reading teacher research', in P. D. Pearson (ed), *Reading: Theory, research and practice.* New York: Mason Publishing.

Kagan, D. (1990) 'Ways of evaluating teacher cognition: inferences concerning the Goldilocks Principle', *Review of Educational Research,* 60 (1): 419–70.

Ketner, C. S., Smith, K. E. and Kaye-Parnell, M. (1997) 'The relationship between teacher theoretical orientation to reading and endorsement of developmentally appropriate practice', *Journal of Educational Research* 70 (4): 212–21.

Lenski, S. D., Wham, M. A. and Griffey, D. C. (1998) 'Literacy Orientation Survey: a survey to clarify teachers' beliefs and practices', *Reading Research and Instruction,* 37 (3): 217–36.

Levande, D. I. (1990) 'Teacher-reported factors influencing reading instruction', *Reading Improvement,* 27: 2–9.

Mergendoller, J. and Sacks, C. (1994) 'Concerning the relationship between teachers' theoretical orientations towards reading and their concept maps', *Teaching and Teacher Education,* 10 (6): 589–99.

Munby, H. (1982) 'The place of teachers' beliefs in research on teacher thinking and decision making, and an alternative methodology', *Instructional Science,* 11: 201–5.

Munby, H. (1984) 'A qualitative approach to the study of teachers' beliefs', *Journal of Research in Science Teaching,* 21: 27–38.

Pajares, M. F. (1992) 'Teachers' beliefs and educational research: cleaning up a messy construct', *Review of Educational Research,* 62 (3): 307–32.

Pesce, R. (1990) 'First-grade reading instruction: current trends in the Northern Valley regional District'. ERIC document No. ED 320 118.

Richards, J. C., Gipe, J. P. and Thompson, B. (1987) 'Teachers' beliefs about good reading instruction', *Reading Psychology,* 8 (1): 1–6.

Richardson, V., Anders, P., Tidwell, D. and Lloyd, C. (1991) 'The relationship between teachers' beliefs and practices in reading comprehension instruction', *American Education Research Journal,* 28 (3): 559–86.

Tabachnick, B. G. and Fidell, L. S. (2001) *Using Multivariate Statistics.* Boston: Allyn and Bacon.

Troyer, S. J. and Yopp, H. K. (1990) 'Kindergarten teachers' knowledge of emergent literacy concepts', *Reading Improvement,* 27: 34–40.

Westwood, P., Allen Knight, B. and Redden, E. (1997) 'Assessing teachers' beliefs about literacy acquisition: the development of the Teachers' Beliefs About Literacy Questionnaire (TBALQ)', *Journal of Research in Reading,* 20 (3): 224–35.

Wideen, M, Mayer-Smith, J. and Moon, B. (1998) 'A critical analysis of the research on learning to teach: making the case for an ecological perspective on inquiry', *Review of Educational Research,* 68 (2): 130–201.

Wray, D. and Medwell, J. (1993) 'The development of student teachers' knowledge, competence and beliefs about the teaching of reading'. Paper presented at the International Conference on Reading, St Martin's College, Lancaster.

Wray, D., Medwell, J., Poulson, L. and Fox, R. (2002) *Teaching Literacy Effectively in the Primary School.* London: RoutledgeFalmer.

Part 3

Meeting the challenge of reporting a review of the literature

Promoting inclusive education: a review of literature on teachers' attitudes towards integration and inclusion

Elias Avramidis and Brahm Norwich

In this chapter, Elias Avramidis and Brahm Norwich outline the process of conducting a critical review of literature on the substantive topic of teachers' attitudes to the inclusion of students with learning difficulties, or disabilities, within mainstream educational settings. They make explicit why it is important to understand teachers' attitudes to including such students in ordinary schools and classrooms. They also identify how the conceptualisation of special educational needs has changed over time, and how this change has been marked by differences in terminology. There has been a move from widespread use of the term *integration* to the more recent one of *inclusion*. The authors indicate that there are differences in the use and understanding of terminology across national and cultural contexts. They make the important point that theories, concepts and methodologies do change over time. In addition, they point out that there is a particular philosophical and value stance implied in the use of the term *inclusion*. This highlights our point in Chapter 1 about the importance of providing stipulative definitions of terms and concepts in writing about research, and of making any value stance as explicit as possible.

Avramidis and Norwich explain the aims and purpose of their review, and describe the stages and procedures they followed in conducting it. They set out the three review questions that guided the study, the sources used to locate relevant work, and their criteria for selecting literature. They outline how they wanted to include studies from as wide a range of national contexts as possible because most earlier reviews had tended to concentrate on a narrow range of contexts. The authors also outline the timeframe they employed for including studies and explain the reasons informing their decision. They indicate how, by progressively narrowing their focus, they were able to identify a framework for answering their review questions and structuring their account.

Avramidis and Norwich highlight what conclusions could reasonably be reached from the evidence reviewed, and also what aspects were less clear-cut. They address the problem of inconsistent or conflicting research findings, and suggest that a lack of clarity or inconsistency on an issue may itself indicate the need for further research. From this review, the authors were able to identify some key research questions to be explored further. A number of issues also arose in relation to methodology, highlighting the methodological limitations of many previous studies on this substantive topic, and indicating that different approaches would be worth pursuing in future work.

Background

Philosophies regarding the education of children with learning difficulties or dis-abilities have changed dramatically over the last two decades. Several countries have led in the effort to implement policies that foster the integration and, more recently, inclusion of these students into mainstream school environments (we define and discuss the terms *integration* and *inclusion* in the following pages). Though the movement towards inclusive education has gained momentum in recent years, a key element in the successful implementation of policy is the views of teachers, the people who have the major responsibility for implementa-tion. Teachers' beliefs and attitudes are likely to be critical for the success of inclusive practices, since teachers' acceptance of the policy of inclusion is likely to affect their commitment to implementing it (Norwich, 1994). Based on this assumption, a body of research has generated important findings that have prac-tical implications for policy makers endeavouring to promote inclusion.

There have been several reviews of this literature (e.g. Hannah, 1988; Jamieson, 1984; Salvia and Munson, 1986; Yanito et al., 1987). But these reviews were based mainly on studies conducted in the early 1980s and, largely, in the USA. A more recent systematic meta-analysis conducted by Scruggs and Mastropieri (1996) included only a small number of American studies. Therefore, we established that there was no comprehensive and up to date research synthesis on the topic.

This chapter reviews the large body of literature on the attitudes of teachers in mainstream school towards the integration and, more recently, inclusion of students with learning difficulties or disabilities. We aim to elucidate some of the factors that might impact on the formation of such attitudes. We outline the criteria used in selecting work to be included; processes involved in con-ducting the review; and the development of the framework that structured it. We also discuss substantive and methodological issues raised by the review and consider possible directions for future research.

The review process

In conducting the review, we adopted a framework outlined by Mertens (1998) consisting of a number of steps or stages. The first two stages consisted of iden-tifying a topic and reviewing secondary sources. We gained an initial overview of what was known about the chosen topic from generic literature relevant to inclusive education and from previously conducted reviews, particularly of teachers' attitudes towards the implementation of the inclusive education policy. From this starting point we identified the following review questions to guide our detailed work:

1 What does empirical research literature tell us about mainstream teachers' attitudes towards integration and, more recently, inclusion?
2 What factors might impact on the formation of these attitudes?
3 What are possible directions for future research?

Once we had identified our review questions we moved on to Mertens's third stage: developing a search strategy. We began by searching databases, including the ERIC (1984–2000), BEI (1986–2000) and PsychINFO (1984–2000), for articles describing teacher attitudes towards the integration and inclusion of students with learning difficulties or disabilities within mainstream schools and classrooms. Reference lists from relevant books (e.g. Jones, 1984; Yuker, 1988a), literature reviews (e.g. Yanito et al., 1987) and any relevant reports were searched for references. Additionally, a number of international refereed journals were hand-searched for suitable articles.

Given that teachers' attitudes toward integration and inclusion have received considerable interest over the last 20 years, the review could not possibly include everything. Thus we needed to identify criteria for selecting work for inclusion in our review (Mertens's fourth stage). We included only work where the main focus was on teachers' attitudes, excluding reports of student teachers' attitudes towards integration and inclusion. Studies conducted before 1980 were excluded since inclusive education has only gained momentum in the 1980s and 1990s. We also excluded unpublished work (including dissertations, theses and conference presentations) and what is known as 'grey' or 'fugitive' literature (like reports to research sponsors, and other work that has not been peer-reviewed).

Since previous efforts had focused mainly on attitude studies conducted in the USA, we decided to include studies from as many national contexts as possible. Our aim here could not extend to deriving firm generalisations because studies conducted in different countries are not directly comparable, given differences in education systems and variations in terms of philosophy and policies. Nonetheless, in spite of these differences there is evidence (e.g. Meijer et al., 1994) that in most OECD countries up to one per cent of the school population is taught in special settings (special schools or classrooms). We identified this small group of children with significant and complex needs as the focus of our literature review, rather than the wider population of students experiencing learning difficulties of a mild to moderate nature who are commonly placed in mainstream settings.

The generic literature served the purpose of clarifying the meaning of the central concepts in this review: *integration* and *inclusion*. We distinguished between studies investigating attitudes to integration and those investigating attitudes to inclusion. The two terms are often used interchangeably, with inclusion recently superseding integration in the vocabulary of special educators as a more radical term located within a human rights discourse. However, it was not at all clear that the terms had common meanings across different national contexts. This terminological distinction was taken into consideration in the identification, selection and presentation of studies. In the UK context, the principle of integration is strongly associated with the publication of the Warnock Report (DES, 1978) where the term was viewed as part of a wider movement in western countries towards 'normalisation'. This idea is widely understood as implying that patterns of life and conditions of everyday living which are as close as possible to the regular circumstances and ways of life of a society should be made available to all persons with disabilities. In the Warnock Report, integration took various forms, which included:

▶ locational integration (placing children with 'special needs' physically into mainstream schools);
▶ social interaction (some degree of social – but not educational – interaction between children with 'special needs' and their mainstream peers);
▶ functional integration (some unspecified level of participation in common learning activities and experiences).

However, whilst the integration movement strongly advocated the placement of children in the least restrictive environment, there was no expectation that every pupil with special needs would be functionally integrated. It was expected that children would be integrated in the manner and to the extent that was appropriate to their particular needs and circumstances. In this respect, integration was seen as a process of assimilation. A full mainstream school placement was seen to depend on whether the child could be assimilated into a largely unchanged mainstream school environment (Thomas, 1997). However, functional integration in the context of whole school policies was clearly intended to change the environment of the mainstream school.

By contrast, inclusion implies a restructuring of mainstream schooling so that every school can accommodate all children irrespective of disability, and ensure that all learners belong to a community (this process is seen as accommodation rather than assimilation). Such an argument locates the discussion in a social-ethical discourse which is strongly focused on values, as witnessed by the *Salamanca Declaration* (UNESCO, 1994). Some people favour the term inclusion because it is thought to embody a range of assumptions about the meaning and purpose of schools and embraces a much deeper philosophical notion of what integration should mean.

Finally, the term inclusion has come to take on a wider significance and popularity in linking up with the recent development of the concept of inclusion or social inclusion as having broader social and political value. Inclusion, in this wider sense, is comparable to equality as a social value in relating to all aspects of social disadvantage, oppression and discrimination. Yet despite these more recent developments towards inclusion, integration has been the main focus of research and we began by examining this body of work.

Overview of research on teachers' attitudes towards integration

The movement towards a system of educational provision that is more inclusive of all kinds of students is part of a broad human rights agenda. But many educators have serious reservations about supporting the widespread placement of pupils with special educational needs (SEN) in mainstream schools. Research undertaken in Australia on professional attitudes towards integration education has provided a range of information in this area. Several studies, undertaken between 1985 and 1989, addressed the attitudes of headteachers (principals) (Center et al., 1985), teachers (Center and Ward, 1987), psychologists (Center and Ward, 1989) and pre-school administrators (Bochner and Pieterse, 1989).

These investigations demonstrated that professional groups varied considerably in their perceptions of which types of children were most likely to be successfully integrated. (Summary data were presented by Ward et al., 1994). Attitudes towards integration were reported to be strongly influenced by the nature of the disabilities or educational problems being presented and, to a lesser extent, by the professional background of the respondents. The most enthusiastic group consisted of those responsible for pre-school provision. The most cautious group comprised classroom teachers, with headteachers, resource teachers and psychologists located in between.

Other studies have also indicated that school district staff who are more distant from students, such as administrators and advisers, express more positive attitudes to integration than those closer to the classroom context. Headteachers have been found to hold the most positive attitudes to integration, followed by special education teachers, with classroom teachers having the most negative attitudes (Garvar-Pinhas and Schmelkin, 1989; Norwich, 1994).

Similarly, work by Forlin (1995) suggested that teachers from Education Support Centres (special centres that cater for the educational needs of children with SEN requiring limited or extended support) were more accepting of a child with intellectual and physical disability than educators from regular mainstream primary schools which co-existed on the same site. Forlin concluded that special education resource teachers tend to have a more positive attitude to inclusion than their mainstream counterparts. This difference was also reflected in a sample of Greek mainstream and special teachers (Padeliadou and Lampropoulou, 1997).

A cross-national UNESCO study (Bowman, 1986) surveyed 14 nations (Egypt, Jordan, Columbia, Mexico, Venezuela, Botswana, Senegal, Zambia, Australia, Thailand, Czechoslovakia, Italy, Norway and Portugal), involving approximately 1,000 teachers with experience of teaching children with SEN. A wide difference was found in teacher opinions regarding integration. Teachers were found to favour different types of children for integration into ordinary classes. Interestingly, Bowman noted that in countries with laws requiring integration teachers expressed more favourable views (ranging from 47 to 93 per cent of teachers). Teachers from countries that offered the most sophisticated forms of segregated educational provision were less supportive of integration (ranging from 0 to 28 per cent).

Another cross-cultural study of teachers' attitudes towards integration (Leyser et al., 1994) in the USA, Germany, Israel, Ghana, Taiwan and the Philippines showed that there were differences in attitudes to integration according to the national context. Teachers in the USA and Germany had the most positive attitudes. Positive attitudes in the USA were attributed to integration being widely practised there as the result of Public Law 94–142. The positive views expressed by the German teachers were seen as surprising because, at the time of the investigation, Germany had no special education legislation. Teachers were not provided with special education training, children with SEN were segregated, and integration was practised only on an experimental basis.

This finding cautions us against the simple relationship between legislative system and inclusive attitudes that Bowman's study had suggested. The authors speculated that the positive views expressed by the German teachers represented the overall sensitivity of Germans toward minorities, including disabled people. Teacher attitudes were significantly less positive in Ghana, the Philippines, Israel and Taiwan. The authors reasoned that this finding might be due to a range of factors: limited or non-existent training for teachers to acquire integration competencies; limited opportunities for integration in some of these countries; and, overall, a small percentage of children who received services at all. (None of these countries had a history of offering children with SEN specially designed educational opportunities.)

Attitude studies within the USA have suggested that general educators have not developed an empathetic understanding of disabling conditions (Berryman, 1989; Horne and Ricciardo, 1988), nor do they appear to be supportive of the placement of special needs learners in their regular classrooms (Bacon and Schulz, 1991; Barton, 1992). Such an attitude can be explained by the fact that integration was often introduced in an ad hoc manner, without systematic modifications to a school's organisation, due regard to teachers' instructional expertise, or any guarantee of continuing resource provision. Center and Ward's (1987) Australian study of mainstream teachers indicated that their attitudes to integration reflected lack of confidence in their own instructional skills and in the quality of support personnel available to them. In this study, teachers felt positive towards integrating only those children whose disabling characteristics were unlikely to require extra instructional or management skills on the part of the teacher.

However a UK study by Clough and Lindsay (1991), which investigated the attitudes of 584 teachers towards integration and different kinds of support, indicated a more widely positive view of integration. This research provided some evidence that attitudes had shifted over the previous ten years or so in favour of integrating children with SEN. The researchers argued that this movement was partly the result of the teachers' experiences. They had developed some degree of competence and had not been 'swamped', as some had feared at the time of publication of the Warnock Report in 1978. Nevertheless, responses still appeared to vary according to the educational needs presented.

Finally, the meta-analysis (synthesis of the results of multiple investigations) by Scruggs and Mastropieri (1996) of American attitude studies included 28 survey reports conducted from at least 1958 through to 1995. These reviewers reported that although 65 per cent of the teachers surveyed (10,560 in total) agreed with the general concept of integration, only 40 per cent believed that integration was a realistic goal for most children. Responses again appeared to vary according to disabling conditions. An important conclusion was that there was no correlation between positive attitudes toward inclusion and the date when studies were undertaken, suggesting that teachers' views have not substantially changed over the years. This conclusion can be contrasted with that of the Clough and Lindsay (1991) study. Their investigation suggested that in the UK at least there was evidence of a change in teachers' attitudes over a period of time.

Overview of research on teachers' attitudes towards inclusion

More recently, researchers have become interested in teachers' attitudes towards inclusion. Early studies in the USA on 'full inclusion' reported results that were not supportive of a full placement of pupils with SEN in mainstream schools. Coates (1989) reported that general education teachers in the state of Iowa did not have a negative view of 'pull-out' (that is, withdrawal of children from the mainstream classroom for additional support) programmes, nor were they supportive of full inclusion. Similar findings were also reported by Semmel et al. (1991) who, having surveyed 381 elementary (primary school sector) educators in the states of Illinois and California (both general class teachers and SEN specialists), concluded that those educators were not dissatisfied with a special education system that operated pull-out special educational programmes.

Another US study by Vaughn and colleagues (1996) examined mainstream and special education teachers' perceptions of inclusion, using focus group interviews. The majority of these teachers – who were not currently participating in inclusive programmes – had strong negative feelings about inclusion. They felt that decision-makers were out of touch with classroom realities. The teachers identified several factors that would affect the success of inclusion, including class size, inadequate resources, the extent to which all students would benefit from inclusion and lack of adequate teacher preparation.

However, in studies where teachers had active experience of inclusion, contradictory findings have been reported. Villa et al. (1996) reported results which favoured the inclusion of children with SEN in the ordinary school. The researchers noted that teacher commitment often emerges at the end of the implementation cycle, after the teachers have gained mastery of the professional expertise needed to implement inclusive programmes. This finding was also reflected in a case study of a senior high and a middle school in Washington School District, Utah (Sebastian and Mathot-Buckner, 1998), where students with severe learning difficulties had been included. Twenty educators were interviewed at the beginning and end of the school year to determine attitudes towards inclusion. The educators felt that inclusion was working well and, although more support was needed, it was perceived as a challenge.

Similar findings were reported by LeRoy and Simpson (1996), who studied the impact of inclusion over a three-year period in the state of Michigan, USA. Their study showed that as teachers gained more experience of children with SEN, their confidence to teach these children also increased. The evidence indicates that teachers' negative or neutral attitudes at the beginning of an innovation such as inclusive education may change over time, as a function of experience and the expertise that develops through the process of implementation.

This conclusion is supported by the results of a recent UK survey of teachers' attitudes in one Local Education Authority (district). Those teachers who had been implementing inclusive programmes for some years held more positive attitudes than the rest of the sample, who had had little or no such experience (Avramidis et al., 2000). But no studies show this move towards more positive attitudes to inclusion leading to widespread acceptance of full inclusion.

Factors influencing teachers' attitudes

The research suggested that teachers' attitudes might be influenced by a number of factors that are interrelated in a number of respects. In the majority of integration attitude studies reviewed earlier, responses appeared to vary according to disabling conditions. In other words, the nature of the disabilities or educational problems presented appeared to influence teachers' attitudes. Using a typology developed by Salvia and Munson (1986) these factors could be termed as *child-related variables*. Examination of demographic and other personality factors – and their influence on teachers' attitudes – suggest that they could be classified under the heading of *teacher-related variables*. The specific context or environment was also found to influence attitudes and these variables could be termed *educational environment-related*. This framework for synthesising research findings was adopted in our review.

Child-related variables

Several of the early integration studies were concerned with determining teachers' attitudes towards different categories of children with SEN and their perceived suitability for integration. (It is worth emphasising that these studies were investigating teachers' attitudes towards *integration*, not *inclusion*, since the latter does not differentiate by category.) Teachers' concepts of children with SEN normally consist of types of disabilities, their prevalence and the educational needs they exhibit (Clough and Lindsay, 1991). Generally, teachers' perceptions may be differentiated on the basis of three dimensions: physical and sensory, cognitive, and behavioural-emotional. Forlin (1995) suggested that educators were cautiously accepting of including a child with cognitive disability, but more accepting of children with physical disabilities. The degree of acceptance for part-time integration was high for children considered to have mild or moderate SEN. The majority of educators in this study (95 per cent) believed that mildly physically disabled children should be integrated part-time into mainstream classes. But only a small proportion of educators (6 per cent) considered full-time placement of children with severe physical disability as acceptable.

Similarly, the majority of educators (86 per cent) believed that only children with mild intellectual disability should be integrated part-time into mainstream classes. A very small number of educators (1 per cent) considered full-time placement of children with intellectual disabilities viable. Most believed that it would be more stressful to cope with children with SEN full-time than part-time. Forlin's findings indicated that the degree of acceptance by educators for the placement of children with SEN in mainstream classes declined rapidly when the severity of the disability increased, across both physical and cognitive categories.

Another study in Australia by Ward et al. (1994) had assessed teacher attitudes towards inclusion of children with SEN whose disabling conditions or educational difficulties were defined behaviourally rather than categorically. With the co-operation of senior staff from the New South Wales Department of School Education, they produced a list of 30 disabling conditions which were defined behaviourally (p. 37). The researchers felt that this type of operational definition would have relevance for school practitioners, since traditional category grouping does not necessarily reflect the child's actual educational needs. In general, teachers in the study showed little disagreement about the inclusion of children with SEN perceived as having mild difficulties, since they were not likely to require extra instructional or management skills. This group included children with mild physical and visual disabilities and mild hearing loss.

There was a common uncertainty about the suitability of including children with disabling conditions that in various ways posed additional problems and demanded extra teaching competencies from teachers. This group included children with mild intellectual disability, moderate hearing loss, visual disability and hyperactivity.

The teachers were unanimous in their rejection of the inclusion of children with severe disabilities (regarded as being too challenging a group and, at the time of the study, normally educated in special schools). These were children with profound visual and hearing impairment and moderate intellectual disability. Children with profound sensory disabilities and low cognitive ability were considered to have a relatively poor chance of being successfully included.

In the UK study by Clough and Lindsay (1991), the majority of teachers surveyed had ranked the needs of children with emotional and behavioural difficulties as being the needs most difficult to meet, followed by those of children with learning difficulties. Third in the ranking were children with visual impairments, and fourth were children with a hearing impairment. Clough and Lindsay attributed the low ranking of children with sensory and physical impairments to the relatively infrequent existence of these children in mainstream classes at that time.

Bowman's (1986) study for UNESCO also indicated that teachers tended to favour different types of children with SEN for integration (in this study note that the focus was on *integration*). Most favoured were children with medical problems (by 75.5 per cent of respondents) and physical difficulties (by 63 per cent). These children were considered the easiest to manage in the classrooms. Half of the teachers involved in the study felt that children with a specific learning difficulty (54 per cent of respondents) and speech defects (50 per cent) were suitable for integration. Around a third thought that children with moderate learning difficulties (31 per cent of respondents) and severe emotional and behavioural difficulties (38 per cent) were suitable for integration. A quarter of teachers perceived children with sensory impairments, visual (23.5 per cent of respondents) and hearing (22.5 per cent), could be integrated in mainstream classes. Very few of the teachers considered that children with severe mental impairments (2.5 per cent of respondents) and multiple handicaps (7.5 per cent) could be taught in mainstream classes.

There was a wide range between individual countries, which indicated considerable national differences in teacher attitudes towards the suitability of children with various types of SEN for integration in mainstream settings. The greatest difference of attitude between countries related to the integration of children with sensory impairments (visual and hearing). The smallest difference of attitude between countries was for the integration of children with moderate learning difficulties. Contrary to the evidence reported in most atti-tude studies, such as Salvia and Munson's (1986) and Jamieson's (1984) reviews, children with moderate learning difficulties – and with severe emo-tional and behaviour problems – were generally more favoured for integration than those with sensory (hearing and visual) impairments.

Overall, our review indicated that teachers generally seemed to exhibit more positive attitudes towards the integration of children with physical and sensory impairments than to those with learning difficulties and emotional-behavioural difficulties (EBD) – although the Bowman (1986) study indicated that the opposite was true. This conclusion was also consistent with Chazan's (1994) review. It was especially relevant to the UK context at this time as there was a dramatic rise in the exclusions from schools of students with emotional and behavioural difficulties.

Teacher-related variables

A considerable amount of research has sought to determine the relationship between teacher characteristics and their attitudes towards children with spe-cial educational needs. Researchers have explored a host of specific teacher variables such as gender, age, years of teaching experience, class grade level, contact with disabled persons and other personality factors which might impact upon teacher acceptance of the inclusion principle. A synthesis of these findings is presented below.

Gender. The evidence with regard to gender appears to be inconsistent. Some researchers noted that female teachers had a greater tolerance level for integra-tion and for special needs students than had male teachers (e.g. Aksamit et al., 1987; Eichinger et al., 1991; Thomas, 1985). Harvey (1985) indicated that there was a marginal tendency for female teachers to express more positive attitudes towards the idea of integrating children with behaviour problems than male teachers. However, other studies (Beh-Pajooh, 1992; Berryman, 1989; Leyser et al., 1994), reported no relationship between gender and atti-tudes, as reflected also in Jamieson's (1984) and Hannah's (1988) reviews. Thus the research evidence indicated that there appeared not to be a clear-cut rela-tionship between gender and teacher attitudes.

Age and teaching experience. Length of experience as a teacher was another teacher-related variable cited in several studies as influencing teachers' attitudes. There was considerable evidence to suggest that younger teachers, and those with fewer years' experience, were more supportive of integration (Berryman, 1989; Center and Ward, 1987; Clough and Lindsay, 1991). Forlin (1995) for example, indicated that acceptance of a child with a physical disability was high-est among educators with less than six years of teaching experience. Acceptance declined with those with between six and ten years' experience of teaching. The most experienced educators (who had taught for more than 11 years) were the least accepting. A similar result was obtained in relation to integrating children with intellectual disabilities. Forlin's study suggested that as educators gained experience in teaching, they became less accepting of integration.

This conclusion was also supported by evidence from a study by Leyser et al. (1994), showing that, overall, teachers with 14 or fewer years' teaching experi-ence had significantly more positive attitudes to integration than those with more than 14 years' experience. Furthermore, a comparison of willingness among teacher trainees and primary (elementary) teachers to accept children with SEN in their classes (Harvey, 1985) indicated a clear reluctance on the part of the more experienced primary teachers to integrate such children, as compared with the teacher trainees.

Whilst there was a strong indication from these studies that younger teachers, and those with fewer years' experience, were more supportive of integration, other investigators have reported no significant relationship between teaching experience and teachers' attitudes (Avramidis et al., 2000; Leyser et al., 1989; Rogers, 1987; Stephens and Braun, 1980). So overall, whilst there was a considerable amount of evidence suggesting that teachers who had the most experience generally held less positive attitudes towards the integration of students with SEN, and those most recently qualified held more positive ones, the evidence was not conclusive.

Grade level taught. Several studies have focused on students' grade level and its influence on teachers' attitudes towards integration. Leyser and colleagues' (1994) cross-national investigation found that senior high school teachers displayed significantly more positive attitudes towards integration than did junior high (lower secondary) school and elementary school teachers. The junior high school teachers, in turn, were significantly more positive about integration than elementary school teachers (but no mention was made of differences across national contexts).

Other studies in the USA revealed that elementary and secondary school teachers differed in their views of integration, and the kinds of classroom accommodations they made for students who were integrated (Chalmers, 1991; Rogers, 1987). Elementary school teachers reported more positive views about integration and its possibilities than their secondary counterparts (Savage and Wienke, 1989). Salvia and Munson (1986) concluded that as children's age increased, teacher attitudes became less positive. They attributed this hardening of attitude to teachers of older children being concerned more about subject matter and less about individual differences between children. Their assertion was supported by Clough and Lindsay (1991), who claimed that for teachers more concerned with subject matter, the presence of children with SEN in the class was a problem from the practical point of view of managing class activity. It could be argued that the ethos of primary schools tends to be more holistic and inclusive, whilst the ethos and structure of secondary schools is more subject-based, and this structural difference might impinge on teachers' attitudes. Although there are studies which have not found a relationship between grade and attitude, such as Jamieson's (1984) and Hannah's (1988) reviews, it is generally believed that an emphasis on subject matter affiliation is less compatible with inclusion than is a focus on student development.

Experience of contact with children who have SEN, or disabled persons, has been mentioned in several studies as an important variable in shaping teacher attitudes towards integration. Here, the 'contact hypothesis' suggests that as teachers implement inclusive programmes, and therefore get closer to students with significant disabilities, their attitudes might become more positive. (See Yuker (1988b) for a comprehensive review of the research on the effects of personal contact on attitudes towards persons with disabilities.) Janney et al.

(1995: 436) also found evidence that experience with low ability children was an important contributing factor to their eventual acceptance by teachers:

> *Already wary of reforms and overloaded with work, general education teachers'*
> *initial balancing of the anticipated high cost of integration against its uncertain*
> *benefit created hesitation or resistance. Following their implementation experiences,*
> *teachers re-evaluated the balance between the cost of teachers' time and energy as*
> *compared to the benefit for students, and judged the integration effort successful.*

Equally, Leyser et al. (1994) found that teachers with more experience of disabled persons held significantly more favourable attitudes towards integration than those with little or no experience. Findings of several other studies conducted in the USA (Leyser and Lessen, 1985; Stainback et al., 1984), Australia (Harvey, 1985; McDonald et al., 1987) and the UK (Shimman, 1990) stressed the importance of increased experience and social contact with children with SEN, in conjunction with the attainment of knowledge and specific skills in instructional and class management, in the formation of favourable attitudes towards integration.

   This body of evidence seems to suggest that contact with students with significant disabilities, if carefully planned (and supported), results in positive changes in educators' attitudes. These studies, combined with more recent ones on teachers' attitudes towards inclusion presented earlier, indicate that as mainstream teachers' experience of children with SEN increases, their attitudes change in a positive direction (LeRoy and Simpson, 1996).

   However, it is important to note here that social contact does not in itself lead to favourable attitudes. Stephens and Braun (1980), for example, found no significant correlation between reported contact with students with significant disabilities and teachers' attitudes toward integrating these students into regular classrooms. Another study by Center and Ward (1987) showed that primary teachers were more tolerant of integration if no special class or unit was attached to their school. These researchers claimed that contact experience with children with SEN did not result in the formation of more positive attitudes.

   Surprisingly, there is evidence in the literature that social contact could even produce unfavourable attitudes. Forlin (1995) indicated that there were differences between teachers who were currently involved with the policy of inclusion and those who were not. Those not involved (but who were aware of the concept of inclusion) believed that coping with a child with SEN and coping with a mainstream child were equally stressful. Those who were involved considered the stress of coping with the child with SEN to be greater than for dealing with a mainstream child. So this study indicated that experience of a child with SEN might not promote favourable acceptance for inclusion, due to the stress factor.

   Training, both pre-service and in-service, and its impact on teachers' knowledge about children with SEN, has attracted considerable attention. This factor was considered important in improving teachers' attitudes towards the implementation of an inclusive policy. Without a coherent plan for training teachers in how to meet the educational needs of children with SEN, attempts to include these children in mainstream educational settings would be difficult.

The importance of training in the formation of positive attitudes toward integration was supported by the findings of Beh-Pajooh (1992) and Shimman (1990). Both researchers studied the attitudes of UK tertiary or further education (FE) college teachers towards students with SEN and their integration into ordinary FE college courses. They showed that college teachers who had been trained to teach students with learning difficulties expressed more favourable attitudes and emotional reactions to students with SEN and their integration than did those who had no such training.

Several other studies conducted in the USA (Buell et al., 1999; Van-Reusen et al., 2000), Australia (Center and Ward, 1987) and the UK (Avramidis et al., 2000) tend to reinforce the view that special education qualifications acquired from pre-service or in-service training courses are associated with less resistance to inclusive practices. Dickens-Smith (1995), for example, studied the attitudes of both mainstream and special educators toward inclusion (not integration). Her respondents were given an attitude survey before and after staff development. Both groups of respondents revealed more favourable attitudes towards inclusion after their in-service training than they did before, with mainstream education teachers showing the strongest positive attitude change. Dickens-Smith concluded that staff development was the key to the success of inclusion.

Teachers' beliefs. More recently, Canadian research has revealed the importance of teachers' views about their responsibility for dealing with the needs of students who are exceptional or at risk. These beliefs influence not only teachers' reported attitudes towards inclusion but their actual teaching styles and adaptations in heterogeneous classrooms. Jordan et al. (1997) found that teachers holding what they term a 'pathognomonic' perspective (where the teacher assumes that a disability is inherent in the individual student) differed in their teaching from those closer to an 'interventionist' perspective (where the teacher attributes student problems to an interaction between student and environment). Teachers with the most pathognomonic perspectives demonstrated the least effective interaction patterns, whereas those with interventionist perspectives engaged in many more academic interactions and persisted more in developing student understanding.

A study by Stanovich and Jordan (1998) further supported this finding. Their investigation attempted to predict the performance of teacher behaviours associated with effective teaching in heterogeneous classrooms. This research was more sophisticated than previous studies because it was based not only on self-reports and interviews but also on observation of actual teaching behaviour. The results revealed that the strongest predictor of effective teaching behaviour was the subjective school norm as operationalised by the principal's attitudes and beliefs about heterogeneous classrooms and his or her pathognomonic–interventionist orientation. Moreover, teachers' responses on the pathognomonic–interventionist interview scale were also found to be important predictors of effective teaching behaviour.

These studies provided evidence that the school's ethos and the teachers' beliefs have a considerable impact on attitudes towards inclusion, which in turn are translated into practice. It can be said that teachers who accept responsibility for teaching a wide diversity of students (thereby recognising the contribution their teaching has on the students' progress) and feel confident in their instructional and management skills (as a result of training) can successfully implement inclusive programmes. (See the study by Soodak et al. (1998) where receptivity towards inclusion was associated with higher teacher efficacy.)

Teachers' socio-political views. There have been a few studies relating attitudes towards integration with educators' wider personal beliefs, including their political outlook and socio-political views. Stephens and Braun's (1980) US study found that attitudes to integration were more positive when teachers believed that publicly-funded schools should educate exceptional children. Feldman and Altman (1985), also in the USA, suggested that classroom teachers with abstract conceptual systems held more positive integration attitudes depending on the ethnic origin of the child to be integrated. Teachers with abstract conceptual systems showed less need for order, less pessimism and less interpersonal aggression, characteristics that have been related to low levels of authoritarianism.

In a comparative study of educators in Devon, England, and Arizona, USA, Thomas (1985) found that educators with low scores on measures of conservatism tended to have less negative attitudes to integration. More recently, Norwich (1994) conducted a comparative study of educators in rural and urban areas in Pennsylvania, USA, and Northamptonshire, England. He examined relationships between integration attitudes and political outlook, socio-political views, and other situational factors (contact with disability, and professional position). In this study, integration attitudes were related to socio-political views only in the UK sample. Norwich concluded that while educators' socio-political or ideological beliefs and values have some relation to integration, attitudes cannot be considered as a strong predictor alone and other situational factors (provision in the two areas, and cultural issues) needed to be taken into consideration.

Educational environment-related variables

Environmental factors and their influence in the formation of teachers' attitudes towards integration or inclusion have been examined in a number of studies. One factor that has consistently been associated with more positive attitudes is the availability of support services at the classroom and the school levels (Center and Ward, 1987; Clough and Lindsay, 1991; Myles and Simpson, 1989). Here, support can be seen as either physical (including resources, teaching materials, information technology equipment, a restructured physical environment) or human (including learning support assistants and speech therapists).

Janney et al. (1995) found that the majority of teachers in their study were initially hesitant to accept children with SEN in their classes because they anticipated a worst-case scenario, where both they and the students with SEN would be left to fend for themselves. Later, the teachers were receptive towards these children after having received necessary and sufficient support. Respondents acknowledged that the support received from the relevant authorities was instrumental in allaying their apprehension that part-time integration would result in extraordinary workloads. A significant restructuring of the physical environment (making buildings accessible to students with physical disabilities) and the provision of adequate and appropriate equipment and materials were also instrumental in the development of these positive attitudes.

In addition to those forms of physical support mentioned by Janney and colleagues, other forms such as availability of adopted teaching materials (LeRoy and Simpson, 1996; Center and Ward, 1987) and smaller classes (Bowman, 1986; Center and Ward, 1987; Clough and Lindsay, 1991; Harvey, 1985) were also found to generate positive attitudes towards inclusion. Support in the form of continuous encouragement from the headteacher or principal also features as instrumental in the creation of positive attitudes to inclusion in several studies. Janney et al. (1995) identified the enthusiastic support from headteachers or principals as a factor contributing to the success of the part-time integration programme in the schools they studied. Chazan (1994) also concluded that mainstream teachers had a greater tolerance of integration if headteachers were supportive. Similarly, Center and Ward (1987) indicated that mainstream teachers whose headteachers had provided some form of support for the integration programme exhibited a more positive attitude towards its implementation than those who had not received any (see also Thomas, 1985).

Support from specialist resource teachers has been identified as an important factor in shaping positive teacher attitudes to inclusion (Kauffman et al., 1989). Janney et al. (1995) reported that the existence of effective support– both interpersonal and task-related – provided by the school's special education teachers was identified by respondents as a factor that had contributed to the success of the part-time integration programme they were implementing. Clough and Lindsay (1991) argued that special education specialist teachers are important co-workers in providing advice to subject specialist teachers on how to make a particular subject accessible to children with SEN. Moreover, Center and Ward (1987) indicated that the experience of working with itinerant teachers, supporting children with a mild sensory disability integrated in mainstream classes, positively affected teachers' attitudes.

The importance of support from specialist resource teachers was also highlighted by Minke et al. (1996) in the USA. They compared the attitudes towards inclusion (and the perceptions of self-efficacy, competence, teaching satisfaction and judgements of the appropriateness of teaching adaptation) of mainstream school teachers who co-taught with resource teachers in inclusive classrooms with those of their counterparts in traditional classrooms. Mainstream teachers in inclusive classrooms reported positive attitudes towards inclusion and high perceptions of self-efficacy, competence and satisfaction. Regular teachers in traditional classrooms held less positive perceptions and viewed classroom adaptations as less feasible and less frequently used than did teachers in classrooms with the protected resource of two teachers.

Other aspects of the mainstream school environment were identified in the studies outlined above as being obstacles to the successful implementation of inclusive programmes. Teachers frequently reported such things as overcrowded classrooms, insufficient pre-prepared materials (differentiated packages of teaching resources), insufficient time to plan with a learning support team, lack of a modified or flexible timetable, inadequately available support from external specialists and lack of regular in-service training (Avramidis et al., 2000).

In particular, the need for more non-contact time to plan collaboratively was stressed in a number of American studies (Diebold and Von Eschenbach, 1991; Semmel et al., 1991). Myles and Simpson (1989) reported that 48 out of 55 teachers (87 per cent) indicated their perceived need for one hour or more of daily planning time for inclusion. Mainstream teachers may therefore feel that implementing an inclusive programme would involve a considerable workload on their part as a result of increased planning to meet the needs of a very diverse population of students. In this respect, human and physical support could be seen as important factors in generating positive attitudes amongst mainstream teachers towards the inclusion of children with SEN.

Conclusion: implications for practice, policy and research

The literature review revealed considerable evidence that mainstream teachers, overall, hold positive attitudes towards the general philosophy of inclusion. Their favourable orientation is consistent with the recent shift in policy in many western countries towards educating children with learning difficulties and disabilities in mainstream educational settings. However, there was also evidence that teachers hold differing attitudes about school placements which are based largely upon the nature of the students' disabilities. In particular, we concluded that there was enough evidence to suggest that:

▶ teachers tend to be more willing to include students with mild disabilities, or physical or sensory impairments, than students who are perceived to have more complex needs;

▶ in the case of the more severe learning needs and behavioural difficulties, teachers tend to hold neutral or negative views about the implementation of inclusion.

Given the consistency of this trend across countries and across time, policy makers wishing to promote inclusive education may have a difficult task convincing educators about the feasibility of the policy. Careful planning and good support appear to be essential in overcoming teachers' initial reservations and concerns. This finding is largely unsurprising given the complexities that the move towards inclusive schooling involves. It is something emphasised in previous reviews of the literature (Scruggs and Mastropieri, 1996) and by commentators in the field (Evans and Lunt, 2002).

But our review differed from previous ones as it identified a small but powerful body of evidence suggesting that teachers' negative or neutral attitudes at the start of implementing an innovation such as inclusive education may change over time. This shift is largely as a consequence of experience and the expertise that develops through the process of implementation. In a number of studies where teachers had been implementing inclusive programmes for some years, positive attitudes were reported. Such a finding contradicts the rather pessimistic conclusions put forward in earlier reviews (Jamieson, 1984; Yanito et al., 1987; Hannah, 1988). The contrast between our review and its predecessors could be attributed to the fact that most of them were conducted in the 1980s. They were based on research which surveyed teachers with little or no experience of inclusive programmes (the number of which considerably increased in the 1990s).

With regard to possible factors influencing teachers' attitudes other than the nature of disability, we identified a number of studies that examined a host of specific teacher variables and environment-related variables. In synthesising the reported findings we concluded that:

▶ the evidence regarding teacher variables (such as gender, age, years of teaching experience, grade level, contact with disabled persons, level of professional development and other personality factors like beliefs and socio-political views) was inconsistent and none of them alone could be regarded as a strong predictor of teacher attitudes;
▶ the level of professional development was the only teacher variable which was consistently associated with positive attitudes to inclusion;
▶ there was considerable consistency regarding educational environment-related variables and teachers' attitudes.

The inconsistent evidence in relation to personality variables indicated that teacher attitudes may be dependent on a number of inter-related factors. There is clearly a need for a holistic exploration of teachers' attitudes in future research efforts (as opposed to a reductionist approach where single variables are isolated and tested). On the other hand, the degree of consistency in relation to professional development suggested that the provision of extensive opportunities for training at the pre-service and in-service levels might be instrumental in the formation of positive attitudes. This finding, which was in accord with previous reviews, suggested that if teachers received assistance in mastering the skills required to implement an innovation such as inclusion, they would become more committed to the change (and more effective) as their effort and skills increased. It has important practical implications for promoting inclusive education, and so merits further research.

Similarly, the degree of consistency in relation to educational environment-related variables suggested that a significant restructuring in the mainstream school environment needed to take place before students with significant disabilities were included. Again, the underlying assumption here was that with the provision of more resources and support, teachers' attitudes could become more positive. Implications for practice are the need to establish appropriate external support systems (or expansion and reorganisation of the existing ones) operating across schools, and learning support teams within educational settings to support individual teachers requesting guidance on aspects of teaching relating to special educational needs.

In sum, despite the useful findings that emerged from this review, it also indicated areas in which research is still needed, particularly to examine additional factors influencing the formation of positive attitudes towards inclusion. We identified that more specific information needs to be gathered about the quality of the training opportunities that teachers have in implementing inclusion. Factors likely to be significant include their duration, content and intensity, as well as the quality of the experiences offered with different groups of exceptional learners. If training is indeed an important factor in modifying teachers' attitudes, how might our future teachers be best prepared? How could the professional development of those currently in schools be facilitated so that they feel more confident in implementing inclusive programmes?

Similarly, if experience of inclusion promotes positive attitudes, how may teachers (the main agents of policy implementation) be supported as schools become more inclusive, so that their experiences are positive? Other school factors that impinge on attitudes and school practices would bear further exploration. They include ethos, policies, organisation, instructional arrangements and the utilisation of resources. However, although research on teachers' attitudes towards inclusion has been on the increase in the last few years, the methodologies employed have been far from unproblematic. In the next section, we consider issues arising from our review relating to methodology and research design in the study of teachers' attitudes in this field.

Towards more sophisticated research

Many researchers investigating teachers' attitudes towards integration have used Likert-type inventories in attempting to ascertain the extent to which respondents agree or disagree with the general concept of integration as related to a range of disabling conditions among students. Such inventories can lead to superficiality. Much of the past research has been represented primarily by acceptance-rejection issues reflecting the traditional categories of disability. But there has been little effort directed at uncovering the factors that may underlie the particular attitudes found.

The use of labels or categories of disability such as 'physically disabled', 'Down's syndrome', or 'autistic', raises the issue that the respondents in a population may have multiple interpretations of the same label. This phenomenon may occur when teachers attribute different characteristics to a label based on their experience or lack of it, which could be positive or negative and be largely unpredictable across a population of teachers. The problem of multiple interpretations might be alleviated by providing specific descriptions (in the form of vignettes or examples) of the behaviours and characteristics of persons with disabilities, rather than referring to a group of persons by a disabling condition.

Moreover, in this area of research, self-report instruments dominated the methodologies used in most studies, and there were few examples that included other sources of data such as teacher interviews, or other unobtrusive measures to validate the measurements taken. A key assumption built into these studies is that reported attitudes will be expressed in behaviour. Given the fact that integration and, more recently, inclusion are considered to be 'politically correct' ideas, there is always the possibility that respondents might give socially desirable answers that have little or no correspondence with their everyday behaviour. Teachers may endorse general statements in favour of having children with difficulties in regular classrooms. But it is another matter entirely how willing they are to make specific adaptations for these children.

For this reason, it may be better to include observations of teachers' actual classroom behaviour and interactions with students. One limitation of direct observation, of course, is that the person being observed may alter his or her behaviour during the observation period. However, one is more likely to observe trustworthy samples of behaviour over periodic observations than by relying solely on questionnaire data.

Overall, our review highlighted the need for adopting alternative research designs for the study of teachers' attitudes towards inclusion or integration. As Eiser (1994) reminds us, mainstream psychological research on attitudes has taken the individual self as both the starting point and focus of analysis. A result may often be to 'psychologise' about social issues without articulating how social interaction makes psychological processes the way they are. Indeed, the vast majority of the studies reviewed here employed traditional quantitative research designs (usually survey) and investigated individualistic experiences of inclusion. But as Eiser argues, the individual and the social are interdependent. In other words, attitudes should not be viewed as solely personal but as arising out of interactions with others in, say, a school.

Given this view of attitude as context dependent and responsive to factors within a particular social and cultural environment, future research might benefit from employing alternative methods. They could include life history, narrative or autobiography to examine teachers' attitudes and how they are formed. Such methods focus on participants' own narratives and can lead to an improved understanding of the complex and interrelated processes of personal experiences, attitudes and practices.

Finally, the review highlighted the need for more longitudinal research studies including qualitative case studies of teachers' attitudes and practices as schools move towards inclusive education. Longitudinal investigations would have the capacity to examine transformation of practices and beliefs over time, and also allow for a more thorough investigation of teachers' attitudes towards the process. Research of this nature has the potential to deepen our understanding of the complexities of inclusion and provide directions for change or continuity of provision as appropriate.

Acknowledgements

An earlier version of this chapter appeared in the *European Journal of Special Needs Education*, 17, 1–19. at http://www.tandf.co.uk. We are grateful to Taylor & Francis for permission to reproduce material from the original article.

References

Aksamit, D., Morris, M. and Leunberger, J. (1987) 'Preparation of student services professionals and faculty for serving learning disabled college students', *Journal of College Student Personnel*, 28: 53–9.

Avramidis, E., Bayliss, P. and Burden, R. (2000) 'A survey into mainstream teachers' attitudes towards the inclusion of children with special educational needs in the ordinary school in one Local Educational Authority', *Educational Psychology*, 20: 193–213.

Bacon, E.H. and Schulz, J.B. (1991) 'A survey of mainstreaming practices', *Teacher Education and Special Education*, 14: 144–9.

Barton, M.L. (1992) 'Teachers' opinions on the implementation and effects of Mainstreaming'. ERIC Document Reproduction Service No. ED 350 802.

Beh-Pajooh, A. (1992) 'The effect of social contact on college teachers' attitudes towards students with severe mental handicaps and their educational integration', *European Journal of Special Needs Education*, 7: 231–6.

Berryman, J.D. (1989) 'Attitudes of the public toward educational mainstreaming', *Remedial and Special Education*, 10: 44–9.

Bochner, S. and Pieterse, M. (1989) 'Preschool directors' attitudes towards the integration of children with disabilities into regular preschools in New South Wales', *International Journal of Disability, Development and Education*, 36: 133–50.

Bowman, I. (1986) 'Teacher training and the integration of handicapped pupils: some findings from a fourteen nation UNESCO study', *European Journal of Special Needs Education*, 1: 29–38.

Buell, M., Hallam, R., Gamel-McCormick, M. and Scheer, S. (1999) 'A survey of general and special education teachers' perceptions and in-service needs concerning inclusion', *International Journal of Disability, Development and Education*, 46: 143–56.

Center, Y. and Ward, J. (1987) 'Teachers' attitudes towards the integration of disabled children into regular schools', *Exceptional Child*, 34: 41–56.

Center, Y. and Ward, J. (1989) 'Attitudes of school psychologists towards the integration of children with disabilities', *International Journal of Disability, Development and Education*, 36: 117–32.

Center, Y., Ward, J., Parmenter, T. and Nash, R. (1985) 'Principals' attitudes toward the integration of disabled children into regular schools', *Exceptional Child*, 32: 149–61.

Chalmers, L. (1991) 'Classroom modification for the mainstreamed student with mild handicaps', *Intervention in School and Clinic*, 27: 40–2.

Chazan, M. (1994) 'The attitudes of mainstream teachers towards pupils with emotional and behavioural difficulties', *European Journal of Special Needs Education*, 9: 261–74.

Clough, P. and Lindsay, G. (1991) *Integration and the Support Service*. London: National Foundation for Educational Research.

Coates, R.D. (1989) 'The Regular Education Initiative and opinions of regular classroom teachers', *Journal of Learning Disabilities*, 22: 532–6.

Department of Education and Science (1978) *Special Educational Needs: Report of the Committee of Enquiry into the Education of Handicapped Children and Young People* (The Warnock Report). London: Her Majesty's Stationery Office.

Dickens-Smith, M. (1995) 'The effect of inclusion training on teacher attitude towards inclusion'. ERIC Document Reproduction Service No. ED 332 802.

Diebold, M.H. and Von Eschenbach, J.F. (1991) 'Teacher educator predictions of regular class teacher perceptions of mainstreaming', *Teacher Education and Special Education*, 14: 221–7.

Eichinger, J., Rizzo, T. and Sirotnik, B. (1991) 'Changing attitudes toward people with disabilities', *Teacher Education and Special Education*, 14: 121–6.

Eiser, J.R. (1994) *Attitudes, Chaos and the Connectionist Mind*. Oxford: Blackwell.

Evans, J. and Lunt, I. (2002) 'Inclusive education: are there limits?' *European Journal of Special Needs Education*, 17 (1): 1–14.

Feldman, D. and Altman, R. (1985) 'Conceptual systems and teacher attitudes toward regular classroom placement of mentally retarded students', *American Journal of Mental Deficiency*, 89: 345–51.

Forlin, C. (1995) 'Educators' beliefs about inclusive practices in Western Australia', *British Journal of Special Education*, 22: 179–85.

Garvar-Pinhas, A. and Schmelkin, L.P. (1989) 'Administrators' and teachers' attitudes towards mainstreaming', *Remedial and Special Education*, 10: 38–43.

Hannah, M.E. (1988) 'Teacher attitudes toward children with disabilities: an ecological analysis', in H.E. Yuker (ed), *Attitudes toward Persons with Disabilities*. New York: Springer.

Harvey, D.H. (1985) 'Mainstreaming: teachers' attitudes when they have no choice about the matter', *Exceptional Child*, 32: 163–173.

Horne, M.D. and Ricciardo, J.L. (1988) 'Hierarchy of responses to handicaps', *Psychological Reports*, 62: 83–86.

Jamieson, J.D. (1984) 'Attitudes of educators toward the handicapped', in R.L. Jones (ed), *Attitude and Attitude Change in Special Education: Theory and practice*. Reston, VA: The Council for Exceptional Children.

Janney, R.F., Snell, M.E., Beers, M.K. and Raynes, M. (1995) 'Integrating children with moderate and severe disabilities into general education classes', *Exceptional Children*, 61: 425–39.

Jones, R.L. (ed) (1984) *Attitudes and Attitude Change in Special Education: Theory and Practice*. Reston, VA: The Council for Exceptional Children.

Jordan, A., Lindsay, L. and Stanovich, P.J. (1997) 'Classroom teachers' instructional interactions with students who are exceptional, at risk and typically achieving', *Remedial and Special Education*, 18 (2): 82–93.

Kauffman, J.M., Lloyd, J.D. and McGee, K.A. (1989) 'Adaptive and maladaptive behavior: teachers' attitudes and their technical assistance needs', *Journal of Special Education*, 23: 185–200.

LeRoy, B. and Simpson, C. (1996) 'Improving student outcomes through inclusive education', *Support for Learning*, 11: 32–6.

Leyser, Y. and Lessen, E. (1985) 'The efficacy of two training approaches on attitudes of prospective teachers towards mainstreaming', *Exceptional Child*, 32: 175–83.

Leyser, Y., Kapperman, G. and Keller, R. (1994) 'Teacher attitudes toward mainstreaming: a cross-cultural study in six nations', *European Journal of Special Needs Education*, 9: 1–15.

Leyser, Y., Volkan, K. and Ilan, Z. (1989) 'Mainstreaming the disabled from an international perspective – perspectives of Israeli and American teachers', *International Education*, 18: 44–54.

McDonald, S., Birnbrauer, J. and Swerissen, H. (1987) 'The effect of an integration programme on teacher and student attitudes to mentally-handicapped children', *Australian Psychologist*, 22: 313–22.

Meijer, C.J., Pijl, S.J. and Hegarty, S. (1994) *New Perspectives in Special Education: A Six Country Study of Integration*. London: Routledge.

Mertens, D.M. (1998) *Research Methods in Education and Psychology. Integrating Diversity with Quantitative and Qualitative Approaches*. London: Sage.

Minke, K.M., Bear, G., Deemer, S.A. and Griffin, S.M. (1996) 'Teachers' experiences with inclusive classrooms: implications for special education reform', *Journal of Special Education*, 30: 152–86.

Myles, B.S. and Simpson, R.L. (1989) 'Regular educators' modification preferences for mainstreaming mildly handicapped children', *Journal of Special Education*, 22: 479–91.

Norwich, B. (1994) 'The relationship between attitudes to the integration of children with special educational needs and wider socio-political views: a US-English comparison', *European Journal of Special Needs Education*, 9: 91–106.

Padeliadou, S. and Lampropoulou, V. (1997) 'Attitudes of special and regular education teachers towards school integration', *European Journal of Special Needs Education*, 12: 173–83.

Rogers, B.G. (1987) 'A comparative study of the attitudes of regular education personnel toward mainstreaming handicapped students and variables affecting those attitudes'. ERIC Document Reproduction Service No. ED 291196.

Salvia, J. and Munson, S. (1986) 'Attitudes of regular education teachers toward mainstreaming mildly handicapped students', in C.J. Meisel (ed), *Mainstreaming Handicapped Children: Outcomes, Controversies, and New Directions*. London: Lawrence Erlbaum Associates.

Savage, L.B. and Wienke, W.D. (1989) 'Attitudes of secondary teachers toward mainstreaming', *High School Journal*, 73: 70–3.

Scruggs, T.E. and Mastropieri, M.A. (1996) 'Teacher perceptions of mainstreaming-inclusion, 1958–1995: a research synthesis', *Exceptional Children*, 63: 59–74.

Sebastian, J.P. and Mathot-Buckner, C. (1998) 'Including students with severe disabilities in rural middle and high school'. ERIC Document Reproduction Service No. ED 417911.

Semmel, M.I., Abernathy, T.V., Butera, G. and Lesar, S. (1991) 'Teacher perceptions of the Regular Education Initiative', *Exceptional Children*, 58: 9–24.

Shimman, P. (1990) 'The impact of special needs students at a further education college: a report on a questionnaire', *Journal of Further and Higher Education*, 14: 83–91.

Soodak, L.C. Podell, D.M. and Lehman, L.R. (1998) 'Teacher, student, and school attributes as predictors of teachers' responses to inclusion', *Journal of Special Education*, 31: 480–97.

Stainback, S., Stainback, W. and Dedrick, V.L. (1984) 'Teachers' attitudes toward integration of severely handicapped students into regular schools', *Teacher Education,* 19: 21–7.

Stanovich, P.J. and Jordan, A. (1998) 'Canadian teachers' and principals' beliefs about inclusive education as predictors of effective teaching in heterogeneous classrooms', *Elementary School Journal,* 98: 221–38.

Stephens, T. and Braun, B.L. (1980) 'Measures of regular classroom teachers' attitudes toward handicapped children', *Exceptional Children,* 46: 292–4.

Thomas, D. (1985) 'The determinants of teachers' attitudes to integrating the intellectually handicapped', *British Journal of Educational Psychology,* 55: 251–63.

Thomas, G. (1997) 'Inclusive schools for an inclusive society', *British Journal of Special Education,* 24: 251–63.

UNESCO (1994) *The Salamanca Statement and Framework for Action on Special Needs Education.* Salamanca, Spain: United Nations.

Van-Reusen, A,K., Shoho, A.R. and Barker, K.S. (2000) 'High school teacher attitudes toward inclusion', *High School Journal,* 84: 7–20.

Vaughn, J.S., Schumm, J., Jallad, B., Slusher, J. and Saumell, L. (1996) 'Teachers' views of inclusion', *Learning Disabilities Research and Practice,* 11: 96–106.

Villa, R., Thousand, J., Meyers, H. and Nevin, A. (1996) 'Teacher and administrator perceptions of heterogeneous education', *Exceptional Children,* 63: 29–45.

Ward, J., Center, Y. and Bochner, S. (1994) 'A question of attitudes: integrating children with disabilities into regular classrooms?', *British Journal of Special Education,* 21: 34–9.

Yanito, T., Quintero, M.C., Killoran, J.C. and Striefel, S. (1987) Teacher attitudes toward mainstreaming: A literature review. ERIC Document Reproduction Service No. ED 290290.

Yuker, H.E. (ed) (1988a) *Attitudes towards Persons with Disabilities.* New York: Springer.

Yuker, H.E. (1988b) 'The effects of contact on attitudes toward disabled persons: some empirical generalisations', in H.E. Yuker (ed), *Attitudes toward Persons with Disabilities.* New York: Springer.

Appendix 1

Useful sources of guidance

The following books are sources of guidance on reviewing literature and other aspects of research relevant to conducting a small-scale investigation. The annotated list is by no means comprehensive: there are numerous other books that address specific methodologies and approaches. However, these texts are a useful starting point for doctoral and masters projects.

Bell, J. (1999) *Doing your Research Project: A Guide for First-Time Researchers in Education and Social Science,* 3rd edn. Buckingham: Open University Press.
> This book has become a well-known text for first-time researchers in education. It serves as a guide to practice for the novice researcher embarking on masters or doctoral study. It takes a step-by-step approach to the research process, and the writing up and presentation of a project. There are plentiful examples of research practice and also helpful checklists to help readers monitor the progress of their projects.

Black, T. (2001) *Understanding Social Science Research*, 2nd edn. London: Sage.
> The book aims to help students to evaluate research, and is clear and straightforward. It is more strongly focused on measurement than other methodologies and research designs.

Blaxter, L, Hughes, C. and Tight, M. (2001) *How to Research*. Buckingham: Open University Press.
> This is a new edition of a book that many masters and doctoral students have found useful. It is primarily about the practice and experience of doing small-scale research in social science. There are sections on using Internet sources for literature searches and for other aspects of the research process.

Cohen, L., Manion, L. and Morrison, K. (2000) *Research Methods in Education*, 5th edn. London: Routledge.
> Something of a classic among the research methodology textbooks in education, this book is comprehensive, covering a wide range of approaches to research. It is also accessible and a useful introductory text for masters and doctoral students.

Coleman, M. and Briggs, A.J. (eds) (2002) *Research Methods in Educational Leadership and Management*. London: Paul Chapman.

> A comprehensive and accessible guide to researching educational management and leadership aimed at relatively inexperienced researchers. There are chapters by a range of well-known people in the field that address topics such as designing a project, reliability and validity, ethics, research methods and instruments, analysing data and presentation.

Denscomb, M. (1997) *The Good Research Guide*. Buckingham: Open University Press.

> Aimed at those undertaking small-scale research projects, the book provides a pragmatic approach to the research process. It aims to help readers with limited time to conduct a rigorous small-scale project, highlighting aspects of good research practice and offering checklists for monitoring research. There is also a companion volume: Denscomb, M. (2002) *Ground Rules for Good Research*. Buckingham: Open University Press.

Fink, A. (1998) *Conducting Research Literature Reviews*. London: Sage.

> A guide to the process of searching and reviewing research literature, this book examines not only the practicalities of literature review, but also how to become a critical reader of research reports. It addresses issues such as research design and sampling strategy, and also data collection, analysis and presentation.

Gorard, S. (2001) *Quantitative Methods in Educational Research: The Role of Numbers Made Easy*. London: Continuum.

> This book provides an excellent introduction to research involving numbers. It is very readable and clear. The author presents examples from his own and other work. There are useful chapters on designing a study, using data from existing sources and on sampling techniques. A helpful appendix lists sources of statistical and numerical data. Strongly recommended for anyone considering doing a study involving survey, experimental or multi-method designs.

Hart, C. (1998) *Doing a Literature Review: Releasing the Social Science Imagination*. London: Sage.

> A thorough examination of the process of reviewing literature. The book makes connections between the literature review in a masters or doctoral study and methodology and research design. It addresses the principles underpinning any literature review; and there is a useful chapter on how to analyse ideas and undertake argumentation analysis. In addition, it covers practical aspects of reviewing literature, such as searching bibliographic databases, and contains a chapter on writing. Examples are taken from a range of sources in social science, and the book is clear and readable. There is now also a companion volume specifically addressing literature searches: Hart, C. (2001) *Doing a Literature Search*. London: Sage.

Knight, P. (2001) *Small-Scale Research*. London: Sage.

> Very much focused on the needs of a graduate student readership, this book is a guide to conducting small-scale research projects for theses or dissertations. It presents systematically the main modes of enquiry and considers

the main strengths and limitations of different approaches. Understanding that small-scale researchers are often short on time and resources, it gives pragmatic practical advice.

Miles, M. and Huberman, M. (1994) *Qualitative Data Analysis: An Expanded Sourcebook*. Thousand Oaks, CA: Sage.
   A classic text on qualitative research approaches. The book is practical and comprehensive – going far beyond data analysis. There are excellent sections on research design, sampling, data reduction, coding and display for qualitative studies. Strongly recommended for anyone considering a study with a qualitative element.

Potter, S. (ed.) (2002) *Doing Postgraduate Research*. London: Sage.
   This book aims to help make the research process as explicit and clear as possible. It addresses the increasing importance of formal research training for graduate students. Taking a practical approach, it provides examples and material to help students develop a range of research skills.

Punch, K. (1998) *An Introduction to Social Research*. London: Sage.
   A comprehensive introduction to both qualitative and quantitative methodologies. It is good on research design, and is very clearly written and presented with good examples of different kinds of research. An excellent all-rounder. There is also a companion volume: Punch, K. (2000) *Developing Effective Research Proposals*. London: Sage. It addresses all aspects of designing a research proposal, and would be useful for planning masters or doctoral research.

Rudestam, K. and Newton, R. (2001) *Surviving your Dissertation: A Comprehensive Guide to Content and Process*. 2nd edn. London: Sage.
   This book covers all dimensions of writing a dissertation or thesis: from choosing a topic and defining research questions through to writing up. A useful section deals with the process of moving from a topic to specifying research questions, something that many masters and doctoral students find quite challenging. Students outside the USA might find the terminology associated with the supervision process a little strange, but otherwise a useful guide to the research and writing process.

Walliman, N. (2000) *Your Research Project: A Step-by-Step Guide for the First-time Researcher*. London: Sage.
   A helpful guide to planning, designing and structuring a research enquiry from the very first stages onwards, which also aims to develop the necessary research skills to conduct a project and considers what makes a successful research project. Another purpose of the book is to help develop skills in critical analysis.

Blank form for the critical analysis of a text

1. **What review question am I asking of this text?** (e.g. what is my central question? why select this text? does the critical analysis of this text fit into my investigation with a wider focus? what is my constructive purpose in undertaking a critical analysis of this text?)

2. **What type of literature is this?** (e.g. theoretical, research, practice, policy? are there links with other types of literature?)

3. **What sort of intellectual project for study is being undertaken?**
   a) *How clear is it which intellectual project the authors are undertaking?* (e.g. knowledge-for-understanding, knowledge-for-critical evaluation, knowledge-for-action, instrumentalism, reflexive action?)

b) *How is the intellectual project reflected in the authors' mode of working?* (e.g. a social science or a practical orientation? choice of methodology and methods? an interest in understanding or in improving practice?)

c) *What value stance is adopted towards the practice or policy investigated?* (e.g. disinterested, critical, positive, unclear? what assumptions are made about the possibility of improvement? whose practice or policy is the focus of interest?)

d) *How does the sort of intellectual project being undertaken affect the research questions addressed?* (e.g. investigating what happens? what is wrong? how well does a particular policy or intervention work in practice?)

e) *How does the sort of intellectual project being undertaken affect the place of theory?* (e.g. is the investigation informed by theory? generating theory? atheoretical? developing social science theory or a practical theory?)

f) *How does the authors' target audience affect the reporting of research?* (e.g. do the authors assume academic knowledge of methods? criticise policy? offer recommendations for action?)

4. What is being claimed?

a) *What are the main kinds of knowledge claim that the authors are making?* (e.g. theoretical knowledge, research knowledge, practice knowledge?)

b) *What is the content of the main claims to knowledge and of the overall argument?* (e.g. what, in a sentence, is being argued? what are the three to five most significant claims that encompass much of the detail? are there key prescriptions for improving policy or practice?)

c) *How clear are the authors' claims and overall argument?* (e.g. stated in an abstract, introduction or conclusion? unclear?)

d) *With what degree of certainty do the authors make their claims?* (e.g. do they indicate tentativeness? qualify their claims by acknowledging limitations of their evidence? acknowledge others' counter-evidence? acknowledge that the situation may have changed since data collection?)

e) *How generalised are the authors' claims – to what range of phenomena are they claimed to apply?* (e.g. the specific context from which the claims were derived? other similar contexts? a national system? a culture? universal? implicit? unspecified?)

f) *How consistent are the authors' claims with each other?* (e.g. do all claims fit together in supporting an argument? do any claims contradict each other?)

5. To what extent is there backing for claims?
a) *How transparent are any sources used to back the claims?* (e.g. is there any statement of the basis for assertions? are sources unspecified?)

b) *What, if any, range of sources is used to back the claims?* (e.g. first hand experience? the authors' own practice knowledge or research? literature about others' practice knowledge or research? literature about reviews of practice knowledge or research? literature about others' polemic?)

c) *If claims are at least partly based on the authors' own research, how robust is the evidence?* (e.g. is the range of sources adequate? are there methodological limitations or flaws in the methods employed? do they include cross-checking or 'triangulation' of accounts? what is the sample size and is it large enough to support the claims being made? is there an adequately detailed account of data collection and analysis? is a summary given of all data reported?)

d) *Are sources of backing for claims consistent with the degree of certainty and the degree of generalisation?* (e.g. is there sufficient evidence to support claims made with a high degree of certainty? is there sufficient evidence from other contexts to support claims entailing extensive generalisation?)

6. How adequate is any theoretical orientation to back claims?

a) *How explicit are the authors about any theoretical orientation or conceptual framework?* (e.g. is there a conceptual framework guiding data collection? is a conceptual framework selected after data collection to guide analysis? is there a largely implicit theoretical orientation?)

b) *What assumptions does any explicit or implicit theoretical orientation make that may affect the authors' claims?* (e.g. does a perspective focus attention on some aspects and under-emphasise others? if more than one perspective is used, how coherently do the different perspectives relate to each other?)

c) *What are the key concepts underpinning any explicit or implicit theoretical orientation?* (e.g. are they listed? are they stipulatively defined? are concepts mutually compatible? is use of concepts consistent? is the use of concepts congruent with others' use of the same concepts?)

7. To what extent does any value stance adopted affect claims?

a) *How explicit are the authors about any value stance connected with the phenomena?* (e.g. a disinterested, critical, or positive stance? is this stance informed by a particular ideology? is it adopted before or after data collection?)

b) *How may any explicit or implicit value stance adopted by the authors affect their claims?* (e.g. have they prejudged the phenomena discussed? are they biased? is it legitimate for the authors to adopt their particular value stance? have they over-emphasised some aspects of the phenomenon while under-emphasising others?)

8. To what extent are claims supported or challenged by others' work?

a) *Do the authors relate their claims to others' work?* (e.g. do the authors refer to others' published evidence, theoretical orientations or value stances to support their claims? do they acknowledge others' counter-evidence?)

b) *How robust is any evidence from others' work used to support claims?* (e.g. – see 5c)

c) *How robust is any evidence from others' research and practice that challenges the authors' claims?* (e.g. – see 5c)

9. To what extent are claims consistent with my experience?

10. What is my summary evaluation of the text in relation to my review question or issue?

a) *How convincing are the authors' claims, and why?*

b) *How, if at all, could the authors have provided stronger backing for their claims?*

Author Index

General Index

academic apprenticeship, 5–7, 25, 37, 53
academic enquiry, 4–7, 156–7, 181
action research, 160
analysis
  case study, 104–7
  correlational, 181–3, 188–9
  data, 68–9, 117
  emic, 117
  multivariate, 173–4, 181–2
  statistical, 73, 195
applying critical reading to research
     questions, 46–8
argument, 5–9, 14, 25–30, 42, 44
Aristotelian ethics, 112, 126
assessment
  convergent, 146–7
  divergent, 146–7
  formative, 129–148
  mathematics, 72–6
  performance, 63–82
  teacher, 75, 130–1, 135–6, 140–2
assumption
  definition of, 13–14

becoming a critical reader, 3–9
bibliographic databases, 203

case studies, 63–82, 77–8, 85–108
classification of educational knowledge, 157
classroom communities, 118–19
classroom interaction, 129, 134–5
coding, 52
concept
  definition of, 10–11
conceptual framework, 63, 85–6, 88–91, 93
critical analysis of texts, 27–36

critical reading and self critical writing, 7–8
critical review exercises, 31–6
cross-case comparison, 77–8

data
  analysis, 68–9, 104–7, 117, 140–5, 180–2
  collection, 116–17, 158–160, 180–2
  primary, 41
  secondary, 41, 51
definitions
  stipulative, 10–11, 15, 47
dimensions of variation among knowl-
    edge claims, 14–16
discussion of findings and conclusion,
    54–6, 59, 107–8, 126, 147–8,
    168–171, 192–5

effective teachers of literacy, 173–97
ethics, 110, 114, 152, 160, 180

focus of research, 42–8
focus of review, 216–19
framing of educational knowledge, 156–7

homework, 85–108
  contexts for, 89–90, 93–5, 97, 101
  tasks, 91, 93, 97, 100
hypothesis
  definition of, 14–15

ideology
  definition of, 13–14
inclusive education, 201–22
  teacher attitudes to, 204–16
instrumentalism
  definition of, 23–4